Choosing Books for Young People, Volume 2:

A Guide to Criticism and Bibliography, 1976-1984

Choosing Books for Young People, Volume 2:

A Guide to Criticism and Bibliography, 1976-1984

by John R. T. Ettlinger and Diana L. Spirt

ORYX PRESS
1987

The rare Arabian Oryx is believed to have inspired the myth of the unicorn. This desert antelope became virtually extinct in the early 1960s. At that time several groups of international conservationists arranged to have 9 animals sent to the Phoenix Zoo to be the nucleus of a captive breeding herd. Today the Oryx population is over 400, and herds have been returned to reserves in Israel, Jordan, and Oman.

Copyright © 1987 by
The Oryx Press
2214 North Central at Encanto
Phoenix, Arizona 85004-1483

Published simultaneously in Canada

Printed and Bound in the United States of America

∞ The paper used in this publication meets the minimum requirements of American National Standard for Information Science—Permanence of Paper for Printed Library Materials, ANSI Z39.48, 1984.

Library of Congress Cataloging-in-Publication Data
(Revised for volume 2)

Ettlinger, John R. T.
  Choosing books for young people.

  Vol. 2 published: Phoenix, Ariz. : Oryx Press.
  Includes indexes.
  Contents: [v. 1] 1945–1975 — v. 2. 1976–1984.
  1. Children—Books and reading—Bibliography.
2. Children's literature—Bibliography.   3. Children's
literature—History and criticism—Bibliography
4. Reference books—Children's literature—Bibliography.
5. Bibliography—Bibliography—Children's literature.
I. Spirt, Diana L.   II. Title.
Z1037.A1E88   1982   [PN1009.A1]   011'.62   82-11659
ISBN 0-8389-0366-5 (v. 1)
ISBN 0-89774-247-8 (v. 2)

The authors wish in this second volume to make a dual dedication, general and particular.

The general repeats, as still appropriate, the dedication of the first, 1945 to 1975, volume.

This work is dedicated to the student assistants, the clerical aides, and the interlibrary loan staff who helped us so much and who rarely get credit for anything in a book (unless they are the author's husband or wife). Although we have already said a personal word of thanks, we would like to add a "literary" thank you for their inestimable help.

The particular dedication is personal, to a friend and sometime colleague held in high personal and professional regard by both of us.

To NORMAN HORROCKS, in recognition of his outstanding and long-standing contributions to library education, to library associations, and to the library profession.

John R.T. Ettlinger
Diana L. Spirt

Contents

Preface

The last line of the verse that initiates the prefatory remarks in the first volume of *Choosing Books for Young People: A Guide to Criticism and Bibliography, 1945–1975* remains true for this volume. "Of making books there is no end." Augmented technology in the publishing industry and an increased interest among adults in books for young people combined in the late seventies and early eighties to provide an endless stream of works that librarians and others should consider when making book selection decisions on titles that will be read by young people. The present volume *Choosing Books for Young People, Volume 2: A Guide to Criticism and Bibliography, 1976–1984* follows faithfully the guidelines of its predecessor and establishes for interested persons and scholars a record of relevant publications that appeared from 1976 through 1984. In agreement with the first volume, a determined effort has been made to locate all of the books and booklists that fit within the delimitations outlined in the Introduction. Each book, including many that were excluded, was personally examined by one or both authors. The searching, from the bibliographic citation in national bibliographies, or failing this, from periodicals, newsletters, or publisher's catalogs, to the examination of the published work, involved a great deal of checking. For each title included, a bibliographic record was thoroughly searched and established, and a description and criticism thoughtfully written. The authors feel fairly certain that they have attained these two primary goals, and they also hope that if any additions or corrections are required, the reader will let them know. This second volume differs slightly from the original in that many more of the included books are still very applicable and useful for current book selection and reevaluation. The book you are about to read and use continues the bibliographic tradition that has existed, no matter how minimally, since 1945 in the field of books for young people.

By examining the booklists in the present volume, one can continue to see the historic trends which were evident in the earlier title. Further, one can continue to witness the changing attitudes of society on certain issues. Although realistic fiction, equal rights, and other issues so popular in publishing in the late sixties and early seventies continue to surface occasionally, an influx of board books or infant materials and other pre-kindergarten title guides display clearly a major societal need that can be related to a higher birth rate in Western Europe and North America since 1976. In America it has been popularly called "a minor baby boom." A close perusal of the lists indicates that teenage romances, reissues of "classics," illustrated fairy tales, and board books for infants predominate for the years covered in the present volume. The latter category is striking, primarily because it is such a new trend. However, librarians can rest assured that a lively balance of categories remains. Even more apparent, especially to the authors, are restrictive economic trends in publishing in North America and Western Europe during the period 1976 to 1984.

These economic trends are easily visible to those predisposed to look for them. Their accumulated dampening influence on the production of books in this speciality during the concluding years of the previous volume was obvious to the authors because of the decreasing numbers of reference books published in the field of books for young people. There was a similar moratorium during the beginning years covered in the present volume. Although this moratorium did not last long, it was real, as anyone in the publishing trade can affirm. By the end of 1984, the publishing of reference books to be used by those who work with young people was again healthy and beginning to boom. Indeed, it is the opinion of one of the authors that there are perhaps too many works about books for young people to the detriment of those very books. That aside, the kind of reference work that this volume treats was in plentiful supply at the close of 1984, with the promise of more to come. There seems to be a potential for another vast outpouring of books for children such as occurred in the early seventies. It is also obvious to those who study the cyclical nature of the book trade that the marketplace follows fairly closely the needs and interests of society as expressed by the populace and understood by the publishers. The years of coverage in this present volume, 1976–1984, supply a fertile field for that thesis. As this volume concluded, it became apparent that the forthcoming titles in the field of books for young people were much more numerous than at the beginning. Again this phenomenon demonstrates a lag of several years duration between the economic cycle and its influence on the publishing industry. Watching the confluence of both societal attitudes and marketplace economic rules on this relatively small section of publishing—reference works and lists about books for young people—has been revealing, to say the least. The authors hope that the use of this monograph of critical and bibliographic control of the works which comment on and select books for young people will be helpful to teachers, librarians, and other interested persons.

"The playwright's mouth, the preacher's jangle,
The critic's challenge and defend,
And Fiction turns the Muses' mangle—"

Diana L. Spirt

Acknowledgments

Many of our obligations from our first volume, *Choosing Books for Young People: A Guide to Criticism and Bibliography, 1945–1975* were renewed and strengthened by this volume. Those recognized, and new friends, have indeed contributed a vast amount of effort for the compilation, research, writing, and publication of this second volume for the years 1976 through 1984. Research and writing change little; they are always painstaking and time consuming. Reminiscent of the aphorism, "It's a life of compensation," one monumental effort that comes immediately to mind and that occasioned great delay, to say nothing of solution, was the "closing of the Library of Congress card catalog" during the working life of this volume. On the other hand, the increasing sophistication of the OCLC database made checking and interlibrary loan service speedier. As in the recent past, our researches were attended by good fortune. There have been innumerable people in key areas who have shared our devotion and interest in providing good bibliographic control and criticism for those who give guidance to young people. We take pleasure in acknowledging the staffs of the following: the B. Davis Schwartz Library, C.W. Post Campus, Long Island University, particularly Conrad Schoeffling (who became Head of Special Collections just before this manuscript was completed), Louis Pisha (who became Head of Circulation and Interlibrary Loan), and Ellen Weinstein (Head of the Library and Information Science Library) and her assistants; the Bodleian Library, Oxford University, England; the Killam Library, Dalhousie University, Canada; the library of the Library Association, England; the library of the National Book League, England; the research committees of both C.W. Post Campus of Long Island University and Dalhousie University, who provided funds to facilitate the research and prepare the material for publication; and James L. Thomas, who recommended us to Oryx Press.

If we have failed to mention your name, be assured that we treasure your kindnesses, and do chide us! However, the authors know that you who do read the following pages will see that your aid has helped us immeasurably in the presentation of this volume, which we now launch with a truly meant, "Bon Voyage!"

Introduction

This annotated bibliography is designed to provide a key to the voluminous output of comment and criticism that has appeared from 1976 to 1984 about all kinds of books for young people of all ages. The listing of titles here goes beyond the treatment of children's books as literature to include works recommending informational and instructional reading in or out of the school environment. The authors' objectives are to be comprehensive in scope, to record and describe any book which selects, criticizes, or lists suitable books for young people, and to comment on their value and usefulness to librarians, teachers, parents, and others who are professionally or personally interested in providing or recommending reading for children and young adults from kindergarten to high-school age. Emphasis has been placed on identifying tools that provide a subject approach or a selective listing chosen by experienced critics and professionals from the increasing number of publications available for juveniles. Besides those titles which offer currently valid selections, there are entries that will demonstrate the criteria for book selection in the recent past. Social and literary historians will be able to perceive that the changes of attitude in choosing children's books have been as rapid as the changes in publication pattern and the style of writing in the books themselves.

INCLUSIONS AND EXCLUSIONS

Date, Language, and Place of Publication: The list includes all relevant books published from 1976 to 1984 in the English language in the United States, Great Britain, and Canada. French-language publications from Canada are included, as are any Australian and New Zealand items that have been located. Titles in other languages and from other countries have been excluded.

Subject: Subject parameters include all monographs and annuals in which at least one of the principal aims is to criticize, to recommend, or to list books for young people. We have included in this category all titles where this criterion forms a major theme or proportion of the text, or where the bibliographical element substantially exceeds a chapter or two or an appendix. On this basis, many titles are listed which ostensibly cover peripheral or related areas, but their inclusion here is due to their bibliographical features or to the degree of relevant comment. Some examples of these related areas are bibliography, black studies, curricular enrichment, disadvantaged readers, folklore, reading guidance, storytelling, and writing and publishing for children. Books on the following topics are excluded from the list: audiovisual materials, except multimedia guides which include books; free and inexpensive materials; anthologies that do not have a substantial proportion of critical or bibliographical material; individual authors and illustrators; teaching methods; and management of school or children's libraries.

Format: Monographs, annuals, and works appearing biennially or triennially of 16 pages or over are included. Excluded are the following formats: items under 16 pages (with one exception); publications processed from typescript; microform publications and paper prints from these; theses not independently published as monographs; periodical titles (except annuals and works appearing biennially or triennially); and periodical articles and offprints from them.

Agency of Publication: The following types of publications are excluded: sales and advertising material by publishers, jobbers, booksellers, and book clubs; documents produced by state agencies or school systems for their own use or purely local distribution; individual library catalogs and lists, except scholarly publications embodying research or critical comment, which are included.

ENTRY

Arrangement by Author or Main Entry: Entries are arranged alphabetically by author or other main entry. Personal author entries take precedence over institutional or title entries where possible, whether the name appears on the recto or the verso of the title page or is identified in the prefatory matter. The form of name used in the book has been preferred. If authors listed as compilers or editors have functioned in fact as authors, they have been so credited without the use of brackets. All co-authors have been credited in the entry, with the exception of committee members. Committee chairpersons have been given editorial credit. Editors of former editions have been identified in the annotation and in the index, as have institutions whose contributions have exceeded their function as publishers.

Edition: Entries describe the last edition published before the close of 1984. The following qualifications to this rule apply. For books published on both sides of the Atlantic within a year, the edition of the country of origin is given. Entry for a full text is preferred over that for a later abbreviated edition. Unchanged reprints by the original publishers are not cited, but reprints of earlier titles by specialized reprint publishers are treated as later editions. All earlier editions are described in the annotation, including editions under different editors or titles. Where noted, editions subsequent to 1984 have been mentioned at the close of the annotation.

ANNOTATION

The primary objectives of the annotation have been to describe the contents of the listed item and to provide bibliographical information. Descriptions have been phrased in terms used by the book's own author, editor, or sponsoring body, whether in direct quotation or in paraphrase. Critical opinions expressed relate particularly to the usefulness of the tool to its potential audience. Readers may presume that standard features such as typographical presentation, illustration, and indexing are of satisfactory quality, unless noted as deficient or as above average in quality or usefulness.

SUBJECT ACCESS

Where appropriate, the subject index uses Sears headings with adaptations for *see* and *see also* references from the Library of Congress. However, considerable variations from these lists have been made to suit the nature of the material. *See* references refer to the whole subject or principal subjects of the books; that is, they will not be analytical in the sense of giving access to individual chapters, etc.

J.R.T. Ettlinger

Annotated Bibliography

References to books annotated in the earlier volume, *Choosing Books for Young People: A Guide to Criticism and Bibliography, 1945–1975* are given, for example, as (E/S 1945–75, p. 155). References to other books annotated in this volume are followed by the entry number in boldface type.

1. Adell, Judith, and Klein, Hilary Dole, comps. *A Guide to Non-Sexist Children's Books.* **Chicago: Academy, 1976. 49p.**

Edited by Waltraud Schacher with a brief preface by Alan Alda, this briefly annotated bibliography is aimed at parents primarily but also to others interested. The compilers offer a wide range of children's and young adult books which do not deal with young people only in the so-called traditional roles. Rather, here are books "that treat boys and girls as people who have the same kinds of frailties and strengths." The approximately 400 entries for youngsters in preschool through junior high are selected largely from publications of the 1960s and 1970s with a few from the 1950s and some out-of-print titles. The list is divided into four age categories: preschool through third grade; third grade through seventh grade; seventh grade through twelfth grade; and titles suitable for "All Ages." Each is subdivided into fiction and nonfiction and arranged alphabetically by author. The descriptive annotations include a brief plot synopsis and a reading grade category. While far from comprehensive, the selection is well chosen for its purpose and does an appropriate job of highlighting relevant publishing efforts in the two decades represented.

2. Algarin, Joanne P. *Japanese Folk Literature: A Core Collection and Reference Guide.* **New York: Bowker, 1982. 226p.**

Young people's titles are strongly, but not exclusively, represented in this scholarly annotated bibliography with accompanying bibliographical essays, intended for researchers, librarians, educators, storytellers, and other interested readers. Three chapters, covering Japanese folklore, Japanese folklore anthologies, and classic folktales of Japan, are arranged alphabetically by author, with helpful indexes for subjects, articles, titles, and particular folktales. Two useful appendices provide access to Japanese-language sources and a glossary. For general readers, for librarians in schools and public libraries, and for the unsophisticated researcher, this is a pioneering and quite comprehensive guide to an intriguing field.

3. Allen, Yvonne, and others. *Ireland.* **(Storylines, No. 8). Birmingham, England: Library Association Youth Libraries Group, 1977. 18p.**

Compiled by a committee of seven members of the Northern Ireland Branch of the Group, this brief annotated list includes 70 books and 12 examples of audiovisual materials, from maps to filmstrips and slides, selected to present a broadly based view of Ireland past and present to young adult readers. Sections cover fairy and folktales, myths and legends, fantasy, contemporary fiction, historical fiction, background information books, and visual material. Most are publications from the British Isles, and each carries a short paragraph of descriptive annotation, with occasional criticisms and recommendations for use.

4. American Library Association. Association for Library Service to Children. *The Arbuthnot Lectures, 1970–1979.* **Chicago: The Association, 1980. 203p.**

The collection prints the text of the first ten of these prestigious lectures by leading writers and specialists in literature for children, with a foreword on the May Hill Arbuthnot Honor Lectureship by Zena Sutherland. Its international caliber is demonstrated by the names of those selected: Margery Fisher, John Rowe Townsend, Mary Orvig, Bettina Hurlimann, Ivan Southall, Mollie Hunter, Jean Fritz, Shigo Watanabe, Uriel Ofek, and Sheila Egoff. An introductory paragraph gives biographical information about each. Most, but not all, chose to comment on aspects of the literature of their own country. The texts often cite particular titles, and some have brief supporting bibliographies. The historical interest of the collection is also increased by a biographical sketch of May Hill Arbuthnot, again by Zena Sutherland.

5. ———. Association for Library Service to Children and Young Adult Services Division. *High Interest/Low Reading Level Information Packet.* **Chicago: The Association, 1978. 38p.**

The material gathered for the Division's preconference, "Dispelling the High-Low Blues," included a brief but carefully selected bibliography of recent "high-low" titles. The YASD later supplemented this with an annotated list of young-adult titles for teenage reluctant readers, *High-Interest-Low Reading Level Booklist*, which appeared in 1980, 1982, 1983, and 1985. Criteria for inclusion consisted of controlled vocabulary, short sentences, short paragraphs, sample plots, and uncomplicated dialog. These were matched against timeliness, maturity of format, content appeal, and a reading level of grade six or under on the Fry scale.

6. ———. Reference Books Bulletin Editorial Board. *Dictionaries for Children and Young Adults.* **Chicago: The Association, 1983. 38p.**

First printed in 1982, this collection of reviews has been reprinted and updated from reviews which appeared in *Reference and Subscription Books Book Reviews.* Prepared for parents, teachers, and librarians considering the purchase of one of the dictionaries published for the young people's market, these assessments of nine of them are full and critical, covering appropriateness of vocabulary, suitability of topical matter, attractiveness of format, and other necessary qualities. Those concerned with the important choice of a dictionary must benefit from this authoritative advice.

7. ———. Young Adult Services Division. *Best Books for Young Adults.* **Chicago: The Association, 1931– . Annual.**

The long-standing, brief, unannotated listing of about 50 titles annually is selected by the Best Books for Young Adults Committee of the Division (E/S 1945–75, pp. 3–4). Titles of "proven or potential appeal and worth" are chosen to "encourage avid and reluctant readers alike." They must meet the following standards: for fiction, believable characters and dialog and plausible plot; for nonfiction, readable text and appealing format. In spite of its ephemeral format, it remains an indispensable selection of the "best of the best" in its field. Back issues retain their value for retrospective research, and often for current acquisition as well.

8. ———. Young Adult Services Division. *Still Alive: The Best of the Best, 1960–1974.* **Chicago: The Association, 1976. 8p.**

Compiled by a committee of the Division in 1975, and first shown in the November number of *Top of the News*, this annotated listing represents a reevaluation of titles previously recommended for these years in the Division's annual selection, *Best Books for Young Adults.* Some titles were dropped after reassessment of their literary merit or current accuracy, or because their popularity had declined; other good titles previously omitted were added. Remaining titles, about two-thirds of the list, carry an asterisk. Of the 73 titles now recommended, 16 were published between 1960 and 1964, 23 between 1965 and 1969, and 34 between 1970 and 1974. The selection documents the growing tendency for young adults to read adult titles. Remaining an authoritative basic checklist, particularly for small libraries, updating can conveniently be made with succeeding annual numbers of *Best Books for Young Adults,* now available in sheet or pamphlet form.

9. Amtmann, Bernard. *A Bibliography of Canadian Children's Books and Books for Young People, 1841–1867/ Livres de l'enfance et livres de la jeunesse au Canada.* **Montreal: Amtmann, 1977. 124p.**

This alphabetical author-and-title checklist is derived from existing Canadian bibliographies, to which references have been provided. There are no annotations or preface or introduction, and the index is incomplete, thus rendering this compilation by a Montreal book dealer of not more than minimal value to the student; but it will serve to supplement the author's previous work in the field.

10. ———. *Early Canadian Children's Books, 1763–1840/ Livres de l'enfance et livres de la jeunesse au Canada, 1763–1840: A Bibliographical Investigation into the Nature and Extent of Early Canadian Children's Books and Books for Young People.* **Montreal: Amtmann, 1976. 151p.**

The author's intent was to examine what was produced and printed in Canada prior to 1840, suitable for and available to juvenile readers, even if not always intended for them. Covering titles in English and French, entered in the language of their composition, it is a bibliographical checklist rather than a work of criticism. Arrangement is in two parts: Part 1 comprises items printed or published in Canada and writings of Canadians published elsewhere; Part 2 includes items by non-Canadians relating to

Canada or the Canadian Arctic, printed or published elsewhere. The latter is a selective listing, intended to show the nature rather then the extent of the relevant publications. The former part is considered by the author, a Montreal book dealer, as "relatively extensive" after consulting published Canadian bibliographies, and doubtless benefits from the examination of examples which passed through his hands. Many reproductions of title pages serve as illustrations to the text. Because of the scarcity of works on the field, this compilation serves as a convenient tool for researchers.

11. Arbuthnot, May Hill; Clark, Margaret Mary; Hadlow, Ruth M.; and Long, Harriet G. *Children's Books Too Good to Miss.* **New York: University Press Books (Press of Case Western Reserve University), 1979. 87p.**

The latest in a long list of editions by Arbuthnot, her collaborators, and successors (E/S 1945–75, p. 7), this respected selection of an "irreducible minimum of choice books" retains the same purpose and arrangement, with a slight change in the order of the editors. With the removal of out-of-print titles and the addition of fresh ones, 211 books that "every child should be exposed to and helped to enjoy" are listed and provided with a paragraph of descriptive and critical comment. The preface by Arbuthnot is retained; a brief new one by Hadlow is added. The chapter on "The Artist and Children's Books" has black-and-white reproductions.

12. Archer, Marion Fuller, regional ed. *The Upper Midwest: Minnesota, Wisconsin, Michigan.* **(Reading for Young People). Chicago: American Library Association, 1981. 142p.**

One of a series of annotated bibliographies of fiction and nonfiction titles compiled for readers from the primary grades through the tenth grade, "designed to focus on the history and character of each region of these United States." Editors for each state within the area have chosen and annotated "approximately 100 of the very best books...available for each state." Criteria for choice were that books should "best portray the spirit, the vitality and diversity of each state of the region" while reflecting overall literary quality and informational accuracy. Out-of-print titles are included if still available in libraries. The annotated bibliography is divided into broad subject groups: fiction, folktales, poetry, drama and music, biography and personal accounts, and other information books. Titles are arranged alphabetically within each group, and carry a brief quotation and a full paragraph of description. Grade ranges are suggested: P for primary, I for intermediate, J for junior, and S for senior high. Supplementary unannotated lists group the titles under each relevant state. The index combines authors, titles, and subjects, and information is given on regional publishers and suppliers. As with all volumes of this series, the selection and commentary are systematic and generous. Its availability is a boon to selectors in school and young people's libraries—indeed in all libraries with local interests—as well as to the region's young people.

13. Armour, Jenny, comp. *Take Off: A Guide to Books for Students Who Are Learning Reading, Writing, Spelling, Maths, Life-Skills, Handwriting.* **London: Library Association, 1980. 180p.**

This selection for adult students with literacy problems, including young adults, inevitably includes some titles originally for children, though books have been excluded if "childish in any way." It succeeds two predecessors more limited in scope, entitled *New Readers Start Here: A Critical Evaluation of Teaching Schemes Used by Tutors of New Adult Readers,* compiled in 1975 by Margaret Redfern and in 1976 by Jean Bell. Completely revised and expanded, this compilation draws on new literacy material, good and bad, and material for teaching numeracy, life skills, and a variety of specific topics, based mainly on information supplied by British publishers. Twelve contributors, adult literacy experts and librarians, have selected almost all items from those tried out by students and tutors. Titles, including series and pamphlets, are arranged within broad subject headings or types of publication with three levels of difficulty indicated: beginners, advancing students, and nearly independent students. The evaluative annotations are intended for instructors. The source of the material makes this more suitable for British than for American users.

14. Aubrey, Irene Elizabeth. *The Animal World in Canadian Books for Children and Young People/Le monde animal dans les livres de jeunesse canadiens.* **Ottawa: National Library of Canada, 1983. 24p.**

This revised and updated version of an earlier list called *Animals in Canadian Books for Children and Young People/ Livres canadiens sur les animaux pour les jeunes,* published in 1978, gives an alphabetical listing, first of English titles and then of French titles, of Canadian publications from 1898 to date. Most are of the 1970s and 1980s, and most are about Canadian animals.

15. ———. *Canadian Children's Books: A Treasury of Pictures/Livres canadiens: Un trésor d'images.* **Ottawa: National Library of Canada, 1976. 18p.**

This selective checklist of Canadian illustrated books for children is divided into two parts: livres français and English books; each title is briefly annotated.

16. ———. *Pictures to Share: Illustration in Canadian Children's Books: Annotated Catalogue/Images pour tous: Illustration de livres canadiens pour enfants: Catalogue annoté.* **Ottawa: National Library of Canada, 1979. 32p.**

This selection, which is new, rather than a revision of Aubrey's previous title, was prepared to celebrate the International Year of the Child, and served as the catalog to an exhibition in the National Library of Canada. The text, bilingual throughout, provides an annotated listing of 119 titles, forming "a representative selection of books whose illustrations serve as a unique contribution to the field." The catalog is arranged in two historical parts, from the beginning of the history of Canadian children's literature in the 19th century to 1959, and from 1960 to the present, the latter comprising the bulk of the entries. The paragraph of annotation on each emphasizes the quality of the illustrations.

17. ———. *Sources of French Canadian Children's and Young People's Books/Sources d'information sur les livres de jeunesse canadiens-français.* **Ottawa: National Library of Canada, 1984. 18p.**

This brief list is an indispensable tool for tracking down young people's titles in this often elusive area.

18. Azarnoff, Pat. *Health, Illness, and Disability: A Guide to Books for Children and Young Adults.* **New York: Bowker, 1983. 259p.**

This annotated bibliography provides librarians and information specialists, mental health and health science professionals, educators, child development specialists, and parents and children with a guide that describes books on young people's experiences with their bodies and disabilities, hospitalization, and medical treatments. It includes 1,000 fiction and nonfiction titles published from 1960 to mid-1983, arranged alphabetically by author. Inclusion indicates approval. A paragraph of descriptive annotation, with occasional brief evaluation, also notes suggested grade level and category of publication. Additional features include a preface, a guide to use, a thematic subject guide, a title index, and a subject index from Abortion to X-Ray. Stress is laid on current terminology; i.e. "spinal disability" replaces "crippling." The selection's up-to-dateness and thorough coverage makes it helpful for all its intended audience. Librarians will find it a useful book-selection aid in this increasingly active area.

19. Bader, Barbara. *American Picture Books from Noah's Ark to the Beast Within.* **New York: Macmillan, 1976. 615p.**

The author of this substantial and detailed account of American picture books for the young from the end of the 19th century to the date of writing attempts to "identify all the picturebooks published; to examine as many as possible; and...to learn of the circumstances of their publication," and does not confine attention to the prize winners and best-sellers. Many chapters, each with full notes and references, examine influences and practices relevant to the development of picture books during the period and their varying genres of publication and also assess the contributions of significant individuals. This comprehensive study, written by a respected and well-known figure in the book world, satisfies the anticipation of both researchers and general readers in providing the best reference work to date on this intriguing area. The extent of biographical and bibliographical information facilitates research on individual authors, illustrators, and books, as the text combines readability and profuse information. Thorough title and author-illustrator indexes and a substantial subject bibliography are provided.

20. Baker, Augusta, and Greene, Ellin. *Storytelling: Art and Technique.* **New York: Bowker, 1977. 142p.**

This manual, which places emphasis on "storytelling as an oral art," is written for librarians, teachers, students, and others by two well-known storytellers and librarians, both long associated with the New York Public Library and both with previous publications in this area to their credit. The text discusses the values of storytelling, types of literature available, principles of selection, techniques of learning and telling a story, and program planning. Also included are a brief history of storytelling in American libraries and short biographical sketches of famous early storytellers. A glossary of storytelling terms is provided, and a 20-page bibliography lists sources for the storyteller. The authors' experience and skill make this a definitive contribution on the essential practices of this notable art, invaluable both to beginning students and to practicing teachers and young people's librarians. These groups will find the bibliographical references additionally valuable as a finding and buying list.

21. Ballin, Ruth; Bleach, Jean; and Levine, Josie. *A Wider Heritage: A Selection of Books for Children and Young People in Multicultural Britain.* **London: National Book League, 1980. 66p.**

Based on a National Book League exhibition, this annotated list of about 70 titles is designed to compensate for "institutionalised racism by schools and publishers" and to contribute to a "normality" where all groups will find themselves represented in strong roles in books for children and young people. The three compilers emphasize that it is a personal list, mainly of fiction, myth, and legend, but also including plays, poetry, autobiography, and biography, with a little nonfiction in a variety of genres. The criterion for choice was to find "reasonably good stories with reasonable illustrations" for an age range from five to sixteen. Titles are mainly current British publications, with a few American and Indian imports. Annotations are descriptive and critical, with an emphasis on the physical characteristics of the books. A final sentence in italics gives appropriate school age or type of library preference. Three divisions comprise books for infants and juniors, divided by age into three sections; books for junior to secondary age; and books for secondary age, divided into sections which include reggae and slavery, Caribbean writing, African writing, and books about South Africa. Although brief, the list does supply titles which will help to minimize the kind of bias in current selection that it seeks to overcome.

22. Balmer, Kathryn J. *Annotated Bibliography of Children's Literature.* **Deerfield, IL: Voices, 1979. 44p.**

This briefly annotated booklist is intended as a source for adults to use in counseling children in a reading guidance situation, when "most often, a child does not know how to select this literature on his or her own and thus requires some assistance from a knowledgeable adult." It aims to include a wide sampling of books for different interests and reading levels, though specific reading levels for the titles are not suggested. About 400 books for young people are listed, primarily for up to eighth grade, though a few young adult titles are included. Arrangement is alphabetical by author within nine broad genres from alphabet books to biography. Annotation is of the reader's note type, suitable for young people and adults. The selection provides a substantial and up-to-date list of superior titles, most being publications from the 1970s, with a few well-respected or prize-winning ones of earlier vintage.

23. Barlow, Richard. *Attitudes and Adventure.* **5th ed. (Reader's Guide, No. 12). Chippenham, England: Library Association Public Librarians Group, 1978. 60p.**

The expanded and completely revised fifth edition of this annotated selection of literature and audiovisual material for teenagers carries on the task of the previous editions of 1965, 1968, 1971, and 1974 (E/S 1945–1975, p. 146). Its objective is to serve as a useful reference tool for librarians and teachers who already have some knowledge of teenage books. Each title now carries a short descriptive and occasionally critical paragraph of annotation. The books on "Attitudes" to self and to others are arranged in 15 groups, extending from relations with the opposite sex to illness and drugs; "Adventure" has eight categories from thrillers to cult books. The two film sections include five thematic divisions and do not avoid controversial films. The rock music on record and tape is not intended to be in any way comprehensive, nor is the listing of periodicals, which includes rock music titles, leisure magazines for boys, and general interest magazines for girls. Basically a list of English publications, this includes many American titles.

24. Barron, Pamela Petrick, and Burley, Jennifer Q., eds. *Jump over the Moon: Selected Professional Readings.* **New York: Holt, 1984. 512p.**

This collection of articles, including some by well-known librarians and educationists, was a development of a "telecourse" given in South Carolina with the same title, but subtitled "Sharing Literature with Young Children." It was compiled "to expose readers...concerned with selecting for young children...to various viewpoints in order to sharpen their critical thinking skills" by including articles "that offer suggestions for introducing children to the joy of books." Twelve parts follow a plan based on children's development in reading; each contains a number of articles which usually deal with traditional genres. These mention relevant titles in the text, and some have brief unannotated lists accompanying them. While it is stated that this anthology of interesting articles can be used independently by nonprofessionals, essentially it will function best as a college-level textbook for professionals in training for education or librarianship.

25. Baskin, Barbara Holland, and Harris, Karen H. *Books for the Gifted Child.* **(Serving Special Populations). New York: Bowker, 1980. 263p.**

Taking account of one of our society's present trends of concern, this selection of contemporary literature for young people is designed to assist in choosing "books that respond to the special capabilities and promote the intellectual growth of gifted children." The scope is limited to contemporary titles mainly of the 1960s and 1970s intended for young people. Introductory chapters discuss the gifted in society, the identification of the gifted, and intellectual aspects of the reading experience. The "Selected Guide to Intellectually Demanding Books" arranges titles alphabetically by author in three gifted reading categories: beginning, intermediate, and advanced. Lengthy annotations on each title summarize contents and analyze special qualities. Titles published in Great Britain are also specified. Title and subject indexes are provided. While occasionally titles might well fit into a different one of the three categories, the overall selection is excellent in quality and suitability for this group of readers. As popular as the authors' two volumes for the handicapped, the list will be helpful for those libraries providing service to gifted youngsters both as a selection and as a reference tool. The publishers reissued it as a paperback in 1981.

26. ———. *More Notes from a Different Drummer: A Guide to Juvenile Fiction Portraying the Disabled*. (Serving Special Populations). New York: Bowker, 1984. 495p.

Written as an extension of the efforts made in the authors' previous title, *Notes from a Different Drummer* (27), to assist educators who needed access to young people's fiction relating to impairment, this continuation examines juvenile titles "written during the early critical years of the mainstreaming experiment and containing characters with impairment." The preface notes that the term "disability" is now used rather than "handicap." The first and second parts examine "Disabled People in Contemporary Society" and "The Disabled in Literature." The third part presents "An Annotated Guide to Juvenile Fiction Portraying the Disabled, 1976–1981." Three hundred forty-eight entries are arranged alphabetically by author, and carry annotations which can extend in length up to a couple of pages; a separate paragraph provides an "analysis" of the title, and reading level and disability are specified. Parameters for selection exclude sectarian press publications and stories adapted from plays and television, but include foreign publications that have U.S. distributors. Title and subject indexes are provided. This volume updates and adds to the usefulness of its predecessor in addressing this current and vital issue.

27. ———. *Notes from a Different Drummer: A Guide to Juvenile Fiction Portraying the Handicapped*. (Serving Special Populations). New York: Bowker, 1977. 375p.

Planned as a "comprehensive guide to juvenile fiction written between 1940 and 1975 that depicts handicapped characters," this annotated bibliography intended for librarians and teachers describes over 300 titles of biographical fiction and some nonfiction suitable for children and young adults. Folklore is excluded. Supporting chapters discuss society and the handicapped, the literary treatment of disability, assessing and using juvenile fiction, portraying the disabled, and relevant patterns and trends in juvenile fiction. The "Bibliographical Guide" arranges entries alphabetically by author; long annotations for each assess the literary quality and reading level, provide a plot summary, and give an analysis of how the impairments referred to are presented. Reading level designations are provided. The work was quickly recognized as an indispensable bibliographical tool in this increasingly significant field of interest.

28. Bator, Robert, ed. *Signposts to Criticism of Children's Literature*. Chicago: American Library Association, 1983. 346p.

This collection of articles has been chosen to help adult professionals recognize the qualities that are basic in good writing. Each part has an introduction by the editor. Part I, "The Domain," introduces articles by authorities on the relation of criticism to children's books: two essays deal with "Definition," eight with "Status," and fourteen with "Approaches." Part II, "The Territories," presents articles on the separate genres: three essays on picture books, four on fairy tales, three on poetry, two on fiction, three on fantasy, four on historical fiction, three on science and fiction, and four on the young adult novel. Contributors include well-known names such as Clifton Fadiman, John Rowe Townsend, Isaac Bashevis Singer, Lillian Gerhardt, Aidan Chambers, and Geoffrey Trease. While some pertinent children's titles are discussed in many of the contributions, and there is a brief bibliography of professional titles, the collection is not directed to the problem of book selection but to the nature of the literature itself. As such, there is much cogent criticism and interesting reading.

29. Bauer, Caroline Feller. *Handbook for Storytellers*. Chicago: American Library Association, 1977. 381p.

The objective of this instructional manual by a well-known storyteller is to show librarians, teachers, and others concerned "how to present literature to children, young adults, and adults through story-telling." Special emphasis is placed on the many different ways of using supportive media. Four parts cover: "Getting Started" (planning, promotion, introducing and closing programs); preparing and telling the story; sources of storytelling (narrative, poetry, nonnarrative); multimedia storytelling (pictures and objects, board stories, overheads, slides, fellowships, film and television, radio, puppetry, magic, and music); and programs, from preschool to adult, including book parties and creative dramatics. Supporting bibliographies are well selected, useful, and up-to-date. This comprehensive manual with its special features constitutes a sound and practical guide to the field.

30. Bennett, Jill. *A Choice of Stories*. (Books in the Primary School). Oxford: School Library Association, 1982. 32p.

This title is the second of three in the British School Library Association series designed to help teachers and librarians develop sound criteria and build up balanced collections that will promote and reward the reading habit among younger pupils. An introductory essay, "Much Ado about Story," leads on to the main text, arranged in three parts in continuous narrative form: "Picture Books" for the youngest and other ages; "Folk and Fairy Tales, Myths and Legends"; and "Story Books," for ages up to about twelve. Titles receive lively comment and advice on their usefulness in the text. Each part concludes with a bibliographical list of books mentioned. An appendix lists some collections of stories for reading aloud in two sections, for first school and for junior school. The over 150 mainly recent British publications constitute a well-constructed selection particularly designed for smaller British primary schools, but also suggestive to other children's libraries and parents.

31. ——. *Learning to Read with Picture Books*. (A Signal Booklist). Stroud, England: Thimble Press, 1979. 46p.

One of a useful series edited by Nancy Chambers, an editor of *Signal*, a specialist journal devoted to children's books, this list provides a full paragraph of descriptive and critical annotation for more than 100 current titles that have been successful with beginning readers from four to seven years of age; a further 150 titles receive briefer mention or citation. The objective of the selection is to help young children become readers and see books as an important part of their lives, continuing to enjoy literature as they grow up. The compiler stresses independent use and believes in using "real" books right from the start, as opposed to specially produced reading schemes. The introduction describes how she puts her ideas into practice. The list is grouped into three stages, each with its own short introduction: "First Steps," "Taking Off," and "Gaining Confidence," each of which carries a supplementary list of additional titles. The list formed the basis of a National Book League exhibit, and mainly British publications are cited; but the selection will suggest some interesting additions or alternatives to current American output.

32. ———. *Reaching Out: Stories for Readers of 6–8.* (A Signal Booklist). Stroud, England: Thimble Press, 1980. 35p.

Another title in the series, following on the author's list for four- to six-year-olds, this selects books for six- to eight-year-olds to read with pleasure. Her choice is based on experience with and response from children. Criteria for inclusion were that the books should be interesting to read, would not be off-putting, and, with one or two exceptions, be under 100 pages long. Titles are grouped into six sections: picture books, all with substantial texts; "I Can Read" type books; traditional tales; poetry and verse; illustrated stories; and storybooks. Each title is accompanied by a paragraph of description and personal assessment indicating its appeal to young readers. This is a suggestive list of good-quality titles, suitable for the intended readership.

33. Bennett, Jill, and Chambers, Aidan. *Poetry for Children.* (A Signal Bookguide). Stroud, England: Thimble Press, 1984. 40p.

This volume in a series edited by Nancy Chambers, editor of *Signal* magazine, covers a wide range of poetry books currently published in both hardback and paperback; these are British "trade" editions, educational publications being omitted. Over 120 titles are listed as main entries, together with recommendations of further titles in the annotations. The compilers chose the books either as suitable for up to eight-year-olds, such as nursery rhyme collections, picture books, and younger anthologies, or to be recommended for use by nine- to fourteen-year-olds. The arrangement is by genre, each grouping with its own paragraph of introduction. The well-written annotations, some brief and some longer, are critical more than descriptive and are directed to adults. Compiled by experienced teachers who have lectured and written on children's literature, this is a quality selection which will be useful to teachers and will be a valuable aid for collection building in British young people's libraries. It will also suggest supplementary choices for North American use.

34. Bernstein, Joanne E. *Books to Help Children Cope with Separation and Loss.* New York: Bowker, 1977. 255p.

This extensive annotated bibliography is meant to serve as a one-volume "reference book," which not only describes books in which young people grieve over separation and loss, but also provides advice on their use in bibliotherapeutic situations. The preface and Part 1, "Using Books to Help Children Cope with Separation and Loss," provide an overview of the problems and the role bibliotherapy can play, with references and comments on previous relevant studies, in addition to explaining the selection criteria and arrangement. Part 2 constitutes the "Annotated Bibliography for Young People," comprising over 400 titles, mainly of the 1970s, arranged in genre groupings. Critical and descriptive annotations are provided which indicate interest level and reading level in accordance with the Fry Readability Graph. Part 3 lists selected reading for adult guides. Indexes are provided for author, title, subject, interest level, and reading level. The volume was the first publication in its specific field to contain such an extensive bibliography. The titles are carefully selected for young people and remain valuable.

35. Bettelheim, Bruno. *The Uses of Enchantment: The Meaning and Importance of Fairy Tales.* **New York: Knopf, 1976. 328p.**

Written by a venerable and respected psychoanalyst whose writings outside this field are well known to the American public, this is fundamentally a treatment of fairy tales from a psychoanalytical point of view. Through analyzing their basic meanings and indicating their appropriateness at certain stages of child development, he conveys a powerful message about their value in the upbringing of children. Chapters, which refer to many individual tales, discuss "Fairy Tale versus Myth," "The Child's Need for Magic," "Transformations," "Bringing Order into Chaos," "Oedipal Conflicts and Resolutions," "Fear of Fantasy," and "On the Telling of Fairy Stories." Notes to each chapter recommend further readings, and a brief bibliography lists the fundamental sources of fairy tales. Originally published for the popular reader who is also a serious student, the book also provided a definitive rationale for folktale and storytelling and thus attracted much attention from teachers, librarians, and storytellers. English editions were published in the same year by Thames and Hudson as a hardbound and by Penguin in paperback. Random House in New York also increased its availability by issuing it as a Vintage paperback in the following year.

36. Bingham, Jane, and Scholt, Grayce. *Fifteen Centuries of Children's Literature: An Annotated Chronology of British and American Works in Historical Context.* **Westport, CT: Greenwood, 1980, 540p.**

The purpose of this compilation is "to provide a single annotated chronological listing of significant or representative books written for or used with or appropriated by British and American children from the 6th century to 1945." The compilers disclaim an elaborate mode of operation and have selected from secondary sources, stating that their main attempt has been to synthesize rather than to judge the worth of works included. For prolific authors primary entry has been made for a significant or first popular title. The listing is chronologically divided into six time segments: 523–1099, 1100–1499, 1500–1659, 1660–1799, 1800–1899, and 1900–1945, with some added titles up to 1969. Each of these periods is placed in context by a description of the historical background, literary developments, and contemporary attitudes toward children and the treatment of children. Additional features include a bibliography of secondary sources, a chronology of children's periodicals, some information on relevant rare-book collections, and a list of facsimile and reprint editions. There are a number of line and half-tone illustrations. Indexing is thorough, including authors, illustrators, translators, printers, and publishers, and a title index comprising 9,700 entries. The authors' interpretation of the history and social attitudes that surround the titles cited is informative and original, though somewhat indebted to the classics in the field, such as Darton and Smith. The very numerous citations to books in the chronology and the index are a most valuable feature of the work, making it a very useful reference tool for researchers.

37. Bisshopp, Patricia. *Books about Handicaps for Children and Young Adults: The Meeting Street School Annotated Bibliography.* **East Providence, RI: Rhode Island Easter Seal Society, 1978. 64p.**

This annotated list, funded by the Rhode Island Department of Education, was planned as a "means of raising readers' awareness about the true nature of handicapping conditions and improving attitudes towards handicapped persons." Intended readers seemingly include teachers, librarians, social workers, parents, and others interested. The 171 fiction and nonfiction titles cover material suitable for pre-K children through to young adults, and can be used to present to handicapped young people situations and characters with which they can identify. They are arranged by author within seven groups of handicapping conditions: deafness and hearing impairment, blindness and visual impairment, orthopedic handicaps, mental retardation and brain damage, learning disabilities, speech problems, and emotional dysfunction. Annotations give critical evaluations, which emphasize a realistic approach to the handicapping condition and literary quality, and include a recommended age level. The appendix contains an author-title index and a list of titles available in paperback. Titles received too late to evaluate are briefly listed at the end. Some of the books annotated receive a "Recommended" or "Not Recommended" rating, which is an especially helpful feature in this valuable selection of well-analyzed titles.

38. Blostein, Fay. *New Paperbacks for Young Adults: A Thematic Guide/New Paperbacks for Young Adults: A Thematic Guide 2.* **Toronto: Ontario Library Association, 1979, 1981. 127p., 149p.**

Both these annotated lists of recent Canadian and American paperbacks for young adults were compiled from a couple of years' issues of a similar title's monthly selection prepared for the Metro Toronto News Company, a paperback distributor. The first part of each volume is intended to "suggest to librarians and teachers ways of looking at the titles...and discussing them with young readers," and lists the titles under appropriate thematic headings. The second part is an alphabetical listing by title, each with a brief descriptive annotation, within three age groups: twelve to fifteen, twelve to eighteen, and sixteen to eighteen. There is a supplementary list of award-winning titles which are also identified in the text.

39. Bodart, Joni. *Booktalk! Booktalking and School Visiting for Young Adult Audiences.* **New York: Wilson, 1980. 249p.**

A guide for young-adult librarians and others concerned, this account of the art of book talking combines a "how-to-do-it" section with a substantial bibliographic commentary on suitable titles. The principal list of titles, chosen as being stimulating for young adults, is arranged alphabetically, with each entry accompanied by a long annotation which describes the content and indicates how it can be used in practical situations. Supplementary bibliographies are provided for junior and high school use. Two lists are provided for junior high, including hi/lo items, and 15 genre and subject lists for high school, each numbering from 20 to 30 items. Most are publications of the 1970s. An additional list is appended of "Books Someone Thought Were Easy to Booktalk," compiled by Alameda County (CA) young-adult library staff members. The guide has come to be regarded as the standard on the subject by practitioners and professional schools, and the supporting choices of books remain current and cogent. A supplementary volume, *Booktalk! 2. Booktalking for All Ages and Audiences*, appeared in 1985.

40. Bogart, Gary L., and Isaacson, Richard H., eds. *Junior High School Library Catalog.* **4th ed. (Standard Catalog Series). New York: Wilson, 1980. 939p. Supplements: 1981, 1982, 1983, 1984.**

First published in 1965, when it was split off from the *High School Catalog*, this basic tool for collection building in school libraries reached a second. edition in 1970, and a third in 1975 (E/S 1945–75, p. 155). As with its companion volume in the series, the *Senior High School Catalog*, to which it is similar in plan and features, the five-year cycle of editions includes annual supplements. Selection, made by an advisory committee with the aid of consultants in different regions of the United States, is planned to cater to grades seven through nine, "encompassing the period of early adolescence...." Out-of-print books have been excluded. Part 1, the Classified Catalog, includes over 3,750 titles, and the supplements each add some 400 titles to this total. These are arranged by the abridged Dewey classification, and have one or more paragraphs of annotation, usually selected from standard reviewing sources. Over 9,000 analytical entries, arranged in a single alphabet with author, title, and subject entries, make up Part 2. This substantial and carefully chosen selection, with its regular updating and its convenient information for processing, has come to be an indispensable tool for school libraries. Designed to be considered a basic collection, its real merits could be a danger in themselves; for like its older cousin, its use as a principal source for a collection, to the exclusion of other ways of locating less "standard" titles appropriate for particular groups of students, would constitute less than adequate practice for building a vigorous school library. As it is designed for American schools, and chosen from American publications, it will be substantially less useful in the Canadian situation. Since efforts have been made in recent editions to minimize duplication between the volumes in Wilson's *Standard Catalogue Series*, junior high librarians are advised to use this title in conjunction with the *Senior High School Catalog* (**41**) and the *Children's Catalog* (**184**).

41. ———. *Senior High School Catalog.* **12th ed. (Standard Catalog Series). New York: Wilson, 1982. 1,299p. Supplements: 1983, 1984.**

With a long history stretching back to 1926, when the title read *Standard Catalog for High School Libraries*, this familiar and indispensable tool for the building of core collections by school librarians reached its tenth edition in 1972 (E/S 1945–75, pp. 58–59). Two years before the ninth edition appeared in 1967, the book had been split into separate volumes for senior and junior high schools. The eleventh edition of 1977, edited by Bogart and Karen R. Carlson, discontinued the separately available Roman Catholic Supplement. But otherwise, the eleventh edition and the current twelfth edition followed closely the pattern of their predecessors, both in the arrangement of the basic volume and in the provision of annual supplements, supplied as part of the service to update the information up to the time of the next edition. Titles are voted in by a group of experienced librarians from a list of books compiled by an advisory committee of consultants. Both these groups are drawn from all regions of the United States. Out-of-print books have not knowingly been included. The first part consists of the basic list of over 5,000 titles, and the annual supplements each add about 500 to this total. These are arranged by the abridged Dewey classification, and have one or more paragraphs of annotation, usually selected from standard reviewing sources. Over 15,000 analytics, arranged in a single alphabet with author, title, and subject entries make up the second part. Ease of use and the provision of criticism, as well as cataloging and ordering information and regular updating, have made this high-quality and continuing selection a favorite tool. All school libraries should, however, be prepared to supplement its choices from other sources of titles appropriate for their own students which are unlikely to be regarded as "standard" for most American schools. For Canadian school libraries, it will necessarily be inadequate as a principal source of a core collection, because of its minimal representation of Canadian publications and books of Canadian interest.

42. Bracken, Jeanne, and Wigutoff, Sharon. *Books for Today's Children: An Annotated Bibliography of Non-Stereotyped Picture Books.* **Old Westbury, NY: Feminist Press, 1979. 33p.**

This list of almost 200 picture books, most of which were published from 1972 to 1977, seeks to provide a critical guide to good titles that avoid stereotyped attitudes, show a wider range of life-styles and more varied images than usual, and present "encouraging examples of humanistic multidimensional characters." Emphasis is given to "the best of alternative press publications which reflect innovative themes and challenge established formulas." Recommended titles meet the compiler's criteria for nonsexism. Items 1–51 are highly recommended; 52–143 are recommended; 144–171 are recommended with some reservations; and 172–193 are not recommended. Each title carries a couple of sentences of descriptive and critical annotation written in a direct style. In addition to an author-title index, there is a subject index which includes "working mothers, handicaps, contemporary grandparents, multiracial titles, single parents, sensitive males, adventurous females, adoption, peer-relationships, and more!" The good coverage including harder-to-find alternative press titles makes this a useful selection tool for those libraries that need to find a place for the unstereotyped presentations that are beginning to be a feature of publishing for children.

43. Bracken, Jeanne; Wigutoff, Sharon; and Baker, Ilene. *Books for Today's Young Readers: An Annotated Bibliography of Recommended Fiction for Ages 10–14.* **Old Westbury, NY: Feminist Press, 1982. 52p.**

This successor to the first two authors' picture-book selection for younger children annotates 73 recommended fiction books chosen with the professional aid of a librarian for an older group of readers. Each is a "good, readable story with sensitivity to stereotype in regard to gender, race, ethnicity, age, class, sexual preference, and physical and mental capability." Seven chapters, each with a preliminary discussion, deal with ten or so titles related to a developmental theme, such as "peer friendships." Paragraphs of annotation directed to adult counselors are devoted to plot and theme. Appropriate age levels are suggested. This small but noteworthy list includes current well-respected titles, and is valuable for librarians and educators to use for collection building and reading guidance.

44. Bratton, Jacqueline Susan. *The Impact of Victorian Children's Fiction.* **London: Croom Helm, 1981. 230p.**

This study is intended to describe and evaluate "the flood of fiction for children which was written during the 19th century with the intention of conveying moral instruction." It investigates who wrote, published, sold, bought, and read these books, and why, and assesses what the readers learned from them. Chapters describe the educational background, the critical approaches, the development of juvenile publishing and children's fiction from 1800 to 1850, the evangelical tradition, books for boys, books for girls, and change and decay at the end of the century. Most major and influential writers of the period receive critical attention. A number of titles are mentioned in the text, but the bibliography is confined to a selection of relevant critical and historical works, intended as an introductory guide to students. While many titles discussed are already well recognized, this study will serve as useful background reading for the student or serious reader. An American edition was issued in New York by Barnes and Noble in the same year.

45. Brewton, John E.; Blackburn, G. Meredith, III; and Blackburn, Lorraine A. *Index to Poetry for Children and Young People, 1970–1975: A Title, Subject, Author, and First Line Index to Poetry in Collections for Children and Young People/Index to Poetry for Children and Young People, 1976–1981: A Title, Subject, Author, and First Line Index to Poetry in Collections for Children and Young People.* **New York: Wilson, 1978, 1984. 471p., 320p.**

Successors to the 1972 volume covering 1964–1969 (E/S 1945–75, p. 17), these additions to the series initiated in 1942 each index over 100 more recent collections of poetry for young people. As with the previous volumes, the titles indexed were chosen through vote by consulting librarians and teachers throughout the United States, bearing in mind the interests of very young children, those in elementary school grades, and junior and senior high school students. Arrangement is in a single alphabet including author, subject, title, and first line. Books indexed have been analyzed and graded. These volumes continue a standard and indispensable reference set for young people's librarians, teachers in elementary and secondary schools, and others concerned with finding poems for children and young adults. In addition, the collections selected constitute a useful list for collection building.

46. Briggs, Nancy E., and Wagner, Joseph A. *Children's Literature through Storytelling and Drama.* **2d ed. Dubuque, IA: Brown, 1979. 201p.**

First published in 1970 by the second author (E/S 1945–75, p. 182) and then covering storytelling alone, this new edition contains an enlarged treatment of creative drama and a chapter contributed by various authors on creative approaches to storytelling and creative drama. The story index includes selections for preschoolers and is now both graded and alphabetized. An appendix contains an evaluation form for college students to use with the books suggested. Still directed to students in speech instruction and other areas who are seeking titles and ideas, the improved organization in this enlarged edition makes it also more useful for teachers and librarians among its intended audience.

47. Broderick, Dorothy M. *Librarians' Guide: Young Adult Paperbacks.* Revised and updated by Mary K. Chelton. New York: New American Library, 1982. 48p.

First published in 1977, this short guide by one experienced young-adult librarian, here brought up-to-date by another, comments on the reading preferences of this age group with frequent references to popular authors and books, and in addition offers practical advice on the promoting of paperbacks in the library. The titles referred to in the text are all significant, and there is a bibliography of more than 100 titles, the majority published by this company. A short list of relevant bibliographic references and addresses concludes this useful pamphlet.

48. ———. *Library Work with Children.* New York: Wilson, 1977, 197p.

Originally planned as a revision of her earlier title, *An Introduction to Children's Work in Public Libraries,* 1965, (E/S 1945–75, p. 18), the preface to this title states that a rereading of the original convinced the author that in view of the changes in society and her own opinions, the text needed to be rewritten as a new book. Addressed to librarians, teachers, students, and anyone who works with youngsters through to twelfth-grade age, the book is divided into two parts: "The Collection" and "Library Services." The first includes chapters on building a collection, selection standards, and sex and sexuality in children's books; the second on the child in the library, programs for children, the library in the community, areas related to work with children, and continuing professional education. Supplementary material gives the text of official statements by the American Library Association's Children's Services Division and the Association for Library Service to Children on the reevaluation of children's material and intellectual freedom for minors, and provides two bibliographical lists, one of adult monographs and periodical articles, arranged by author within such categories as child development, and the other of 50 children's titles discussed in the text. Footnotes and index entries give further references. The author's well-known acerbic wit and keen intelligence are evident in many of her opinions and statements. These enhance a plain-spoken text that is good reading, especially for nontraditional practitioners, and would-be practitioners, of library service to children.

49. Brown, Christopher Richard. *Kentish Tales.* Maidstone, England: Kent County School Library Service for the School Library Association, Kent Branch, 1976. 37p.

This selection of books set in one of the better-known English counties mainly comprises fiction written for children, though there are some adult titles suitable for children. A number are of more than local interest. There is quite lengthy annotation and an index to the localities connected with the stories.

50. Brownhill, Sue. *Starting Point.* **3d ed. London: National Book League, 1979. 56p.**

This annotated booklist, designed primarily for adult illiterates, was first published in 1975 (E/S 1945–75, p. 150), with a second edition in 1977, both being selected by Betty Root and Sue Brownhill. The introduction to this revised edition states: "Inevitably this list has still to be selected largely from books written for children, albeit teenagers and young adults." The lengthy critical annotations on each item, including many series, are intended for teachers. The list provides an access point for British publications which are useful for young adults with reading difficulties.

51. Buckinghamshire County Library. *Guide to Reference Books for Middle Schools.* **Aylesbury, England: The Library, 1981. 26p.**

Similarly arranged to the same county library's selection for secondary schools, this short annotated list caters to the reference requirements of students from eight to twelve years of age.

52. ———. *Guide to Reference Books for Secondary Schools.* **Aylesbury, England: The Library, 1982. 26p.**

First published in 1980, this clearly presented selection by local librarians and teachers is intended to help school librarians select a good basic collection of accurate and up-to-date reference books in the traditional sense, mainly for the twelve to sixteen age group. Titles are in-print British publications, with a few American ones, arranged within broad subject groups in Dewey order, with brief descriptive annotations.

53. ———. *Seven to Nine: Stories for Younger Readers.* **Aylesbury, England: The Library, 1982. 36p.**

Revising a list first published in 1980, the compilers of this British selection—local children's and school librarians—made a thorough assessment of currently available stories for seven- to nine-year-olds, to help parents and teachers choose books that appeal to children at the "in-between" stage of reading development. One hundred sixty-five titles judged lively, interesting, and well written each receive a brief descriptive annotation, and most receive a sentence of critical comment.

54. ———. School Library Service. *Outstanding Fiction for Young People, 1970–1976.* **Aylesbury, England: The Library, 1978. 29p.**

Planned to help teachers and parents select or suggest good modern fiction to be read and enjoyed by young people from about ten to fifteen years of age, this carefully annotated booklist includes many titles which will be enjoyed by the more adult. Originally compiled from the county's annual list of suggestions for the Carnegie Medal, with some additions originally published outside Great Britain, all selection has been reassessed in the light of children's reception of the books.

55. Bush, Margaret, and others. *Storytelling: Readings, Bibliographies, Resources.* **Chicago: American Library Association, 1978. 16p.**

The chairperson of an ad hoc committee of the Association for Library Service to Children and her colleagues prepared this minimal selection of "materials that will help storytellers learn the craft and identity and locate good stories," including books, articles, recordings, films, and videotapes. Arrangement is under three categories: "Background Reading, Listening and Viewing"; "The Art of Storytelling"; and "Sources of Stories." The last section can barely skim the surface, but items cited are traditional and proven to be worthwhile. With the exception of the inevitable dating of the audiovisual material, this remains a helpful basic beginning list.

56. Butler, Dorothy. *Babies Need Books.* **London: Bodley Head, 1980. 190p.**

Written in the firm belief that books should play a prominent part in children's lives from babyhood, the author of this carefully structured selection seeks to persuade parents and other adults that access to books, through their guidance, will greatly increase a child's chances of becoming a happy and involved human being. The introduction discusses how to introduce books to babies, and which books, and when. Succeeding chapters pose the questions "Why Books?" and "Too Little to Look?," and are followed by year-by-year analyses from age one to age four to five, with a concluding chapter, "Now We Are Six." Interspersed are relevantly chosen lists of titles, carefully matched but with no apology for personal favoritism. Most of these titles carry descriptive and critical comment, and others are mentioned in the text, explaining ways that they can be introduced. All were used with children by the author. The great majority of the titles are British or American publications in English; some are translations. Originally addressed to interested lay persons, this book has been widely adopted by librarians, many of whom have always shared the viewpoint of the author. For a ready reference list of titles for very young children, this list has gained preeminence. An American edition was published by Athenaeum in the same year, and an English paperback reprint was issued by Penguin in 1982.

57. ———. *Cushla and Her Books.* **London: Hodder, 1979. 128p.**

Based on a thesis describing how a personal book-based compensatory program was provided for a child with serious developmental handicaps, this study-in-depth of one child provides not only creative ideas, but also a substantial bibliographical element useful for those who deal with children in similar circumstances. Excellent full-size color and black-and-white illustrations supplement the text, which analyzes many titles and their usefulness. Chapters follow chronologically from birth to three years and nine months. One appendix codifies the child's reactions to individual books, and another lists over 100 titles in her library, grouped according to the age when they were introduced to her. An American edition was published by Horn Book in the following year.

58. ——. *Reading for Enjoyment for 0 to 6 Year Olds*. 5th ed. Cranleigh, England: Baker Book Services, 1984. 32p.

This series of informal guides designed to help parents choose books for their children was initiated by the National Book League in 1970. Divided into age groups, and selected by children's literature specialists from current British publications, all editions maintain retrospective interest. Each was based on one of the League's traveling exhibitions. In 1970 the division for two- to five-year-olds was selected by Elaine Moss, with a second edition in 1975 and a third in 1977; and the division for six- to eight-year-olds by Brian Alderson, Joan and Alan Tucker taking over that age group in 1975 and 1977 (E/S 1945–75, pp. 126, 176). The present compiler prepared the division for this age group in the completely new fourth edition published in 1981. The fifth edition, as was the fourth, is based on Butler's *Babies Need Books* (**56**), about 100 titles being selected from the 400 cited there. A brief introduction offers guidance to parents and relates young children to various genres of publications. Many of the recommendations are old titles rather than new, though all were in print. The list is grouped into alphabet books, number and counting books, nursery rhymes, songs and jingles, titles for the youngest children, traditional stories, collections, and poetry. Brief annotations are descriptive and critical. This is a limited but quality British selection. In this fifth edition, the companion volume for seven- to eleven-year-olds was prepared by Vivien Griffiths (**141**), and for twelve-year-olds and up by Christine Kloet (**200**).

59. Butler, Francelia. *Sharing Literature with Children: A Thematic Anthology*. New York: McKay, 1977. 492p.

Purportedly designed for use in college classes, as a source book in libraries and schools, and for parents, this imaginative anthology of stories and other material for children includes a number of reprinted critical essays which serve as introductions to the various genres. Written by specialists in their fields, these are carefully chosen to support course work or independent study. An unannotated bibliography of reading for children is provided, and also a list of further readings for adults.

60. Butler, Francelia, and Rotert, Richard, eds. *Reflections on Literature for Children*. Hamden, CT: Library Professional Publications, 1984. 281p.

This anthology of scholarly articles about children's literature written mainly from a critical standpoint is introduced in a foreword by Leland B. Jacobs. The 26 articles by a wide variety of contributors are grouped in four divisions: "A Note on Story..." (five articles); "Some Meanings in Children's Literature" (five articles); "Poetry Can Say It Best" (four articles); and "Some Extraordinary Writers and Their Characters" (twelve articles). A number of the essays are by well-known authors and critics. The subject matter concentrates on the more famous 19th- and 20th-century figures and general themes relating to writing for children considered as literature. Bibliographic citation of children's books is limited to references in the text, but there is a selected list of anthologies of critical essays and bibliographies.

61. Butts, Dennis, ed. *Good Writers for Young Readers.* **St. Albans, England: Hart-Davis Educational, 1977. 144p.**

Fourteen critical essays make up a survey of recent British writing for children. Most were published in the periodical *The Use of English*; some appear originally here. Thirteen are articles on individual authors, from Joan Aiken to Ivan Southall and Rosemary Sutcliffe, by contemporary British critics of the field, such as Edward Blishen, Peter Hollindale, and Winifred Whitehead. The remaining essay by Dennis Sanders is an examination of British picture books since 1960. All include a list of books mentioned and there are useful supplementary lists at the end of the volume. The introduction puts the essays in focus by commenting on critical principles applied to children's literature. The book is a very readable collection of perceptive assessments on some of the best children's authors currently writing in Great Britain.

62. Cadogan, Mary, and Craig, Patricia. *You're a Brick, Angela. A New Look at Girls' Fiction from 1839 to 1975.* **London: Gollancz, 1976. 397p.**

A scholarly, historical, and critical survey of the extensive and influential fiction written especially for adolescent girls in the last 150 years, with particular attention to the popular series which started to flourish in Great Britain at the end of the last century. American books are noted and compared if they attracted a large readership in Great Britain. Thorough critical assessment is made of the major figures, such as Angela Brazil, and the "near-classics" are analyzed for their literary values as well as for their place in the social context of their time. A wide variety of titles is discussed in the text and these are also cited in a concluding bibliography. A short bibliographical list of relevant critical and historical works is included. This carefully reasoned and entertaining study is an important contribution to the knowledge of this significant sex-differentiated body of literature.

63. Campaign to Impede Sex-Stereotyping in the Young (CISSY). *Non-Sexist Picture Books: Compiled and Produced by CISSY, Campaign to Impede Sex-Stereotyping in the Young.* **London: Women in Print, 1979. 28p.**

Four women experienced in teaching, bookselling, and library work examine here what is wrong with picture books, which they find in general blatantly sexist. The introduction voices a demand for fantasy and picture books that present possibilities of adventure and excitement for girls as well as for boys. The bibliography in two parts includes mainly British publications of the previous 20 years, only a few exceptional picture books from outside Great Britain being included. The first part lists 33 positively nonsexist books which are essentially enjoyable for young children; these can be recommended without reservation as showing the potential for both sexes, or as actively challenging conventional depiction of males and females. The second, longer, part lists about 100 books arranged in three sections: "unstereotyped females; unstereotyped males; and undifferentiated males and females." These are considered worth reading from a nonsexist point of view, but with reservations which are brought out in the descriptive and critical annotation. The titles cited in both parts could function as an aid for selection—or rejection—but others appropriate to the topic have been published since on both sides of the Atlantic.

64. Canada. Indian and Eskimo Affairs Program. Education and Cultural Support Branch. *About Indians: A Listing of Books.* **4th ed. Ottawa: Minister of Indian and Northern Affairs, 1977. 400p.**

First published in 1973 with a second edition in 1974 and a third in 1975 (E/S 1945–75, pp. 20–21), this bibliography has been compiled for teachers, librarians, and others interested, but particularly "to create in young persons an early awareness of some of the complex problems faced by Indians in North America today." The features of the third edition are maintained, as is the excellent production with its attractive layout and numerous color pictures. In several ways this is one of the best bibliographical references dealing with North American Indians. Since Indian cultures are often artificially divided by political boundaries—both in reality and in many reference works—the many entries covering Indians as a whole make this work an important source for American as well as Canadian libraries, good for general readers as well as for a juvenile audience.

65. Carlsen, G. Robert. *Books and the Teenage Reader: A Guide for Teachers, Librarians, and Parents.* **2d rev. ed. New York: Harper, 1980. 290p.**

This influential and much-consulted guide first appeared in 1967, with a second edition in 1971 (E/S 1945–75, p. 23.) The updated version reflects comparative changes of interest in teenage reading. New chapters include literature by and about women, drama, and science fiction and fantasy; chapters dropped are reading for the college-bound, ethnic experiences in literature, and a guide to reference books. The bibliographies were compiled by a nationwide team of librarians including prominent practitioners such as Dorothy Broderick and Regina Minudri, the latter the compiler of the science fiction and fantasy list. Other bibliographical features include an appendix of bibliographical tools and sources and a basic list of paperbacks. The overall selection of titles is extensive and excellent, and keeps the new edition a convenient and current source, useful for all types of users.

66. Carlson, Ruth Kearney. *Enrichment Ideas.* **2d ed. (Literature for Children). Dubuque, IA: Brown, 1976. 166p.**

This examination of the variety of purposes which literature can serve in the curriculum was first published in 1970 (E/S 1945–75, p. 24). Essentially similar to the first in purpose and organization, this edition contains "more ideas...and more suggestions for using literature to enrich each facet of the curriculum", and suggests numerous ways in which children can interact with an author. The five chapters each contain bibliographies for children and for adults. The helpful index of activities is increased and there are some new emphases, such as on oriental poetry, controversial books, and loneliness. Children's titles cited are relevant and are good choices for the use of teachers.

67. Carpenter, Humphrey, and Prichard, Mari. *The Oxford Companion to Children's Literature.* **Oxford: Oxford University Press, 1984. 586p.**

This encyclopedic dictionary follows the tradition of the Oxford Companion series of reference books in covering all aspects of its field in a large number—here nearly 2,000—of medium-length and short entries which blend factual information with scholarly criticism. The genesis of this volume lay with Iona and Peter Opie, to the latter of whom it is post-humously dedicated by the authors, who have followed their example of writing all the articles, rather than compiling contributions by outside experts. The authors' preface explains that coverage extends from the beginnings to May 1983 and that the original intent to center on British and American children's literature has been modified to cover the literature of foreign countries more briefly, not confining the latter to those works naturalized in the English-language environment. The alphabetical sequence of articles includes country and period surveys; genres; a very strong biographical representation covering authors, illustrators, and others concerned with the production of children's books; and also characters and important individual works, usually with a brief plot summary or description. Very many other titles are mentioned in other articles. Cross-referencing is full and systematic. Well over 100 small, functional, and appropriate illustrations are provided, though it is not primarily an illustrated book. There is no index to supplement the alphabetical arrangement of the text entries. Although there are not separate supplementary biographical listings of titles, collection builders will find it useful because of both the selectivity and the comprehension provided in the text. While such use would be particularly appropriate for an historical collection, the authors' choice of current authors is shrewd and not parochial. This volume lives up to the publisher's reputation for one-volume reference tools that are equally useful for the scholar and the researcher, for teachers and librarians, for the general reader, and for students of all ages from the secondary level up. It succeeds in being an interesting and entertaining book in itself, a book to own and read, as well as an essential reference tool.

68. Carr, Jo, ed. *Beyond Fact: Nonfiction for Children*. Chicago: American Library Association, 1982. 224p.

This collection of essays, all reprinted, was chosen to stimulate interest in nonfiction writing for children and to explore the meaning of quality in nonfiction writing for them. The scope includes informational writing for kindergarten through eighth grade, and the focus is on trade books to the exclusion of textbooks. The authors, largely but not exclusively American, including widely known figures such as Zena Sutherland, N. Hentoff, and Margery Fisher, present varied themes to adult audiences, mainly on subject areas, but some on current issues. The editor contributes several essays and a short but enthusiastic preface, countering the denigration of the value of nonfiction writing. Five essays address "Nonfiction Writing: Books as Instruments of Intelligence"; seven, "Science and the Excitement of Discovery"; five, "History: The Past Realized, Remembered and Enjoyed"; five, "Biography: Facts Warmed by Imagination"; and seven, "Controversy: An Active Healthy Skepticism." Many of the articles discuss recommended books, and further references can be found in the concluding notes, but as there is no index to these titles, bibliographic access is restricted. Appendices list awards for nonfiction and professional books and journals. The selection is well chosen and thoughtful; the contributors share a high quality of writing and bring informed critical judgment to present their views of "the best." Well worth reading now, in the future the collection will be a valuable document for research into current attitudes.

69. Carroll, Frances Laverne, and Meacham, Mary. *Exciting, Funny, Scary, Short, Different, and Sad Books Kids Like about Animals, Science, Sports, Families, Songs and Other Things.* **Chicago: American Library Association, 1984. 193p.**

This annotated bibliography emphasizes fiction and nonfiction for second to fifth graders, but contains a few titles suitable for up to a maximum range of eighth grade. Picture books are almost totally omitted. Almost 1,200 titles that librarians can suggest in answering children's requests for books are listed in a unique and special arrangement that the compilers designed to provide a format that could express "our ideas on how to entice children to read the popular books recommended by librarians." Thirty-five main topics are subdivided into almost 80 areas of interest, and are geared to children's typical inquiries. The lists of titles in each associated group were submitted by practicing librarians, and the short annotations are original and written in a popular style. The majority of books are hardbacks from the 1970s with some from the early 1980s and a few earlier titles from the 1950s and 1960s, all recently in print. Inclusions are popular with youngsters. This practical presentation provides a useful and practical tool for librarians and others, such as parents, particularly in responding to the constant inquiry for another book just like one previously enjoyed.

70. Cass, Joan E. *Literature and the Young Child.* **2d ed. Harlow, England: Longman, 1984. 130p.**

First published in 1967 (E/S 1945–75, p. 26), the second edition carries a short introduction by Anne Wood, editor of *Books for Young Children* magazine. The author, an educationist and social worker well known in Great Britain for her books for children, has written here for parents and teachers, and "in fact anyone who reads and tells stories and poetry to young children, or who shares the delights of picture books with them." She has tried to show what children about two to seven want to enjoy. Chapters discuss genres of publication with a new chapter on nursery rhymes, another new chapter on storytelling, and some practical points; there are also five stories to tell. A bibliography of about 100 titles for young children represent her selection of books "which not only possess quality but are also ones they will like." Most have stood the test of time and, it is suggested, should be a part of every boy's and girl's experience. All are British publications, though not necessarily of British authorship. There are supplementary lists of background books about children. This brief guide is enhanced by attractive style and presentation. Written from a British point of view, its ideas will be of interest to North American readers, as will be the careful selection of British titles.

71. Caughey, Margaret, ed. *Children's Choices of Canadian Books. A Practical Guide to Canadian Children's Books, Prepared by Parents and Children for the Benefit of All Who Want to Know More about What Is Worthwhile and Appealing to Canadian Children.* **3 vols. Ottawa: Citizens' Committee on Children, 1979, 1981, 1984. 89p., 119p., 167p.**

This project by a private citizens' organization was prepared to draw the attention of concerned Canadians to good Canadian books currently published for young people. Carefully collated reader input by many children of different ages and both sexes is incorporated in the annotations. Titles initially selected by professionals are grouped in six categories according to popularity, ranging from those enjoyed by 90% and over of the respondents to those not generally enjoyed. Each volume is indexed, with a cumulative index in the third volume. Canadian children's books have not been sufficiently recognized inside or outside the country, and these well-organized and attractively presented lists make critical assessment available for about 700 titles.

72. Cech, John. *American Writers for Children 1900–1960*. (Dictionary of Literary Biography, v. 22). Detroit: Gale, 1983. 412p.

A bibliographical and biographical dictionary planned to present a representative and comprehensive view of the range of writers who played vital roles in creating "Childhood's Golden Era" in American children's literature. Almost all writers and illustrators included produced their most famous work prior to 1960. Introduced by a concise overview of the period, the alphabetical arrangement of entries for each author provides a photograph, a list of works, and a text giving some biographical information, more descriptive information about the books, and critical comment, original and quoted. The selection of authors is full and appropriate, making this bibliographically oriented reference tool most appropriate for the literary researcher, but, as many of the authors are still alive and their books in print, it will also serve as a suggestive source for current selection as well as for retrospective development.

73. Chambers, Aidan. *Introducing Books to Children*. 2d ed., completely revised and expanded. Boston: Horn Book, 1983. 223p.

First published in 1973 (E/S 1945–75, p. 27), this edition has been fully revised and the contents reorganized. It is still written for teachers and librarians, especially for beginners in those professions, and "for anyone who is concerned about how to help children grow into avid, willing, enthusiastic readers of literature." The author, an experienced teacher as well as a literary critic of children's books, attempts to take a straightforward and practical look at ideas, methods, and varying approaches which bring books and young people into contact. Four parts examine "Why Literature?," "The Reading Environment," "Time to Read," and "Response." New material is presented about criticism and about children's responses to what they read. This British contribution remains a sound guide to introductory reading. A British paperback reprint was published by Heinemann in 1984.

74. ———. *Plays for Young People to Read and Perform*. (A Signal Booklist). Stroud, England: Thimble Press, 1982. 82p.

The cover title adds that the plays are "considered as literature as well as theatre." This critically annotated guide to plays written for and performed by young people lists over 80 plays and collections. Both professional theatrical productions and theater intended for the educational field are covered. An historical introduction outlines theatrical, educational, and publishing developments and places children's theater in the context of children's literature as a whole. Arrangement is in four progressive sections, each with an introductory note. "Touchstones of Quality" establishes critical attitudes and prescribes an order of reading age suitability. "Starting Where

Young People Are" suggests plays which make an immediate appeal and which are suitable for performance by the less experienced. "Going On" comprises the main body of titles, and is divided into plays for younger ages (eight to fourteen) and plays for older ages (fourteen to eighteen). "Adaptations" lists plays originally in book form or from other media. Not all the plays are recommended, but rather form a selection from the range and nature of plays available that would have a place in a comprehensive collection. Full annotations vary in length from a paragraph to a couple of pages, and combine description with personal criticism, often offering comparisons with other titles. In addition to bibliographic information, reading age, performing age, time of performance, and casts of male and female characters are noted. A final short list for adult specialists includes four books and a magazine for those professionally involved. This "first time study" by a drama teacher and author of children's plays presents appropriate titles originally selected for a National Book League exhibition. It also contributes significant literary criticism about a relatively unexplored field.

75. Chambers, Dewey W. *The Oral Tradition: Storytelling and Creative Drama*. 2d ed. (Literature for Children). Dubuque, IA: Brown, 1977. 102p.

This title in a series under the general editorship of Pose Lamb was originally published in 1970 as *Storytelling and Creative Drama*. The objective is the encouragement and stimulation of oral literature in the form of storytelling, by providing a "how to" manual, primarily for teachers. The text is divided into two parts, "Storytelling" and "Creative Drama." Chapters in Part 1 discuss "The Oral Tradition," "Guidelines in Selection and Preparation," "About Technique," and "Storytelling and the Curriculum." Chapters in Part 2 cover "Creative Drama, a Natural Part of Childhood," "Getting Started with a New Technique," "Creative Drama in Action," "Analysis," and "Educational Implications." Each part has a list of selected references, and each chapter a list of "Points for Discussion" and "Things to Do." The author acknowledges indebtedness to the fourth edition of May Hill Arbuthnot's *Children and Books*. This reorganized activity guide for the classroom storyteller, though slight, is fundamentally sound.

76. Chambers, Joanna Fountain. *Hey Miss! You Got a Book for Me?: A Model Multicultural Resource Collection Annotated Bibliography*. 2d ed. Austin, TX: Austin Bilingual Language Editions, 1981. 91p.

First published in 1977, this bibliographical list of titles primarily selected to appeal to young readers, listeners, and viewers in multicultural environments was compiled to be used as a selection and cataloging aid for resource centers, public and college libraries, classroom teachers, parents, and students. Consideration for inclusion was based on educational value and the stressing of "variety of culture and language as a positive feature of a healthy world view." Representative in scope, titles were selected for children from preschool age through the middle grades. Most are in English, but some are provided in Spanish, and others in English bilingually with Chinese, French, Greek, Filipino, and Vietnamese. Brief critical annotation aimed at teachers accompanies the cataloging and ordering information, and illustration is noted. Symbols indicate language and grade level. Although many additional titles are included in this edition, as a multicultural selection aid it is still very limited in scope. However, sources are few for appropriate books in what are now necessary language adjuncts for schools and libraries in many North American regions, and within the limits of this list the recommendations will be found useful.

77. Chambers, Nancy, ed. *The Signal Approach to Children's Books: A Collection.* **Harmondsworth, England: Kestrel, 1980. 352p.**

The periodical *Signal*, published by Aidan and Nancy Chambers, aims to provide a forum for people with ideas about and interests in literature for children, where they can write at greater length than is possible in reviews or brief articles. This is a selection from articles which appeared in the magazine, written by British critics who are looking at the literary and social values of today's writing for children, rather than offering practical advice to teachers, librarians, or parents. Contributors include John Rowe Townsend, Alan Tucker, Irene Whalley, and Jay Williams; Elaine Moss's article, "The Seventies in Children's Books," may be singled out for special mention. A short biographical note on the author precedes each article. The keynote of the anthology is thoughtful consideration of children's books, their authors, and their illustrators. An American edition was published by Scarecrow in the same year.

78. Child Study Association of America. *Children's Books of the Year.* **New York: The Association. 1930– . Annual**

With variant titles and edited by several committees under a number of chairpersons, this selection from the previous year's children's publications has appeared for over 50 years (E/S 1945–75, p. 23). Since 1980 it has been jointly issued with the Bank Street College of Education. Its purpose has remained essentially the same, "to help parents, teachers, librarians, and others find their way through an overwhelming number of new books" by selecting those "which reflect positive values in facing life's difficulties, triumphs and aspirations." The volunteer selectors include parents, writers and illustrators, and specialists in related fields, besides teachers and librarians. Their annual choice of recent years has numbered 500 titles from some 3,000 considered. Arrangement is by title within age group—from nursery age through thirteen—and genre categories. Some titles are specified as easy to read, and books of outstanding merit are starred. Annotations are brief. Selected by a sensitive and concerned group, the current list constitutes a useful buying tool, and perusal of previous selections over the years is of value for retrospective collecting and research.

79. ———. Children's Book Committee. *Reading with Children through Age Five: A Selected Book List.* **3d ed. New York: Bank Street College, 1980. 44p.**

First published with a slightly different title in 1970 in cooperation with Project Head Start, a second edition appeared in 1972 (E/S 1945–75, p. 30). In this third edition, a selection of new and recently published books have been added and many long-loved titles retained. The primary audience of parents remains the same, and the committee members' long experience with children's books and with parents' concerns for their children lies behind the philosophy and criteria for choice. Arrangement is by title grouped within informal topics, such as "About Children and Families" and "Inexpensive Books," with a brief annotation for each book. The selection is a solid one, trustworthy for parents. If by chance librarians and teachers do not already know the majority of titles, it can serve as a finding list for staples.

80. Children's Book Council. *Children's Books: Awards and Prizes.* **New York: Children's Book Council, 1981. 215p. Biennial.**

This volume of the title, now discontinued as a biennial, is essentially the same as the previous editions in 1969, 1971, 1973, 1975 (E/S 1945–75, p. 94), 1977, and 1979. The series has been regarded as an official list of major international and foreign book awards and all those located in English-speaking countries, including organizational and publishers' prizes. Only those child-selected awards are listed "in which young voters representative of a whole state or province or more than one state have participated." In this edition, discontinued awards have been dropped and others added to show a slight overall increase. Since its inception the book has been a boon to librarians and other concerned individuals, the gap caused by its loss was temporarily filled by Dolores B. Jones's *Children's Literature Awards and Winners* (**189**). All editions retain major research value for historical reference. However, a major revision of the Council's list appeared in 1985.

81. Children's Books International. *Proceedings and Book Catalog.* **Boston: Boston Public Library, 1976–78. Annual.**

The proceedings of these international meetings, managed by the staff of Boston Public Library, contain many references to children's authors, illustrators, and books in the papers given and their accompanying bibliographic lists, though the phrase "book-catalog" was dropped from the title with the third number. Many of these citations would be difficult to locate elsewhere.

82. Children's Rights Workshop. *Sexism in Children's Books: Facts, Figures, and Guidelines.* **London: Writers and Readers Publishing Co-operative, 1976. 56p.**

The Co-operative's Paper No. 2 is a collection of introductory articles on sexism in children's literature. Paper No. 1 appeared in 1975 (E/S 1945–75, p. 145). The introduction refers to relevant guidelines developed by some publishers. Four articles discuss sex-role socialization for preschool children, sexism in award-winning picture books for preschool children, sex roles in reading schemes, and the McGraw-Hill guidelines. Strong criticism is voiced by this British group about a problem which is only beginning to be remedied. While a few titles are cited in the text, there is more attention given to matters relating to general principles.

83. Christensen, Jane, and others. *Your Reading: A Booklist for Junior High and Middle School Students.* **New ed. Urbana, IL: National Council of Teachers of English, 1983. 764p.**

Having a long history as a well-pedigreed selection for junior high schools sponsored by one of America's most prestigious educational associations, with previous editions appearing from 1946 to 1975 (E/S 1945–75, p. 183), the new edition with its slight change of title was prepared by the Council's

Committee on the Junior High and Middle School Booklist, correspondingly renamed, which consisted of seven teacher members and three Council officers, chaired by Jane Christensen. Entries have increased to over 3,000 and only include appropriate titles published from 1975 to 1983, so there is no duplication of choice with the previous edition. Fiction, over half the total, takes priority in the arrangement, subdivided by type of situation or genre, such as "Family Situations" and "The Supernatural," followed by other creative writing and collections. The nonfiction is arranged in an informal subject breakdown, followed by an "Information Please" section and author and title indexes. Entries, alphabetical by author within the section, carry a paragraph of lucid descriptive annotation with relevant curricular emphasis, addressed to and often contributed by students of the age bracket eleven to fourteen. The "Introduction to the Student" is written to them directly and gives intructions for use. For the teachers and librarians in school libraries who will use most copies, this substantial annotated bibliography remains a standard source; in fact all libraries for young people can find a use for this thorough selection tool.

84. Cianciolo, Patricia Jean. *Illustrations in Children's Books.* **(Literature for Children). 2d ed. Dubuque, IA: Brown, 1976. 210p.**

Essentially the same as the first edition, which appeared in 1970 (E/S 1945–75, p. 31) as one of the publisher's series for elementary school teachers, this edition updates material and adds new sections on surrealism and naive art. Included are a finely selected bibliography of quality illustrated books and a useful briefer one of professional readings. The black-and-white illustrations are well chosen, if not outstanding. This revision of her elementary text maintains the author's reputation as a specialist in the field.

85. ———. *Picture Books for Children.* **2d ed., revised and enlarged. Chicago: American Library Association, 1981. 237p.**

First published in 1973 (E/S 1945–75, p. 32) with the assistance of a committee, this major revision by the now sole author carries over a few titles from its predecessor and makes 1980 the cut-off date for inclusion. The new introduction "explores the values and uses of the variety of picture books being produced today, examines and describes current trends in styles of writing and illustration for picture books, and discusses criteria for evaluating them." While the age range for the books' audience remains the same, from three to sixteen years, the selection of over 700 entries has been "categorized to reflect the basic concerns of all people regardless of age and culture." Within such categories as "Me and My Family" and "The Imaginary World," arrangement is alphabetical by author, and each title receives a paragraph of descriptive and critical annotation. Full indexing includes authors, illustrators, translators, publishers, and titles, and the 36 illustrations are apposite and well reproduced. Valuable reading for students of the variety of artwork in children's books, the titles also form a splendid current basic list of picture books.

86. Ciani, Alfred J., ed. *Motivating Reluctant Readers.* **Newark, DE: International Reading Association, 1981. 104p.**

Of the nine articles in this compilation, six were first presented to professionals at the Association's 1978 convention. They represent "views on many facets of why some youngsters refuse to read and what may be done to get them to want to read" and provide "suggestions for working with those students who function at a frustration level." Articles are included on "Building Language Experiences," "Home Remedies," "Motivating through the Top Twenty," "Recent Adolescent Literature," and "Book Sharing." Titles discussed in the text and listed in the bibliographies at the end of each chapter are those familiar to teachers and librarians and will be suggestive to the specialist student.

87. Clark, Catherine, and Widutis, Florence, eds. *Books for New Age Children and Youth.* **College Park, MD: Beautiful Day Books, 1977. 47p.**

An annotated booklist chosen to aid parents, teachers, and librarians, in the hope that they will "help children to become citizens of the New Age we all hope for." About 200 titles ranging in date from 1856 to 1977 are reviewed by Pam Atherton and others. Age recommendations are provided and especially recommended titles are starred. The reviewers' perception of the "best of the best" in children's books in over a hundred years makes for an eclectic selection which will be familiar to teachers and librarians.

88. Cline, Ruth K.J., and McBride, William G. *A Guide to Literature for Young Adults: Background, Selection, and Use.* **Glenview, IL: Scott, Foresman, 1983. 200p.**

Primarily a textbook for library school and other students, this guide addresses general issues and describes types of publication, rather than discussing individual titles. Some chapters, such as "A Brief History of Literature for Young Adults," "Contemporary Literature for Young Adults," and "Literature in Other Disciplines," have citations, and there is a lengthy account of comic books and strips.

89. Clish, Douglas. *Teaching Science.* **London: National Book League, 1979. 69p.**

This exhibition catalog of pupil-oriented books selected and annotated by the compiler was arranged with the aim of helping teachers to find the specific science teaching areas in which they are interested. Eight sections, corresponding to areas of modern school science, are divided into sub-sections according to age or level in the British school system, with minimal attention to the under-nine age group. "Course books" are emphasized. Items carry a paragraph of descriptive annotation directed to the teachers.

90. Colwell, Eileen. *Storytelling.* **London: Bodley Head, 1980. 83p.**

The distinguished British storytelling specialist offers this account as a very personal contribution based on her own experience for over 40 years. Chapters discuss: "What is Storytelling?," "Storytelling Then and Now," and "What Shall I Tell?" for preschool children and for five- to twelve-year-olds;

concluding chapters mainly emphasize the "how-to-do-it." The stories are discussed in the text, and the booklist of about 100 titles—mostly British publications—indicates the sources of those mentioned, rather than forms a comprehensive list of recommended books. Colwell's reminiscences and comments make this an original and valuable contribution.

91. Commire, Anne, ed. *Something about the Author: Facts and Pictures about Contemporary Authors and Illustrators of Books for Young People.* **Detroit: Gale, 1971– .**

Extended to 36 volumes by the close of 1984, this continuing series (E/S 1945–75, p. 35) documents the lives and works of the authors and illustrators of children's books, primarily but not exclusively from English-speaking countries. They include less prominent figures. The emphasis is on detailed factual information, incorporating much autobiographical material. Illustration is plentiful, and is not confined to portraits. There have been slight changes of objectives and coverage over the years. The original primary direction to a young audience has been expanded to serve librarians, teachers, students, researchers, and parents. With volume 15, following the discontinuation of *Yesterday's Authors of Books for Children* (**92**), major writers who had died before 1961 received entries. Volume 25 began numerous revised entries for authors previously included. A brief entry format, not precluding the appearance of the usual full form, was introduced in volume 27. Obituaries are a regular feature, and each volume carries cumulative indexes. The series has become an increasingly valuable tool. Both researchers and younger readers will not find an adequate substitute for locating the minor facts and figures that do not find their way into more discriminating reference works.

92. ———. *Yesterday's Authors of Books for Children: Facts and Pictures about Authors and Illustrators of Books for Young People, From Early Times to 1960.* **2 vols. Detroit: Gale, 1977–78. 274p., 335p.**

Begun as a continuing series as a companion to the publisher's series *Something about the Author* (**91**), which was then confined to authors still living in 1961, only two volumes appeared before that series absorbed coverage of the earlier period, from 1979 onward. Associate editors were Adele Sarkissian and Agnes Garrett. Each volume covers between 30 and 40 authors who died before 1961, giving primary attention to those who are still being read by children. Children and students of children's literature were the intended readership, and the style is designed to be interesting to read. Entries, arranged alphabetically, give thorough overviews of careers and personal information, usually with extensive quotations of an autobiographical nature. The authors' works are listed in chronological sequence, and further bibliographical references are noted. The many illustrations aid the comprehensive presentation and include portraits as well as pictures relative to the books or to an author's background. Movie stills figure on occasion. Both volumes are indexed, the second cumulatively. Full and scholarly as these are as far as they extend, complete benefit for reference purposes will require consultation of the companion series.

93. Commonwealth Institute. *Commonwealth Children's Literature* **(Checklists on Commonwealth Literature). London: The Institute, 1979. 56p.**

This annotated checklist is based on the holdings of the Institute and was originally selected for a joint exhibition with the National Book League. Areas covered include Africa, Antarctica, Asia, Australia and New Zealand, Canada, the Caribbean, and Oceania. The 500 titles exhibited have been increased to about 850, mainly local publications published during the 1960s and 1970s. Some audiovisual material is included. Because bibliographical information is hard to locate for many of the smaller territories covered, this is a valuable source.

94. Coody, Betty. *Using Literature with Young Children.* **3d ed. Dubuque, IA: Brown, 1983. 239p.**

First published in 1973 (E/S 1945–75, p. 35) with a second edition in 1979, this third edition of an introductory textbook for prospective teachers adds new features. Fifty extra reviews of books suggested for classroom use have been added to the more than 250 in the second edition; new chapters are included on poetry experiences, holidays, and puppetry, besides the second edition's additional coverage of reading aloud, creative writing, art projects, bibliotherapy, and other topics. Treatment of the parental role in storytelling is expanded, and Dorothy Butler's *Cushla and Her Books* (**57**) is reviewed in relation to bibliotherapy. The final chapter discusses the selection and use of children's books, including hints on how parents can help. It provides a cogent chart on "Books and Concept Development" up to the age of six. The bibliographies of related professional books at the end of each chapter have been updated. Appendices include a list of Caldecott awards and an author, title, and subject index. This textbook for teachers will also be useful for introductory courses in childhood education.

95. Coody, Betty, and Nelson, David. *Teaching Elementary Language Arts: A Literature Approach.* **Belmont, CA: Wadsworth, 1982. 390p.**

This teaching aid is a useful reference for college students, elementary school teachers, and librarians. The authors state that books for children can and must become an integral part of the language arts curriculum. Procedures for teachers are discussed in 12 chapters that cover the language arts program, including poetry, drama, and folklore. At the end of each chapter, children's books are listed and reviewed, and a bibliography of further reading for the professional is provided. The children's titles that are listed are adequate for the purpose of the book, but fall short of the quality and comprehensiveness required for library selection. The book will best serve the librarian as a liaison between the language arts classroom and the library.

96. Cook, Elizabeth. *The Ordinary and the Fabulous: An Introduction to Myths, Legends and Fairy Tales.* **2d ed. Cambridge, England: Cambridge University Press, 1976. 182p.**

First published in 1969 (E/S 1945–75, p. 36), this plea for the value of myth and legend for children has a revised and enlarged booklist in its second edition, which includes "some of the important writing for children that has appeared in the genre since 1968." The text has not been materially altered from the first edition, but the author notes that "a fabulous storyteller has different obstacles and opportunities" six years later and comments on new literary trends. Valuable both for background and recommending titles for library selection, this account has become a standard on both sides of the Atlantic since its original appearance. However, it does demonstrate an age difference in prescribed reading preferences between British and American children; to the former, myths are recommended up to fourteen years; in America they are made a speciality of a younger age.

97. Cott, Jonathan. *Pipers at the Gates of Dawn: The Wisdom of Children's Literature*. New York: Random House, 1983. 327p.

Well known as editor of the periodical *Rolling Stone*, the author brings his obvious delight in children's literature to describe his "reflections and encounters with six extraordinary creators of children's literature and a man and woman who studied it." They are Dr. Seuss, Maurice Sendak, William Steig, Astrid Lindgren, Chinua Achebe, P.L. Travers, and the Opies, Iona and Peter. His discussions and interpretations combine many conversational asides with sociological and psychological insight. His own personal views are reflected in his sensitive, autobiographical introduction, which leans heavily on the examples of William Blake, Carl Jung, and C.S. Lewis. Significantly, his title is taken from *The Wind and the Willows*. Six pages of bibliographies include each of the books of each of the authors interviewed. This is interesting and entertaining writing, set down with a scholarly charm. It was reprinted in London by Viking in 1984, and in 1985 McGraw-Hill published it in paperback format in New York.

98. Crago, Maureen, and Crago, Hugh. *Prelude to Literacy: A Preschool Child's Encounter with Picture and Story*. Carbondale, IL: Southern Illinois University Press, 1983. 294p.

This account of the ways in which one child experienced and responded to the picture books and stories she met between the ages of twelve months and five years offers the opportunity of commenting more generally on preschool children's interactions with books. A number of titles are examined, some closely, in the text, and there is a selected bibliography of those mentioned.

99. Croft, Ann. *Wales*. (Storylines, No. 9). Birmingham, England: Library Association Youth Libraries Group, 1977. 16p.

This short annotated booklist is one of the Group's series of pamphlets presenting books for young people about particular places in the British Isles and periods in their history. Some 70 English-language titles have been selected to present as broad a picture of Wales as possible, particularly to readers outside the country. Five categories cover myths, legends, and folktales; fantasy; contemporary fiction; historical fiction; and background information books. The brief descriptive annotations include some age recommendations.

100. Crosland, Alan. *North American Indians.* **(Pamphlet No. 16). Birmingham, England: Library Association Youth Libraries Group, 1975.**

An annotated list of over 60 titles, including some audiovisual material, about Native Americans north of Mexico, excluding Inuit, chosen for young people's librarians, teachers, and others. Arrangement is by region, culture, and tribe followed by sections on biography, crafts, folklore, and Indian wars. Criteria for choice were authenticity, presentation, and illustration. A short paragraph of descriptive annotation on each item gives age recommendations. British and American imprints are included, with a number of out-of-print books. The selection of books, although limited, is well made and provides a useful topical list for young people for both sides of the Atlantic.

101. Crouch, Marcus, and Ellis, Alex, eds. *Chosen for Children: An Account of the Books Which Have Been Awarded the Library Association Carnegie Medal, 1936–1975.* **3d ed. London: Library Association, 1977. 180p.**

First published in 1957, with a second edition in 1967 compiled by Marcus Crouch (E/S 1945–75, pp. 37–38), this account of the titles that won the most prestigious of British library awards for children's literature has been brought up to 1975. The two sections on earlier winners to 1965 have not been revised, but the new editor has given a general account of developments over the decade and has followed the same formula for each new title—a critical note on the book and the author, an extract from the text, a description of the book, how it came to be written, and an illustration in black-and-white. Small portraits of the winners are provided. The list of winners will serve as a useful selection source for large or retrospective American collections wishing to include the best of British children's books over the years.

102. Cullinan, Bernice E., and Carmichael, Carolyn, W., eds. *Literature and Young Children.* **Urbana, IL: National Council of Teachers of English, 1977. 180p.**

This collection of 11 essays, four of them by the editors, was compiled to emphasize the value of literature for the young and to illustrate aspects of children's literature apposite to early childhood education programs. The editors were chair and associate chair of an NCTE Committee on Literary Experiences for Preschool Children, which assisted in the compilation, as did consultant readers Charlotte Huck and Eileen Tway. Chapters designed to share experience of the effects of good literature on children discuss various aspects of the relationship of young children and books, such as "Illustrated Books in the Life of the Young Child" and "Children's Legacy: Avoiding Sex and Race Stereotypes in Children's Books." Each chapter appends a list of references to children's books and professional readings. Nearly 40 illustrations supplement the text. A final list of "100 Best Books for Young Children," which the editors found "most popular with children," is accompanied by brief annotations. Addressed by specialists to professionals, this volume makes interesting reading, and the excellent, though limited, selection of titles recommended is valuable for teachers and parents.

103. Cullinan, Bernice E.; Karrer, Mary K.; and Pillar, Arlene M. *Literature and the Child.* **New York: Harcourt, 1981. 594p.**

This substantial textbook is primarily addressed to an audience of elementary school teachers and librarians, educational specialists, those training for one of these professions, and parents. The scale and objectives can be generally related to the pattern established by Arbuthnot's *Children and Books.* The authors take a "child-centered approach," and within this parameter "discuss outstanding books of yesterday and today, and offer ways they can be introduced to readers through creative interaction." They also outline a comprehensive activity-based literature program appropriate to children at the nursery, elementary, and junior high school levels. The text is divided into three parts. Part 1, "The Child," includes chapters on "The Study of Literature for Children," "A Historical View of Children and Books," and "Expanding Language through Literature." Part 2, "The Books," devotes a chapter to each of seven major literary genres. Part 3, "The Child and the Books," examines "Literature and Children with Special Needs," "Using Books in the Classroom," "A Literature Curriculum," and "Issues in the World of Children's Books." Children's books mentioned in the text are listed at the end of each chapter, and there is a list of professional readings. Appendices include awards, selection aids, books on authors and illustrators, publishers, and holiday and birthday lists. Though not written for the sophisticated reader, for the audience envisaged this is a sound and competent expository text, and the children's books cited are generally important.

104. Cullinan, Bernice, and Weiss, M. Jerry, eds. *Books I Read When I Was Young: The Favorite Books of Famous People.* **New York: Avon, 1980. 192p.**

This collection of famous people's favorite titles was initiated as a project of the Commission on Literature of the National Council of Teachers of English. Students chose the famous people in a national survey, selecting each as "a central personage taking an admirable part in any remarkable action or event, a person regarded as a model." Those chosen on this basis were each asked to name three books or authors who had influenced his or her life. The alphabetical arrangement of the subjects usually includes a photograph, brief comments, and a signature. It is interesting to note that of the celebrities chosen, authors, actors, and politicians responded most frequently. Titles selected were read mainly between the ages of ten and eighteen, and the list is liberally sprinkled with then popular series books and traditional classics. For the librarian, they are a motley collection of usually predictable authors and titles. The real value of the project may be for teachers, who will use the results of this student survey to stimulate other students.

105. Culpan, Norman, and Waite, Clifford. *A Symposium, Variety Is King: Aspects of Fiction for Children.* **Oxford: School Library Association, 1977. 173p.**

The editors have selected relevant periodical articles considered to be of lasting value from a wide variety of British and American journals, primarily for working librarians and teachers, as well as for a wider readership. A number were reviewed or noticed in the *School Librarian.* This collection makes more readily available and permanent some useful and significant contributions to the field. Eight groups present: "A Mixed Diet," "Reading and Development," "Roughage—Comics," "More Roughage—Books," "Writing for Children," "The Illustrator's Contribution," "Young Adult Novels," and "Reviewing Children's Fiction." The authors include Gillian Avery, Edward Blishen, Aidan Chambers, Clifton Fadiman, Rumer Godden, Margaret Meek, and Nicholas Tucker. It makes interesting reading for American librarians, as well as for the intended British audience of most articles. The valuable booklists appended to many of the articles have been brought up-to-date, but the lack of an index is a hindrance to use for collection building.

106. Daniel, Elouise. *A Treasury of Books for Family Enjoyment: Books for Children from Infancy to Grade 2.* **Pontiac, MI: Blue Engine Express, 1983. 122p.**

This annotated booklist of young children's titles is addressed to parents. The author's introduction stresses the importance of family reading. Three sections are each divided into a number of topical lists: (1) "Basic Books for Family Enjoyment"; (2) "Books for Special Interests," with many holiday-related lists; and (3) "Special Interest Books for Adults." Arrangement is alphabetical by author within these subdivisions. This is an inspirational list, composed by the author during a period of chemotherapy and encouraged by teacher friends. The choice reflects her commitment to the practice of parents reading to and with children, and there are some accompanying photographs which illustrate this. The titles will also be suggestive for teachers and librarians who assist this age group.

107. Darton, F.J. Harvey. *Children's Books in England: Five Centuries of Social Life.* **3d ed., revised by Brian Alderson. Cambridge, England: Cambridge University Press, 1982. 398p.**

One of the major accounts of English children's literature, a milestone when first published in 1932 and revised in 1958 (E/S 1945–75, pp. 41–42), has here been fully and systematically revised by a leading British scholar in the field. Both substantial alterations and minor amendments have been made throughout the text, and supplementary information, including an additional chapter of notes on Victorian and Edwardian books, has been supplied in the appendices. The editor's notes give a "miscellany of editorial asides" and there are numerous footnotes, mainly bibliographical. An extensive bibliographical element has been provided; additions have been made to Darton's brief booklists at the end of each chapter, particularly for later periods, and at the end of the book a more formal bibliography of works on the history of English children's books has been provided. Critical biographical and bibliographical material on Harvey Darton himself has not been forgotten. Alderson's own erudite and stylish contribution has been blended with Darton's classic original so as to form a scholarly work that is both delightful to read and invaluable for reference by all serious and interested students, and has confirmed the work as an authoritative and indispensable work in the field.

108. Davis, Enid. *A Comprehensive Guide to Children's Literature with a Jewish Theme.* **New York: Schocken, 1981. 177p.**

Prepared for those who relate to Jewish young people from preschool through junior high, as professionals or otherwise, this annotated guide attempts both comprehensive listing and critical recommendation. To be included, fiction had to have good characterization and an interesting plot, contain an appreciable amount of Jewish content, be available either through purchase or loan, and be appropriate for the age range; nonfiction had to be lucid, well organized, accurate, and relevant in providing information on Jewish life and history. Some textbooks written in an accessible style are included for subjects where trade publications are lacking, as are some adult-market books in areas where young people's literature is scarce. Chapters, each with the compiler's comments, cover the Hebrew alphabet, the Bible, biographies, fine and domestic arts, history, holidays, fiction, folktales and anthologies, music and dance, theology, and multimedia. Entries, arranged by author, carry annotations which are primarily descriptive and age recommendations. Citations to reference books follow each chapter; appendices give acquisition information; author, title, and subject indexes are provided. Creditably combining coverage and selectivity, this bibliography will be a helpful source to librarians, not only in Jewish institutions, but also in public or school libraries in communities with substantial numbers of Jewish young people.

109. De Montreville, Doris, and Crawford, Elizabeth D. *Fourth Book of Junior Authors and Illustrators*; **Holtze, Sally Holmes.** *Fifth Book of Junior Authors and Illustrators.* **New York: Wilson, 1978, 1983. 370p., 357p.**

These two volumes are supplements to the publisher's long-established reference series (E/S 1945–75, pp. 102–03), the first volume of which appeared in 1934, and they continue its features. However, the *Fourth Book*, succeeding the *Third* of 1972, was the first to include illustrators in the coverage, who make up about a third of the entries, and the *Fifth Book* is similar. The stated objectives are to provide "young readers with a direct way of learning more about their favourite authors, and librarians and teachers with access to information that will pique the interest of children in reading." The *Fourth* has 242 sketches, and the *Fifth* has 239 sketches, of authors and illustrators who have come to prominence since publication of the previous volume. An advisory committee of specialists in children's literature which voted on the names included Britons and Canadians as well as Americans. Articles consist largely of autobiographical material, biographical sketches being supplied when that is lacking, and are usually accompanied by a small photograph and a facsimile signature. The text is followed by two bibliographical lists—"Selected Works" and "About." Cross-references are now provided in the index, rather than in the text, and indexing is provided to both current and all previous volumes. With its overall coverage increasingly full and current, the set makes a truly indispensable tool, useful to scholars but giving its most important service to children.

110. Detroit Public Library. *Books to Own: Recent Books and Old Favourites for Any Child's Bookshelf.* **Detroit: The Library, 1938– . Annual.**

This long-standing annual selection (E/S 1945–75, p. 45), recently titled *Children's Books to Own*, has presented to parents and others the considered choice of one of America's largest library systems. Because of the expertise and experience of its young people's librarians, this will also be useful as a brief checklist for small libraries elsewhere.

111. deWit, Dorothy. *Children's Faces Looking Up: Program Building for the Storyteller.* **Chicago: American Library Association, 1979. 156p.**

Suggesting guidelines and source material, this practical manual aims "to strengthen and develop skills in programming, so that telling stories to boys and girls may be more meaningful, more enjoyable." There are four parts: Part 1 gives a brief background on storytellers and storytelling, indicates selection sources, shows how to modify tales, and gives tips for tellers; Part 2 outlines six demonstration programs, each with an extensive list of citations; Part 3 explains program enrichment. Part 4, the bibliography, is arranged under five headings: the books cited in the text; authors and lists of books suitable for storytelling; books on holidays; basic sources (such as Kipling's *The Jungle Book*); and professional sources, including relevant research. This delightfully written book is full of practical pointers, models for programs, and useful bibliographical citations.

112. Dikty, Alan S. *The American Boys' Book Series Bibliography, 1895–1935.* **San Bernardino, CA: BBC Publications, 1977. 167p.**

Primarily intended as a reference source for collectors and dealers, this annotated bibliography was compiled by a private collector who formerly had edited the serial *The Boys Book Collector*, and was intended to supplement Harry K. Hudson's *A Bibliography of Hardcover Boys' Books, 1965*. Preface and introduction discuss this field of collecting. Preliminary sections list dealers and publishers. The main section records series containing 4,700 titles, a total stated by the compiler to be probably incomplete. Lists in appendices relate authors to series and publishers to series. Also reprinted is a descriptive essay by Franklin K. Matthews, author of many boys' books, entitled "Blowing Out Boys' Brains." A few poor-quality reproductions neither enhance nor limit the usefulness of this specialist bibliography, which will be helpful to rare-book librarians as well as to collectors and dealers.

113. Dixon, Bob. *Catching Them Young.* **2 vols. London: Pluto, 1977. 141p., 176p.**

A hostile analysis of conventionally sexist children's literature and its authors, some 19th century but mainly current, much of the material being identified as antisocial, if not antihuman. Intended as a literary study for all those interested, rather than as a social or psychological one, the overall aim is "to increase the awareness of what happens in children's literature, and to try to ensure that a lot of it doesn't happen any more." The examination of the ideas, attitudes, and opinions that authors convey to children through novels and stories (but not poetry or folktales) does not spare usually respected writers, such as C.S. Lewis and Richard Adams, and savages Enid Blyton. The first "synthetic" volume covers sexism ("Birds in a Gilded Cage"), class ("Snakes and Ladders"), and racism ("All Things White and Beautiful"). The second "analytic" volume carries on into the political sphere with "Comics: More EEK than TEE-HEE," "Enid Blyton and Her Sunny Stories," "Empire: Fiction Follows the Flag," and "The Supernatural: Religion, Magic and Mystification." So that readers can make informed choices, a bibliography, (the same in both volumes) lists 100 inexpensive books in print considered largely free from sex, class, and race bias, which the author believes will help children enter into a meaningful relationship with the world around them. This is divided into three age groupings—up to eight, eight to twelve, and twelve onward. A select bibliography is added of works most useful for background information. Most titles cited are British publications, and the author's criticism is more apposite to Great Britain, but some of the observations can also apply to the American scene, where sexual and racial problems surface for young people in a different way and at a different age.

114. Donelson, Kenneth L., and Nilsen, Aileen Pace. *Literature for Today's Young Adults.* **Glenview, IL: Scott, Foresman, 1980. 484p.**

This substantial textbook for teachers is designed to give a framework and background information for classes, supplying "first an introduction to young adult literature, then a history of the field, then a look at contemporary books and finally a view of the professional's role." These four parts comprise 14 chapters with thematic headings such as "Life Models" and "Of Heroes and Hopes" which suggest criteria for evaluation. Each carries an annotated list of recommended titles, beside extensive citations in the text. Concern for young adult reading is shown, for instance, in the debunking of nine myths about its nature, long treasured even in the professional field; the last of these, that "girls read about girls and boys; boys read only about boys," is confuted by examples such as *Island of the Blue Dolphin* and *Go Ask Alice.* Appendices include a book selection guide and a sample selection policy. Subject and author-title indexing is thorough. While the text is a treasure trove for professionals, its frequent bibliographic recommendations make up a valuable checklist for library selection. The second edition appeared in 1985 with the authors listed in reverse order.

115. Dorsett, Cora Matheny, regional ed. *The Mississippi Delta: Arkansas, Mississippi, Louisiana.* **(Reading for Young People). Chicago: American Library Association, 1984. 150p.**

One of a series of annotated bibliographies of fiction and nonfiction titles compiled for readers from the primary grades through the tenth grade, "designed to focus on the history and character of each region of these United States." Editors for each state within the area have chosen and annotated "approximately 100 of the very best books...available for each state." Criteria for choice were that books should "best portray the spirit, the vitality, and diversity of each state of the region" while reflecting overall literary quality and informational accuracy. Out-of-print titles are included if still available in libraries. The annotated bibliography is divided into broad subject groups: fiction, folktales, poetry, drama and music, biography and personal accounts, and other informational books. Titles are arranged alphabetically within each group, and carry a brief quotation and a full paragraph of description. Grade ranges are suggested: P for primary, I for intermediate, J for junior high, and S for senior high. Supplementary unannotated lists group the titles under each relevant state. The index combines authors, titles, and subjects, and information is given on regional publishers and suppliers. As with all volumes of this series, the selection and commentary are systematic and generous. Its availability is a boon to selectors in school and young people's libraries—indeed in all libraries with local interests—as well as to the region's young people.

116. Dreyer, Sharon Spredemann. *The Bookfinder: A Guide to Children's Literature about the Needs and Problems of Youth Aged 2-15.* **2 vols. Circle Pines, MN: American Guidance Service, 1977, 1981. 649p., 519p.**

Written for adults "who want to identify books that may help children cope with the challenges of life," this substantial reference work describes over 1,000 current children's books in the first volume, with almost 750 more published between 1975 through 1978 in the second volume. They are categorized according to more than 450 psychological, behavioral, and developmental topics of concern to children and young adolescents. Arranged by principal topics, the books are easily accessible through author, title, and subject indexes. The subject index in the second volume is expanded with contemporary topics. Bibliographical information is accompanied by annotation giving a synopsis of the book, a commentary on the theme, strengths and limitations, and a recommended reading level. Use by teachers and librarians for bibliotherapy and book selection is a primary function of this popular reference tool; but its extensive store of titles and descriptions makes it also an excellent source for other kinds of research into current children's literature. These two volumes used a "split-page" format that facilitated consultation of the indexes while leafing through the annotations. A new edition published in 1985 abandoned this peculiar format.

117. Egoff, Sheila A. *Thursday's Child: Trends and Patterns in Contemporary Children's Literature.* **Chicago: American Library Association, 1981. 323p.**

The book is an "attempt to identify and assess the main trends, features, and accomplishments of the last quarter century." It is addressed to teachers, librarians, students, and interested readers. The well-known and respected author applies her critical skills to the recent sociological era which saw a booming publication of titles for young people—over 100,000, she states in her introduction. The approach is by time period and literary genre, excluding informational books, titles in foreign languages, and all titles published before 1957. The first chapter gives a brief history of children's literature, while the remaining chapters examine children's literature from a critical viewpoint. Many titles are discussed in each chapter and also cited at the conclusion of the chapter. The book demonstrates the author's skill in discussing the literary qualities of titles and relating them to the times. The book is thoughtful reading, and makes an excellent selection tool.

118. ———, ed. *One Ocean Touching: Papers from the First Pacific Rim Conference on Children's Literature.* **Metuchen, NJ: Scarecrow, 1979. 252p.**

Based on a 1976 conference at the University of British Columbia, the papers of the guest speakers from ten different countries center around the general theme of the child and the book, usually with attention to their own areas. Divided into two parts, "International" and "Canadian Composite," the whole, perhaps inevitably in a conference format, makes a random rather than a systematic approach to the world picture. The papers are original and lively, and the distinguished international contributors often present fresh information and cite less well known local titles in the text and in the booklists which conclude a number of the articles.

119. Egoff, Sheila A., and Belisle, Alvine. *Notable Canadian Children's Books/Un choix de livres Canadiens pour la jeunesse.* **Revised and updated by Irene E. Aubrey. Ottawa: National Library of Canada, 1976. 94p. Supplements: 1975– , 1980, 1977– , 1982. 8 vols.**

The first edition of 1973 (E/S 1945–75, p. 52) was based on a National Library exhibition and was representative of significant books, in English and French, of "creative literature" for children from the early period to 1972, which were briefly annotated. The second reprints its historical essay on the development of Canadian children's literature, and continues and indexes the bibliographical selection through 1974. The supplements by Irene Aubrey, assisted by others, extend the record to 1980. All subsequent to the first edition are in typescript.

120. Egoff, Sheila A.; Stubbs, G.T.; and Ashley, L.F., eds. *Only Connect: Readings on Children's Literature.* **2d ed. Toronto: Oxford University Press, 1980. 457p.**

The first edition of this collection published in 1969 (E/S 1945–75, pp. 51–52) became successful in finding an audience not only as a textbook for students, but also with practitioners and interested general readers, because of its appropriate choice of distinguished North American and British experts to cover significant areas within the field. For the revision about a quarter of the material has been replaced and updated in order "to pay due attention to the changes in attitude towards children that have characterized the ten years from 1970 to 1980." The criteria have remained the same, "to promote interest in children's books, old and new, and to give the reader stimulating ideas and fresh insights." With 11 articles deleted and nine added, the total is now 38, arranged under five headings: "Books and Children"; "Fairy Tales, Fantasy, Animals"; "Some Writers and Their Books"; "Illustration"; and "The Modern Scene." The last contains almost all new material, including Sheila Egoff's "The Problem Novel" and "Percepts, Pleasures, and Portents: Changing Emphases in Children's Literature." Notes on the contributors, a selected bibliography, an index, and a few illustrations complete the volume. The new edition maintains the same appeal as the first to all classes of its readers.

121. Elkin, Judith Laikin. *Multi-Racial Books for the Classroom: A Select List of Children's Books.* **(Pamphlet No. 22) 3d ed., revised. Birmingham, England: Library Association Youth Libraries Group, 1980. 134p.**

First published in 1971 (E/S 1945–75, p. 52) and revised in 1976, this third edition incorporates much new material while retaining a few outstanding out-of-print titles. The objective remains to recommend to librarians, teachers, social workers, and parents worthwhile children's books, including picture books, fiction, and nonfiction that deal positively with life in a multicultural society, and also those that show the geographical, cultural, and religious backgrounds of the Indian subcontinent and West Indies factually and with understanding. There is, in addition, a short complementary section of African picture books and folktales. Annotations describe the value of individual titles and code for suggested reading levels. Publications are not only from Great Britain, but also from the United States, Jamaica, and elsewhere. This is a well-tried select list for British libraries, and, just because of the different, but overlapping, mix of minorities in North America, will offer libraries there valuable suggestions for supplementary titles.

122. Elleman, Barbara. *Popular Reading for Children: A Collection of the "Booklist" Columns.* **Chicago: American Library Association, 1976–1981. Annual.**

The children's book reviewer of ALA's important book reviewing journal has cumulated and rearranged the books evaluated in her "Popular Reading" columns into annual issues of about 60 pages each. Choices were made from her "own repertoire of books successfully used with children," with suggestions from librarians and recommendations from other selection tools. A "popularity quotient" was the foremost selection criterion, although a measure of quality was deemed necessary. Titles were suitable for youngsters in grades two to nine, with a concentration in grades four through seven, with supplementary lists covering "Light Romance" for young adults and a "Fourth Grade Connection" specifically for nine- and ten-year-olds. Each received a brief sentence of descriptive annotation and a grade level. Arrangement is alphabetical within informal subject groups, with an author-title index. The quality of selection made the annual an important listing for teachers, day-care workers and parents, and for those librarians who could not consult the regular issues of *Booklist* on a monthly basis. *Popular Reading for Children II*, covering 1981 to 1985, appeared in 1986.

123. ——, ed. *Children's Books of International Interest.* **3d ed. Chicago: American Library Association, 1984. 101p.**

Virginia Haviland first edited this list under the present title in 1972 (E/S 1945–75, p. 81) and revised it in 1978, her interesting preface to the second edition being retained here. It stems from an initial list, *Books Recommended for Translation*, issued in 1955 by the International Relations Committee of the American Library Association's Children's Services Division, and augmented annually. The third edition expands the scope of its predecessors beyond the objective of making librarians and the book trade aware of American publications for children that are suitable for translation. The present selection of 215 new titles in addition to 136 retained from the second edition were all in print at the time of publication. It now has as objectives collection development and individual reading guidance, "in the hope that teachers and librarians both here and abroad will use the bibliography to help children realize their place as world citizens." Books that "incorporate universal themes or depict the American way of life" were eligible. Titles are arranged alphabetically by author within general genre or subject sections, such as "Picture Books," "Poetry," and "The Arts." The separate age groupings of the previous editions have been omitted in favor of a single category extending to age fourteen, but age recommendations are provided with the brief annotations. The new edition is a current high-quality list, albeit limited by its selectivity, and of value both to the publishing world and to practicing librarians and teachers.

124. Fader, Daniel N.; Duggin, James; Finn, Tom; and McNeil, Elton. *The New Hooked on Books*. New York: Berkeley, 1976. 321p.

First appearing as *Hooked on Books* in 1966, with a revised edition in 1968 (E/S 1945–75, pp. 54–55), this radical reevaluation of preconceived notions about young people's reading attained a wide popularity with an audience that extended beyond teachers and librarians. The new title is, in fact, a new edition of the old which continues its emphasis on talking about ways in which to get young adults to read, and citing titles of "interest to young readers." Sections on writing and the environment for the book's program have been expanded, and a new reading list of "A Thousand Authors" has been prepared. Titles are listed under topical categories for young adults such as "career challenges." Some seem dated, e.g., Hope Newell's *A Cap for Mary Ellis*, but generally they still appeal to less interested or less able readers. A number of tables have been eliminated. The new edition does not seem so sensational, because the idea of matching paperbacks with delinquency is no longer a novel concept. But it will appeal as its predecessor did, because youngsters are still around and paperbacks are still a potentially powerful medium for them. One could hope that the quality of the choices could improve, but that may be vain as a short-term prospect. The book appeared as a Berkeley Medallion paperback in the same year, and this was reprinted in 1981.

125. Favat, F. Andre. *Child and Tale: The Origins of Interest*. (Research Report, No. 19). Urbana, IL: National Council of Teachers of English, 1977. 102p.

Sponsored by the Council's Committee on Research, this examination of children's reading interests reconsiders them within the context of fairy tales and children six to eight years old. The examination of the interest phenomenon is made by research into the interrelationship of reader characteristics and tale characteristics. The author describes his methods and his findings. Some fairy-tale titles investigated are discussed in the text, with implications for teachers, parents, and researchers. Further adult readings are listed.

126. Feaver, William. *When We Were Young: Two Centuries of Children's Book Illustration*. London: Thames and Hudson, 1977. 96p.

This anthology of illustrations is introduced by a brief history of the genre. The period covered extends from Blake to Sendak. Almost half of the over 100 plates are in color. European as well as British and American examples are reproduced, and the accompanying list provides annotations for the titles chosen. Because of the large size and good quality of the reproductions, this is a valuable selection for the student, as well as a pleasure to the general reader. It was published in hard-bound and paperback editions by Holt in New York in the same year.

127. Field, Carolyn W., ed. *Special Collections in Children's Literature.* **Chicago: American Library Association, 1982. 257p.**

First published in 1969 as *Subject Collections in Children's Literature* (E/S 1945–75, p. 59), the new edition of this directory of North American institutions with specially organized collections of children's books increases the total to 267, compared with 133 thirteen years before. It is again the project of the National Planning for Special Collections Committee of the Association for Library Service to Children. Consultants for the edition were Margaret N. Coughlan and Sharyl G. Smith, and Peggy Sullivan contributed the three-page introduction on collectors and collections. The arrangement remains similar, enabling the researcher to find collections or topics geographically or by specific name. Remaining an indispensable tool for researchers, the revision also documents the increase of interest in children's literature and bibliographic support for research in the field over the past several decades.

128. Fitzgerald, Michael J. *Reading Provision for Immigrant Pupils: Primary and Secondary.* **Reading, England: University of Reading School of Education Centre for the Teaching of Reading, 1977. 28p.**

An annotated list designed to help immigrant pupils in British schools to "read their way" into their new environment. The preface contrasts the needs and problems of immigrants with English-speaking students. Reader series from British publishers are mainly stressed. Each level, elementary (with vocabulary up to 500 words), intermediate (500 to 1,000 words) and advanced (1,000 to 2,500 words), is divided into three sections: books suitable for all nationalities and for a wide range of primary and secondary pupils; books suitable for only one nationality because of their cultural content; and suitable periodicals and selections of stories that are accompanied by tapes. Obviously chosen to be useful in Great Britain, some titles may be appropriate for schools and libraries serving young immigrants in other countries or in their lands of origin.

129. Flemming, Carolyn Sherwood, and Schatt, Donna, eds. *Choices: A Core Collection for Young Reluctant Readers.* **Evanston, IL: Burke, 1983. 554p.**

The compilers of this substantial annotated bibliography "set out to provide teachers, librarians, reading specialists, and parents with a tool to use while working with reluctant second through sixth grade readers." They regard "reluctant" readers as falling into two groups: the first consisting of children who read below their own grade level, and the second of children who get no satisfaction from reading. Three hundred sixty titles were finally chosen to meet their needs out of 700 seriously considered. Five thousand were initially considered, of which 1,400 were tested for readability level, the Spache formula being used below the fourth grade and the Dale-Chall above the third grade. Choice was purposely concentrated on general literature rather than on specific hi-lo material. Arrangement of the bibliography is in two parts: an alphabetical author sequence, and a subject sequence, the headings being adapted freely from the Sears list of subject headings and arranged alphabetically. Annotations extend to two or more paragraphs; a descriptive note, which emphasizes the action, being followed by an evaluative note, which emphasizes interest level and use. Grade notations are made for interest level and reading level, and "further search topics" are indicated. The subject section repeats the annotation, rearranging entries under each topic, divided into nonfiction and fiction. These lists will make up short subject bibliographies for professional use. Stemming from the compilers' cogent distinction between reading and interest levels a "Group Two" notation has been provided here for books considered to have great interest for children who are unsatisfied readers. Titles selected are excellent for their purpose; the compilers have drawn on recent trade publications for young-adult reading that followed the appearance in 1977 of a seminal article on the need for books for reluctant readers written by Barbara Bates for *School Library Journal*. Use as a collection-building tool might be facilitated by a conventional author-title index to the excellent subject section of the bibliography, rather than the duplication of all the entries in the author section. The cover title indicates that this is the first volume, and triennial publication is promised.

130. Fox, Geoff, ed. *Writers, Critics and Children: Articles from "Children's Literature in Education."* **New York: Agathon, 1976. 245p.**

Twenty-one contributions from the first six years of this British journal about the place of children's literature in education have been selected by a team of five, Geoffrey Fox, Graham Hammond, Terry Jones, Frederick Smith, and Kenneth Sterck, to make them more accessible. In Part 1, "Writers," individual authors consider challenges and choices in writing for children; Part 2, "Critics," is concerned with evaluation and critical discussion of children's fiction; Part 3, "Children," deals with the relation of books to young readers, suggesting methods of presentation and of deepening enjoyment and appreciation. The selection is strongest on writing for children, particularly novels, but educational and psychological aspects are also considered. Most contributors are British practitioners, including Gillian Avery, Ted Hughes, Geoffrey Trease, and Nicholas Tucker, and the essays are well written and often stimulating. First printed in the United States, the volume was issued in England in the same year by Heinemann Educational.

131. Fraser, Dorne. *Sequels.* **7th ed. Vol. 2. Junior Books. London: Association of Assistant Librarians, 1984. 108p.**

Sequels in its first four editions was a tool for adult titles only; the fifth edition of 1967 was the first with a separate section for young people's books, and the sixth edition of 1976, compiled by Frank M. Gardner and Lisa-Christine Person, gave them a separate volume. To qualify as a sequel, titles must feature the same character or groups of characters, or have a connected narrative or developing theme, or have an interior connection, usually topographical or historical. In this edition, many authors and titles present in previous editions have been omitted, as it was felt they were no longer of current interest or not easily available. An effort has been made here to give original British dates of publication. Substantially, this is a list of British books, though some American titles are included. Arrangement is by author, then by series, and then by title; place and publisher are not noted. There are very occasional notes, to show the relationship of some titles. A list of award winners has been included. A tool for British public libraries, its use would be necessarily limited in North America, though this and its preceding editions serve for occasional reference use.

132. Freeman, Judy. *Books Kids Will Sit Still For: A Guide to Using Children's Literature for Librarians, Teachers, and Parents.* **Hagerstown, MD: Alleyside Press, 1984. 210p.**

This annotated and graded bibliography of more than 1,000 recent titles for kindergarten through grade six was compiled by an elementary school librarian, and was obviously written primarily to help and encourage teachers to include creative literature for children in curricular activities within the classroom. Her introduction stresses her belief that "children's books, read aloud daily, profoundly affect children"; and she has chosen "only those books...found to be winners when read aloud." Titles are arranged in 12 sections, the first six of which contain "Read–Aloud Fiction" for grades K–1, 1–2, 2–3, 3–4, 4–5, and 5–6. These are followed by three on folk and fairy tales, two on poetry, and a final section on "Fifty Ways to Celebrate Books." Annotations for each title give short descriptions and suggestions for curricular use. A brief, but current, professional bibliography with brief annotations is added and there are author and title indexes. The advice in the two introductions relates to practical considerations and how to accomplish specific tasks and will be especially helpful to beginning children's librarians, as well as to teachers. Titles are an excellent choice within the wide general range available for this age span, and form a good checklist for selection purposes for school and public librarians.

133. Frend, Patricia M. *Junior Fiction Index.* **4th ed. London: Association of Assistant Librarians, 1981. 50p.**

First appearing in 1964, with succeeding editions in 1971 (E/S 1945–75, p. 64) and 1977, the scope of this edition has been slightly widened to cover many recently published titles designed for young readers up to the age of sixteen. Books for the under-eights are still generally excluded, as are pre-1970 out-of-print books except much used titles. Arrangement is by subject headings matching those in the *Cumulated Fiction Index*, including types of literature, such as adventure stories, and then by author and title. Publisher or date information is not provided. This simple library reference tool, mainly for current British books, fills a need in British public and school libraries. A fifth edition appeared in 1985, edited by Trevor Knight.

134. Gawith, Gwen. *Children's Paperbacks, 11–16.* **London: National Book League, for the School Library Association, 1977. 44p.**

A companion volume to Margaret Marshall's *Children's Paperbacks, 5–11,* **(240)** this booklist of nearly 200 paperbacks, selected, annotated, and illustrated by the compiler, is not oriented toward the curriculum in British schools, as its sponsorship might suggest, but is aimed to provide for "the catholicity of adolescent reading." Titles have been selected to reflect teenage interests, "absorbing stories, memorable heroes and heroines, with content that is emotionally relevant to the teenager," to cater to a wide range of reading levels and reading interests among eleven- to sixteen-year-olds. Some titles have been added for them that reach back into younger children's reading and forward into adult reading, but few of the "obvious" adult books which teenagers enjoy have been included. The criterion for the inclusion of the nonfiction titles was that they should not be textbooks but be fun to read and worth owning. A secondary aim was to recommend a basic stock for a secondary school bookshop. Publications, but not necessarily authors, are British. The arrangement is alphabetical by author, each title receiving a paragraph or two of descriptive and critical comment, usually with an age or interest recommendation. This is a stimulating selection, albeit British oriented; but because British paperback publishing for young people is vigorous and different from American, it will suggest some good additional titles to North American school and children's librarians.

135. Gersoni-Edelman, Diane. *Work-Wise: Learning about the World of Work from Books: A Critical Guide to Selection and Usage.* **(Selection Guide Series, No. 4). New York: Neal-Schuman; Santa Barbara, CA: ABC-Clio, 1980. 258p.**

This annotated bibliography represents a critical look at approximately 500 books on careers and the working world that can be read by children and teenagers. Fiction and nonfiction, dealing with specific careers or the world of work in general, including books for adults that are accessible to young people from preschool through teenage, are listed. Arrangement is alphabetical by author within related categories. Annotations are detailed and critical, and grade levels are given. Recommendations, sparingly used, are indicated by an asterisk. Titles selected are representative of the best available in the field of work, always a fundamental topic for libraries and one extremely popular in the current decade. This excellent and handy guide will help those concerned with young people's reading to meet an international societal concern.

136. Gillespie, John T. *More Junior Plots: A Guide for Teachers and Librarians.* **New York: Bowker, 1977. 253p.**

This successor to *Juniorplots,* by the same author and Diana Lembo, published in 1967 (E/S 1945–75, p. 67), remains the same in organization and in its primary purpose as a booktalking manual that provides models for booktalks. The preface states that "the need for active reading guidance by teachers and librarians appears even more acute today." Seventy-two books are analyzed here; there were 80 in the previous title. Titles selected were chosen from questionnaires administered to young adult librarians and direct consultations with teachers, librarians, and library school students, "organized under nine developmental goals associated with adolescence." Each carries a plot summary with relevant thematic material and booktalk material, with suggestions for related books and biographical material about the author. The last feature is a new addition to this volume, as is an essay on booktalking by Mary Kay Chelton reprinted from *School Library Journal.* The selection is apt and the features retain the same usefulness as in its predecessor. Both are currently valuable and have become indispensable aids for booktalking with junior high and senior high pupils.

137. Gillespie, John T., and Gilbert, Christine B. *Best Books for Children: Preschool through the Middle Grades.* **2d ed. New York: Bowker, 1981. 635p.**

A successor to the annual paperback *Best Books for Children* published from 1959 to 1972 (E/S 1945–75, p. 12), the new title first appeared as a monograph in 1978, and this revision followed three years later, with an increase in titles from about 10,000 to about 13,000. The aim is to present to librarians, teachers, and others working with children a "list of books that are highly recommended to satisfy both a child's recreational reading needs and the demands of a typical school curriculum." Ages catered to extend from preschool through sixth grade. Criteria for inclusion were availability, up-to-dateness, accuracy, usefulness, relevance, and three references in sources consulted. The majority of titles included are American trade titles of the 1970s; the second edition adds publications from 1978 to 1980 and omits out-of-print titles. The list is divided into types of publication and subject areas, arranging the numbered entries in alphabetical order by author. The bibliographic citation is followed by a brief annotation. Professionally executed under the direction of its editors, both previously practicing librarians, the formerly useful annual trade list has been transformed into a creditable and worthwhile addition to the standard sources that young people's and school libraries will keep on hand. A third edition was published in 1985.

138. Gilliland, Hap. *Indian Children's Books.* **Billings, MT: Montana Council of Indian Education, 1980. 257p.**

This annotated guide, primarily designed for teachers, lists 600 children's books chosen by Indian evaluators, who have graded the alphabetically arranged titles with symbols for five ratings, from "outstanding" to "completely rejected," which are explained in an insert. Two introductory sections describe using the guide and comment on problems when using available Indian books. Following the annotated list, supplementary sections provide a breakdown of titles by tribe, region, and subject; a list of publishers of Indian books; an author index; and appropriate maps. All these, as well as the basic title arrangement, are helpful to the searcher and reference worker unused to the idiosyncrasies of Indian nomenclature. Acquisition librarians, as well as teachers, can make excellent use of this substantial, if not exhaustive, list when building up this important area, since Native American material is hard to assess within the dominant culture.

139. Gillis, Ruth J. *Children's Books for Times of Stress: An Annotated Bibliography.* **Bloomington, IN: Indiana University Press, 1978. 322p.**

"Designed to help children and their parents cope with a wide range of emotionally stressful situations," this guide to "books in the affective area" lists 261 titles arranged alphabetically by author within seven broad subject categories, usually with subheadings. These correspond to situations encountered "from death to shyness," including terms such as anger, behavior, family, friendship, jealousy, and self-concept. The selection criteria, using accepted standards of excellence in characterization, plot, theme, style, and story, required titles to be thematically relevant, appropriate for an age group from preschool through nine years, and reviewed in standard review sources. Each entry is followed by a full paragraph of descriptive and evaluative annotation and a list identifying other relevant problem areas. Title, author, and illustrator indexes are provided. The computerized type-face offers a barrier to easy reading, but otherwise the list makes an excellent selection tool that assesses "the increasing number of books for young children dealing with the emotional aspects of a child's life." It will be helpful, as the author claims, "to teachers, parents, librarians, and others working with children in the clinical setting, classroom, or social agency," and for professional education.

140. Griffin, Barbara K. *Special Needs Bibliography: Current Books for/about Children and Young Adults Regarding Social Concerns, Emotional Concerns, the Exceptional Child.* **DeWitt, NY: The Griffin, 1984. 72p.**

The compiler explains that "this bibliography has been compiled as an instrument for professionals in their search for and acquisition of specialty books." The concerns and problems treated have been classified into 12 headings, such as "Handicaps-General," "Gifted," "Divorce-Adoption-Foster Care," and "Death and Dying." Under each, fiction and nonfiction are interfiled alphabetically by author. Factors considered in selection were appropriateness for the category, suitability for children through the teenage years, in-print status, and publication since 1980, though many titles from the 1970s were included, if they had received "wide critical acclaim" and filled a void. There seem as many books selected for the professionals as for the younger readers. Annotation is brief and includes references to review sources and a recommended interest level by grade. Titles unavailable for examination are starred. Format is looseleaf with heavy paper tabbed dividers; this is to provide "a means of maintaining currency," as the publisher plans annual update. While there is a present need for this type of resource, this aid offers much less to use with young people than the similar title published by the American Guidance Service, Sharon Dreyer's *The Bookfinder* (**116**).

141. Griffiths, Vivien. *Reading for Enjoyment for 7 to 11 Year Olds.* **5th ed. Cranleigh, England: Baker Book Services, 1984. 32p.**

This series of informal guides designed to help parents choose books for their children was initiated by the National Book League in 1970. Divided into age groups, and selected by children's literature specialists from current British publications, all editions maintain a retrospective interest. Each was based on one of the League's traveling exhibitions. In 1970, the division for six- to eight-year-olds was selected by Brian Alderson, and the nine- to eleven-year-olds by Jessica Jenkins, Joan and Alan Tucker taking over the six- to eight-year-olds and Janet Hill the eight- to eleven-year-olds in 1975 (E/S 1945–75, pp. 2, 86). The third edition with the divisions by the same editors was published in 1977. Ann Bartholemew prepared the division for seven- to eleven-year-olds in the completely new fourth edition in 1981. This fifth edition was intended to complement rather than replace its predecessor. Using quality of writing or illustration as the criterion, the compiler chose "books that can be recommended with confidence as a passport to reading" and will also capture imagination or engender enthusiasm. The introduction offers some guidance to parents and other adults who are in daily contact with children. Tastes from the hesitant beginner to the mature fluent reader are served by picture books, easy readers, poetry, folktales, classics, and contemporary novels. As in its predecessor, the list of a little over 100 titles is split into a seven-to-nine and nine-to-eleven group, and a loose age level or, rather, "level of understanding," is indicated. Lively annotation on each title is descriptive, with critical asides. This limited but quality British selection will suggest to North American libraries worthwhile overseas titles to supplement their collections. The companion selection for zero- to six-year-olds was made by Dorothy Butler (**58**), and for twelve-year-olds and up by Christine Kloet (**200**).

142. Griffiths, Vivien, and Barlow, Carole. *Ghostly Encounters.* **(Pamphlet No. 19) Birmingham, England: Library Association Youth Libraries Group, 1978. 24p.**

The compilers of this annotated selection of novels and anthologies with ghostly themes admit that there is a fine dividing line between the supernatural and time fantasy. They include titles for all ages, the majority in print. The arrangement sections novels and picture books, collections, poetry collections, and information books. A paragraph of descriptive and critical annotation, initialed by one of the selectors, indicates suitability for approximate age groups. Titles in this slim suggestive list are mainly British publications, but many will be of lively interest across the water.

143. Griffiths, Vivien, and others. *Peace at Last: Books for the Pre-School Child.* **(Pamphlet No. 24) Birmingham, England: Library Association Youth Libraries Group, 1983. 25p.**

The annotated book list of British publications for preschool children was selected by the Birmingham Public Library's Children's Services Team, in the belief that it is important that under-fives come in contact with books as soon as possible. The books are for their pleasure; the selection is as simple and uncluttered as possible. There were four criteria for choice: illustrations should be bright and clear, and suitable for the very young; sentence structure should be simple; situations should be everyday; and the stories should be such that "we ourselves" should enjoy transmitting them to the children. Arrangement is alphabetical by author; annotation gives a paragraph of description with some criticism. Some of the British titles for reading to the very young will make novel choices for North American libraries, for this is an increasingly active area.

144. Grindea, Carola, and Walter, Christopher. *Music Books for Schools: An Annotated List.* **(School Library Association Booklists). Oxford: School Library Association, 1977. 32p.**

Primarily directed to music teachers as well as librarians, this annotated list of over 200 British publications is intended to serve as a guide to borrowing as well as for buying. The arrangement groups titles into sections covering general books, composers, particular works, instruments, textbooks, Christmas, music making, and the very youngest. Each is divided into books suitable for seniors from fifteen to eighteen and "the main range" for pupils from seven to fourteen or fifteen except the last, which is split into books about music and books with music. Annotations are brief and factual, with occasional critical notes on use. This scholarly and balanced selection

provides for more mature as well as younger students, and can serve as a basic acquisitions list for school libraries.

145. Grylls, David. *Guardians and Angels: Parents and Children in Nineteenth Century Literature.* **London: Faber, 1978. 211p.**

This academic study in 19th-century literary history examines the stereotype of Victorian parents and children, and the development of thought on family relationships. It traces the growth of childhood independence as an underlying theme and indicates positive developments from the early part of the century onward. Chapters discuss parents and children, periodical articles, children's books, Jane Austen and Dickens, Butler and Gosse, and conclusions. While references to individual publications are minimal, the book contributes to the interpretation of children's literature in the 19th century.

146. Haining, Peter. *Movable Books: An Illustrated History.* **London: New English Library, 1979. 141p.**

An entertaining and lavishly illustrated study of a minor, though fascinating, genre of children's literature, which includes many early children's classics. The author's preface gives a historical introduction and the remainder of the text comments on individual items. The large oblong format permits the reproductions, many in folded and unfolded states, to be examined alongside the relevant passages. Almost all items are in English, but the publications come not only from Great Britain and America but also from color printers in France and, notably, Germany. A bibliography of titles mentioned is appended.

147. Haley, Frances; Hustleby, Susan; and McCormack, Regina. *Ethnic Studies Handbook for School Librarians.* **(Publication Series, No. 232). Boulder, CO: Social Science Education Consortium, 1978. 67p.**

This annotated booklist was designed to help school librarians identify, analyze, and select appropriate and useful ethnic studies library materials. It was developed by the Ethnic Studies Project for School Librarians at a series of workshops funded by the U.S. Office of Education Ethnic Heritage Studies Branch. These studies aimed to develop community ethnic profiles, identify print and nonprint material, produce acquisition lists, and "brainstorm" relevant ideas. An introduction, followed by a four-part evaluation questionnaire, precedes the bibliography. Approximately 1,500 entries, divided by format, are listed as suitable for use at the elementary and secondary levels. As a basic up-to-date list of ethnic studies material it will be indispensable to educators and librarians. The wealth of ethnic studies material provided will be of particular value to school librarians.

148. Hallworth, Grace. *My Mind Is Not in a Wheelchair: Books and the Handicapped Child.* **Huddersfield, England: Woodfield and Stanley, for Hertfordshire Library Service, 1978. 16p.**

A therapeutically designed selection of titles about children with disabilities. The selector has "steered clear of books with mawkish sympathy for a handicapped child" and chosen well-written and sensitive fictional and biographical books with which child readers can identify and which can provide "a pointer to all concerned." Besides mentally and physically de-

prived children, those with emotional and social disabilities have been provided for. The text is arranged alphabetically under the disabilities concerned, with the relevant titles cited and commented on within the text. There is an author index and a classified index, also under disability, which repeats the titles and notes the appropriate age range for each. This is a limited but helpful selection of British publications.

149. Hallworth, Grace, and Marriage, Julia. *Stories to Read and to Tell.* **2d ed. (Pamphlet No. 16). Birmingham, England: Library Association Youth Libraries Group; London: National Book League, 1978. 16p.**

First published in 1973 (E/S 1945–75, p. 76), the second edition of this YLG pamphlet retains some items from the previous edition and some out-of-print titles, but chiefly aims to introduce more recent and unfamiliar material which has proved successful with children of different ages from three to nine and over, and of varying abilities and interests. An increase of demand for preschool material has been provided for. Arrangement is in five sections: preschool activities, picture stories, anthologies, verse songs and nonsense, and three titles to form a storyteller's bookshelf. A paragraph of descriptive and critical annotation accompanies each of the titles, which are British publications. If filmstrip versions are available, they are noted, as is particular success with a specific age group. There is a title index.

150. Harmon, Elva A., and Milligan, Anna L., regional eds. *The Southwest: Arizona, New Mexico, Oklahoma, Texas.* **(Reading for Young People). Chicago: American Library Association, 1982. 245p.**

One of a series of annotated bibliographies of fiction and nonfiction titles compiled for readers from the primary grades through the tenth grade, "designed to focus on the history and character of each region of these United States." Editors for each state within the area have chosen and annotated "approximately 100 of the very best books...available for each state." Criteria for choice were that books should "best portray the spirit, the vitality and diversity of each state of the region" while reflecting overall literary quality and informational accuracy. Out-of-print titles are included if still available in libraries. The annotated bibliography is divided into broad subject groups: fiction, folktales, poetry, drama and music, biography and personal accounts, and other informational books. Titles are arranged alphabetically within each group, and carry a brief quotation and a full paragraph of description. Grade ranges are suggested: P for primary, I for intermediate, J for junior high, and S for senior high. Supplementary unannotated lists group the titles under each relevant state. The index combines authors, titles, and subjects, and information is given on regional publishers and suppliers. As with all volumes of this series, the selection and commentary are systematic and generous. Its availability is a boon to selectors in school and young people's libraries—indeed in all libraries with local interests—as well as to the region's young people.

151. Harms, Jeanne McLain. *Comprehension and Literature.* **Dubuque, IA: Kendall-Hunt, 1982. 146p.**

Designed to serve as a reference for classroom teachers and school curriculum development committees, and as a basis for school in-service programs, this study examines how children in kindergarten through grade eight

develop comprehension abilities through literature. Chapters cover attention, literal understanding, interpretation, evaluation, and application. The examples of the children's responses, all from actual happenings, are related to representative tasks and to experiences with literature. Suggestions can be used to supplement existing readings and language programs, or as a guide for revision. Many bibliographical references appear in the 21 appendices; while some are for professional reading, the majority contain substantial lists of children's books in areas such as contemporary poetry for children, picture books with no or minimal text, books to read aloud to older children, and literature for children in grades two and three. Most titles will be familiar to librarians. The book should be helpful to all, but especially to the teacher, parent, or librarian looking for successful titles to use with preschool children.

152. Harrah, Barbara K. *Sports Books for Children: An Annotated Bibliography.* **Metuchen, NJ: Scarecrow, 1978. 526p.**

This bibliography, designed to assist librarians and students to choose books wisely to fit their interests as well as their reading abilities, contains over 3,500 titles considered acceptable and of interest to children from preschool through grade twelve. Seventeen chapters cover individual sports or groups of sports, often subdivided into smaller "categories" such as "Frisbee." The arrangement is alphabetical by author within these subdivisions. Many of the titles carry a phrase or sentence of annotation; the numerous unannotated ones are suggested for further reading or were not available to examine. Publishers' suggested interest level is noted and titles examined personally have Fry gradings. A selected guide to appropriate periodicals corresponds to the subject divisions. Author and title indexes complete this list of sports books which were in print as of January 1977. Most titles are from the 1970s, but a few more important and available titles from the 1940s to the 1960s are included. While there are some British books listed that have American distributors, this is an American selection, as can be instanced by the miscellaneous chapter on team sports; cricket is not one of the 11 chosen, though rugby is. This extensive list, which leans toward inclusiveness rather than selectivity, is of some value currently, but fast-moving publication in the field is making it more of an historical and sociological record.

153. Harris, Linda, and others. *Conceptions and Misconceptions: Sexuality in Children's Books.* **Oakland, CA: Association of Children's Librarians of Northern California, 1978. 34p.**

This annotated booklist of both recommended and rejected fiction and nonfiction for young people is an outgrowth of an institute on "Sexuality in Children's Fiction" held in Berkeley. Chairpersons for this final choice were Linda Harris, Neel Parikh, Susan Rowe, and Holly Willett. It is designed as a selection and reevaluation tool for public and school libraries, parents, teachers, counselors, pediatricians, bookstore purchasing agents, or anyone who provides access to sexual information for children. Arrangement is in three divisions: "Birth and Reproduction," "Puberty and Adolescence," and "Relationships"; each is subdivided by level—primary, intermediate, and junior high. Grades for use are also given with each of the titles, which are carefully analyzed according to criteria and critically evaluated in the annotations. Out-of-print titles are included, and, for a recommended few of

these, suggestions are made to the publisher for a new edition. Some "standard" titles are rejected for reasons given. Although the list is a small one, the field covered is substantial for an area that has received scant attention at this age level. The guide presents a lucid viewpoint that deserves attention by all the groups of its intended readers.

154. Haviland, Virginia. *The Best of Children's Books, 1964–1978, Including 1979 Addenda.* **New York: University Press Books, 1981. 126p.**

This retrospective compilation from the titles selected annually for Haviland and Coughlan's *Children's Books* (**155**) was first published by the Library of Congress in 1980; this hardbound edition adds a further year's selection. Using the same general selection criteria as the annual, "this selection from some 3000 works...will serve...to bring a broad range of outstanding titles to the attention of those who stand in various relationships to the reading needs and interests of children and young people." As the reconsidered judgment of specialists in the field about the best children's publications over a 15-year period, it remains a very useful checklist for back acquisitions.

155. Haviland, Virginia, and Coughlan, Margaret N. *Children's Books.* **Washington, DC: Library of Congress, 1964–1984. Annual.**

The volume for 1983 concludes, under this title, the series of selected and annotated listings of the previous year's output of children's titles (E/S 1945–75, p. 80), chosen with the assistance of a committee of children's librarians. Arranged in subject and age categories, the graded entries were chosen for literary merit, usefulness, and enjoyment. For its primary audience of librarians who deal with youngsters from preschool through junior high school age, it has served as a valuable current checklist of about 150 titles annually, and the series as a whole is of considerable retrospective interest. In 1985, it was superseded by a new list of 100 choices entitled *Books for Children,* under the editorship of Margaret N. Coughlan, assisted by a committee of local specialists in children's literature.

156. ———. *Children's Literature: A Guide to Reference Sources.* **Second Supplement. Washington, DC: Library of Congress, 1977. 413p.**

The last supplement to appear to date, this adds 929 more references to the 1,819 cited in the original volume of 1966 and the *First Supplement of 1972* (E/S 1945–75, p. 81). Sections have been included to cover new emphases in the field, such as nonprint materials and research in children's literature. "French Canada" is a new heading. This comprehensive and annotated bibliographical guide has been a major resource in the field, but further supplements will be required to maintain its usefulness to its wide audience of researchers, teachers, and librarians.

157. Haviland, Virginia, and Smith, William Jay, eds. *Children and Poetry: A Selective Annotated Bibliography.* **2d ed. rev. Washington, DC: Library of Congress, 1979. 84p.**

In this revision of their annotated bibliography, first published in 1969 (E/S 1945–75, p. 83), the former head of the Children's Section in the Library of Congress and a poetry specialist have again provided a selection of available

poetry titles for children, for consultation by teachers, parents, and librarians. New annotations and extracts are included on the same organizational plan as previously in this helpful checklist. The literary and physical presentation enhance the appeal to its audience of this delightful bibliographical essay.

158. Haycock, Anne. *Bibliotherapy: Recommended Titles for Personal and Interpersonal Problems and Situations, Grades K-9.* **Vancouver, BC: British Columbia School Library Association. 1978. 21p.**

An "Occasional Paper" of the Association, this annotated and graded list, derived mainly from standard Canadian and American selection and reviewing sources, is intended for teachers and librarians. Sections cover adoption, alcoholism, siblings, childbirth, deafness, death, divorce, and foster homes, with emphasis on fiction titles.

159. Hazard, Paul. *Books, Children and Men.* **Boston: Horn Book, 1983. 196p.**

Hazard's classic and inspirational commentary on the qualities of children's literature has appeared in three American editions, translated from the French by Marguerite Mitchell (E/S 1945-75, pp. 83–84). This reprint carries a new insightful introduction by Sheila Egoff.

160. Heald, Dorothy, regional ed. *The Southeast: Virginia, North Carolina, South Carolina, Alabama, Georgia, Florida.* **(Reading for Young People). Chicago: American Library Association, 1980. 176p.**

One of a series of annotated bibliographies of fiction and nonfiction titles compiled for readers from the primary grades through the tenth grade, "designed to focus on the history and character of each region of these United States." Editors for each state within the area have chosen and annotated "approximately 100 of the very best books...available for each state." Criteria for choice were that books should "best portray the spirit, the vitality and diversity of each state of the region" while reflecting overall literary quality and informational accuracy". Out-of-print titles are included if still available in libraries. The annotated bibliography is divided into broad subject groups: fiction, folktales, poetry, drama and music, biography and personal accounts, and other informational books. Titles are arranged alphabetically within each group, and carry a brief quotation and a full paragraph of description. Grade ranges are suggested: P for primary, I for intermediate, J for junior high, and S for senior high. Supplementary unannotated lists group the titles under each relevant state. The index combines authors, titles, and subjects, and information is given on regional publishers and suppliers. As with all volumes of this series, the selection and commentary are systematic and generous. Its availability is a boon to selectors in school and young people's libraries—indeed in all libraries with local interests—as well as to the region's young people.

161. Heald, Dorothy W., and others. *Excellent Paperbacks for Children*. Washington, DC: Association for Childhood Education International, 1979. 52p.

A successor to the Association's *Good and Inexpensive Books for Children*, 1972 (E/S 1945–75, p. 16), itself with a bibliographical history dating back to 1947, this briefly annotated selection of outstanding children's paperbacks was compiled by an ad hoc committee, chaired by Heald, and edited by Monroe D. Cohen, assisted by Sara Hadley. Arranged alphabetically by author, subject access is provided by an index of 11 topics—broad subject areas or types of literature—each arranged alphabetically. The brief sentences of annotation carry an indication of developmental, not grade levels: nursery, primary, intermediate, and adolescent. A useful "Resource Guide for Parents, Teachers and Librarians" by Elizabeth Thompson is included. As with the other lists sponsored by this prestigious association, the titles that remain in print still provide a sound checklist for teachers and for school and other libraries.

162. Hearne, Betsy Gould. *Choosing Books for Children: A Commonsense Guide*. New York: Delacarte, 1981. 150p.

This inspirational guide for all who deal with youngsters "tells how, what, when, and where" to relate to the young "over a bridge of books." Eleven chapters with topical titles such as "Trying to be Human" are followed by short lists of the author's favorite children's titles, to be used as a starting point for anyone interested in exploring books for children. There are annotations in some of the lists, as well as discussion of individual children's titles in the text. Common sense does blend with inspiration in this personal approach by the well-known former children's book coeditor of *Booklist*.

163. Hearne, Betsy Gould, and Kaye, Marilyn, eds. *Celebrating Children's Books: Essays on Children's Literature in Honor of Zena Sutherland*. New York: Lothrop, 1981. 244p.

The editors have collected 22 essays explaining various aspects of the craft of writing, illustrating, and publishing for children and young adults by contributors described as an outstanding group of individuals who have achieved success in the field; these include well-known figures such as Lloyd Alexander, Robert Cormier, and Ursula Nordstrom. The graceful introductory tribute to Zena Sutherland is by Sophie Silverberg. Sections group essays under the topics of "Creating the Books," "Producing the Books," "Understanding the Books," and "Reaching the Readers." Many discuss children's titles and some have appended booklists, often with annotations. Contributions are informative and will provide useful data for literary and sociological research.

164. Heeks, Peggy. *Choosing and Using Books in the First School*. (Language Guides). London: Macmillan Educational, 1981. 146p.

This essentially practical guide for British elementary teachers by an experienced children's librarian provides a substantial bibliographical element. Chapters cover "Interpreting Pictures," "What's in a Story," "Traditional

Tales," and "Finding the Facts." At the end of each chapter is a booklist of appropriate titles with annotations indicating their usefulness.

165. ——. *Ways of Knowing: Information Books for 7 to 9 Year Olds.* (A Signal Bookguide). Stroud, England: Thimble Press, 1982. 54p.

This annotated list of over 100 reference and informational titles for younger children formed the basis for a National Book League exhibition. It was planned to be useful as a book selection tool, as a basis for workshop collections, and as an aid to subject work with seven- to nine-year-olds. Arranged in subject groupings in Dewey order, each section has an introduction of its own. The annotations to each book are described by the author as "thumbnail sketches" that may also be useful for book-selection training. Final pages sum up the criteria for finding suitable nonfiction for the junior school age group. This useful British list will suggest alternative titles for North American school libraries.

166. Heins, Paul, ed. *Crosscurrents of Criticism: Horn Book Essays, 1968-1977.* Boston: Horn Book, 1977. 359p.

The noted former editor of *Horn Book* has here assembled a collection of articles from the magazine which follows in the tradition of two former collections, Norma Fryatt's *A Horn Book Sampler* of 1959 (E/S, 1945–75, p. 64) and Elinor Field's *Horn Book Reflections* of 1969 (E/S, 1945–75, p. 60). "As unhackneyed a selection as possible" was chosen to address the "various problems, attitudes, and possibilities faced by the critics of children's literature." The editor's brief but erudite introduction, discussing the history of children's literature, precedes the arrangement of essays under the themes of: "Status"; "Classification"; Standards' (with the editor's seminal article of the sixties, "Out on a Limb"); "At Critical Crosspurposes"; "In Defense of Fantasy"; "Humor"; "Making the Past Understandable"; "The International World of Children's Books"; "Translation"; and "Books and Authors." The articles thus reprinted and made more available contain much of interest both to the researcher and the general reader.

167. Hinman, Dorothy, and Zimmerman, Ruth, regional eds. *The Midwest: Iowa, Illinois, Indiana, Ohio, Missouri.* (Reading for Young People.) Chicago: American Library Association, 1979. 250p.

One of a series of annotated bibliographies of fiction and nonfiction titles compiled for readers from the primary grades through the tenth grade, "designed to focus on the history and character of each region of these United States." Editors for each state within the area have chosen and annotated "approximately 100 of the very best books...available for each state." Criteria for choice were that books should "best portray the spirit, the vitality and diversity of each state of the region" while reflecting overall literary quality and informational accuracy". Out-of-print titles are included if still available in libraries. The annotated bibliography is divided into broad subject groups: fiction, folktales, poetry, drama and music, biography and personal accounts, and other informational books. Titles are arranged alphabetically within each group, and carry a brief quotation and a full paragraph of description. Grade ranges are suggested: P for primary, I for intermediate, J for junior high, and S for senior high. Supplementary unannotated lists group the titles under each relevant state. The index combines authors, titles, and subjects, and information is given on regional publishers and suppliers. As with all volumes of this series, the selection and commentary are systematic and generous. Its availability is a boon to selectors in school and young people's libraries—indeed in all libraries with local interests—as well as to the region's young people.

168. Hirst, John. *Victorians*. (Storylines). Birmingham, England: Library Association Youth Libraries Group, 1977. 16p.

This brief annotated booklist brings together a number of historical novels which taken together form a fictional background to the development of Great Britain during the 19th century. Though chosen primarily as support- ive material to historical study, each title satisfies the criteria of being enjoyable as fiction and as gaining a positive impetus from being set in an authentic period background. Most titles are suitable for children in the upper years of primary school and the lower years of secondary school. Sections cover domestic life, social and industrial change, Great Britain overseas, and some stories of the period, as well as background information books. Most titles were in print in Great Britain. Each title receives an extensive descriptive and critical annotation with frequent bibliographical references to other authors and titles. Because of the careful choice and presentation, this selection transcends local interest and is valuable beyond the school environment.

169. Hodowanec, George V., ed. *The May Massee Collection: Creative Publishing for Children, 1923–1963, a Checklist*. Emporia, KS: Emporia State University, William Allen White Library, 1979. 316p.

This limited first edition catalogs the "majority of books published under the aegis of May Massee." One of the early famous editors of children's books, she devoted many of her career years to developing the children's department at Viking. It provides an "access tool for scholarly research" on the "various aspects of the publishing of children's books." The editor is the curator of the Collection. Nine hundred thirty entries arranged by author are included with brief annotations. These have been prepared by Jeanne Frederickson. Correspondence, manuscripts, typescripts, and articles by and about May Massee also appear. There are two indexes—title-author and audiovisual—and a bibliography for researchers.

170. Hopkins, Lee Bennett. *The Best of Book Bonanza*. New York: Holt, 1980. 243p.

This compilation of material culled from the monthly feature column "Book Bonanza," appearing in *Teacher* magazine from 1974 to 1980, has been reedited, updated, and reorganized into eight sections: "Understanding Life"; "Children and Culture"; "The Seasons"; "Getting Involved"; "More than Just Fun"; "Plants, Pets, and Beasts"; and "Last but Certainly not Least." The column emphasizes "the everyday use of books in elementary and junior-high school classrooms and libraries" and is directed to "everyone interested in bringing children and books together." Citations of titles follow each section, and these, as well as numerous references in the text, constitute a good source for classroom teachers.

171. Hopkins, Linda. *World War Two.* **(Storylines). Birmingham, England: Library Association Youth Libraries Group, 1976. 17p.**

This annotated list aims to introduce a selection of the novels written for children set during the second world war, and also includes personal narratives. Criteria for choice were a well-written story and understanding of human situations. Except where specified, the novels were judged more suitable for children of eleven years and older. Two sections cover stories and narratives arranged alphabetically by author, and a brief list of information books. The descriptive annotations are often quite lengthy and include careful critical assessment. Apart from a few out-of-print titles believed to be available in libraries, all were in print in Great Britain. This is a stimulating selection that does not avoid the tragic element and reflects many aspects of the conflict in many areas.

172. The Horn Book. *Children's Classics: A Booklist for Parents.* **Boston: Horn Book, 1984. 19p.**

Since 1947, this outstanding children's literature periodical in America has issued short lists of children's classics with varying titles and different editors intended for parents and for use in bookstores. (E/S 1945–75, pp. 96–97). The last edition by editor Alice M. Jordan with assistance by Paul Heins appeared in 1976. A successor was prepared by Jane Manthorne in 1982, with a change in subtitle that emphasized its use by parents. Each contains a short inspirational introduction and a revision of the list of titles regarded as classic. This issue presents "old friends from childhood along with great new selections." The pamphlet is organized to help choose books for children from infancy to early adolescence. Entries do not cite date of publication but titles could be presumed to be in print. An invaluable guide for the group for which it is intended, the selection will be too brief to be of use for current selection by librarians. A comparison of the choices made over the years in succeeding editions is of retrospective interest.

173. Horner, Catherine Townsend. *The Aging Adult in Children's Books and Non-Print Media.* **Metuchen, NJ: Scarecrow, 1982. 242p.**

Similar in approach to the author's *The Single Parent Family in Children's Books* (**174**), this title seeks "to communicate the responsiveness of contemporary authors to the inherent problems of aging, to introduce some of the books they are promulgating to sensitive children...and demonstrate the increasing practice of portraying senior adults realistically and positively." The introduction comments on agism, surveys the genre and its stereotypes, and notes some recent findings. The entries are divided into an annotated bibliography of 337 titles in three reading levels—preschool and primary, intermediate, and middle and high school—and an unnumbered multimedia section which includes textbooks and nonfiction as well as articles, slides, films, videotapes, records, and games. Annotations are lengthy and carefully descriptive, but avoid direct criticism, the author wishing "to allow every interested individual to decide from one's own particular perspective or bias what is constructive or relevant in a given situation." Grade levels or recommended reading levels are indicated, though the author advises that these are arbitrary and overlapping. A "ready reference profile" and a title index facilitate access. This topic has become extremely popular in the late 1970s and 1980s, and the bibliography is correspondingly useful, both in the school situation and also in providing a potential for sociological and historical research.

174. ———. *The Single Parent Family in Children's Books: An Analysis and Annotated Bibliography, With an Appendix on Audiovisual Material.* Metuchen, NJ: Scarecrow, 1978. 172p.

Developed from a thesis, this bibliographical monograph attempts to identify as many as possible of the titles in children's fiction involving a single parent. The introduction describes bibliotherapy and the relevant research. Further introductory parts give an analysis of the literary genre, a summary of conclusions, and a listing of evaluative criteria, with a corresponding coding chart for the book. The annotated bibliography of 215 titles, dating from 1925 to 1975 with a majority in the last two decades, is classified by cause of single parenthood, e.g. widowed, divorced. The lengthy descriptive annotations give careful plot summaries but avoid direct criticism. Recommendations for grade level are included. The brief appendix of 25 audiovisual items is provided as a useful adjunct and is briefly annotated. Indexes include listings for "Predominant Parent," as well as author-title and subject. Those with an avowed interest in bibliotherapy will find this bibliographical study extremely helpful, but it will also be helpful to other librarians for acquisition purposes.

175. Hoyle, Karen Nelson. *Danish Children's Literature in English: A Bibliography Excluding H.C. Andersen.* Minneapolis, MN: University of Minnesota Center for Northwest European Language and Area Studies, 1982. 75p.

This annotated bibliography of some 400 Danish children's books was compiled by the curator of the Kerlan Children's Literature Research Collections as a part of the celebration of the "Scandinavia Today" theme adopted by the state of Minnesota in 1982–83. The numbered listing by author of children's titles by Danish authors and about Denmark is supplemented by a list of articles about Danish children's authors and illustrators, references to Danish children's literature, and full indexing of titles, translators, and illustrators. An appendix lists Danish illustrators of non-Danish children's books. As this rich children's literature is largely unknown to librarians, with the exception of the works of Hans Christian Andersen, this careful booklist will be suggestive for collection building, as well as an invaluable aid for research.

176. ———. *Girls' Series Books: A Checklist of Hardback Books Published, 1900–1975.* Minneapolis, MN: University of Minnesota Libraries Children's Literature Research Collections, 1978. 121p.

This unannotated bibliography was compiled by the curator of the Kerlan Children's Literature Research Collections, whose informative introduction provides a survey of the genre. The series, all American publications, are listed alphabetically, followed by entries for individual titles within the series chronologically arranged. A chronological index is provided, as well as indexes for authors and publishers, a short selected bibliography of references, and a few attractive illustrations. The list is invaluable for bibliographical research into an immensely popular field of American writing for children.

177. Huck, Charlotte S. *Children's Literature in the Elementary School.* **3d ed., updated. New York: Holt, 1979. 788p.**

First published in 1961, with a second edition in 1968 (E/S 1945–75, p. 90) and a third in 1976 after the death of its coauthor, this latest edition of a now familiar work remains essentially faithful to its predecessors in objective, audience, and organization, and reflects the tremendous growth of children's literature over recent years. The author states "My primary purpose was to share my knowledge and enthusiasm for the literature of childhood with students, teachers, and librarians." While emphasizing the joys of reading rather than the skills, she also wanted to show how books can become an integral part of the curriculum. Over 80% of this edition has been rewritten, while every chapter has been expanded. Updating has removed out-of-print books except particularly worthy ones; the updated work includes over 250 new titles of children's books and references, adding fresh poems and a color section of pictures of children in the learning environment. Appendices on awards and selection aids have been brought up-to-date. The work has again proved its value for its intended audience.

178. Hunt, Abby Campbell. *The World of Books for Children: A Parent's Guide.* **New York: Sovereign, 1979. 242p.**

Written to help the parent or child who wants to find a good book, with a secondary purpose to aid teachers in finding books for classroom use, this approach, based on personal experience by a mother of five, gives hints for encouraging a child to read and discusses the needs of different age levels. Chapters cover from birth to age three, ages three and four, first and second grades, and third and fourth grades. There is a corresponding bibliography for each chapter in a subject arrangement; entries carry a brief annotation summarizing the plot, a grade recommendation from the publisher, and a note as to availability in paperback. Appended is a brief but sound list of references to books about children's literature designed for parents, and a list of "100 Books for a Basic Library." These are all worthwhile titles for parents, though the recommendations are necessarily too limited a selection for library use.

179. Hunt, Mary Alice, ed. *A Multimedia Approach to Children's Literature: A Selective List of Films (and Videocassettes), Filmstrips, and Recordings Based on Children's Books.* **3d ed. Chicago: American Library Association, 1983. 182p.**

First appearing in 1972 (E/S 1945–75, p. 73) with a second edition in 1977, both compiled by Ellin Greene and Madalynne Schoenfeld, the third edition, as its predecessors, was "designed as a buying guide to a quality collection of book-related non-print materials for use with children from preschool to grade six," and its purpose remains "to assist libraries, teachers and others who wish to introduce a book or story in non-print form to locate appropriate material quickly." The basic list, arranged in an alphabetical title sequence no longer separated into format categories includes 568 books, 153 16-mm films, 365 filmstrips, and 348 recordings, up to a cut-off date of January 31, 1983, all with brief annotation and buying information. The selection in this edition was based on the knowledge and experience of committee members drawn from the Association for Library Service to Children. Unavailable nonprint material and titles with more appeal for young adults than for the younger age group are no longer listed. This remains a substantial and high-quality selection, but, nevertheless, as a standard source, it is necessarily limited, due to the size and complexity of the area covered. In particular, the rapidity of the out-of-print phenomenon in the audiovisual field will make it progressively more important for libraries and schools to supplement this edition with current listings and selection aids.

180. Inglis, Fred. *The Promise of Happiness: Value and Meaning in Children's Fiction.* **Cambridge, England: Cambridge University Press, 1981. 333p.**

This academic study of moral values in the children's literature of this century and the last examines the interaction of children's fiction with popular culture and social imagination, centering on "some very intelligent men who have written for children." The text is divided into three parts: the first of which is theoretical and examines the necessity of fiction in the creation of values; the second—"The Old Books"—looks at authors of the late 19th and early 20th centuries, while the third—"The New Work"—examines selectively the later generations, including the present generation's harking back to its predecessors. This original work of literary criticism makes frequent references to individual titles and their place in the development of well-known authors of children's literature.

181. International Youth Library, Munich. *Bibliography of Books for Handicapped Children.* **(Studies on Books and Reading). Paris: United Nations Educational, Scientific, and Cultural Organization, 1981. 197p.**

Compiled by the Library's staff as a part of UNESCO's contribution to the International Year for Disabled Persons, 1981, this annotated bibliography was intended to focus attention on the vital part books can play in the integration of handicapped children into the everyday world around them. It lists "a vast range of children's books currently available worldwide, published for and about handicapped children." Entries are arranged in alphabetical sequence of national groupings. They are cited in the original language, followed by an English translation, and include bibliographical data, an age recommendation, a brief description of the contents, and the nature of the handicap treated. Libraries in North America and Great Britain will find the foreign language titles particularly valuable for immigrant and non-Anglophone children, and for those who deal with them.

182. ———. *New Zealand Books for Children.* **Munich: The Library, 1981. 16p.**

An exhibition committee of the Children's Literature Association, convened by Joan Brock, was responsible for the exhibition and its catalog of about 100 selected titles. The booklist, with descriptive annotations by Jill MacLaren, is divided into three groups: picture books, books for younger children, and books for older children. It is supplemented by three essays by Jill MacLaren and Alison Grant: "New Zealand Children's Literature," "New Zealand Awards for New Zealand Children's Books," and "A New Survey of New Zealand Junior Fiction," which document the story from 1833 to 1978. This catalog brings together information about New Zealand children's literature that is difficult to locate elsewhere.

183. Ireland, Norma Olin. *Index to Fairy Tales, 1973–1977, Including Folklore, Legends, and Myths in Collections. Fourth Supplement.* **Westwood, MA: Faxon, 1979. 259p.**

The most recent addition to the long-established reference series which originated with Mary Huse Eastman's *Index to Fairytales* and carried on with three previous supplements (E/S 1945–75, p. 93). To this very large body of references to popular tales and folklore found in collections, the current supplement adds 130 new titles of collections published from 1973 to 1977, selected on the basis of availability and favorable reviews in professional journals. Arrangement remains the same, the first part being a list of the collections, which also can be used as a selection tool, and the second part the alphabetical subject analysis of the stories themselves, which functions as a day-to-day finding source. There are a few changes in the subject headings previously used. Again, the intended audience is one of public and school librarians and teachers, rather than scholarly researchers, and, again, for them it is an indispensable tool.

184. Isaacson, Richard H., and Bogart, Gary L. *Children's Catalog.* **14th ed. (Standard Catalog Series). New York: Wilson, 1981. 1,277p. Supplements: 1982, 1983, 1984.**

This edition marked the seventy-fifth anniversary of the first appearance of this volume in the publisher's series of basic library acquisition tools. It succeeds the thirteenth edition of 1976, edited by Barbara E. Dill, and its annual supplements. The present editors also edited, in reverse order of precedence, the corresponding fourth edition of the *Junior High School Library Catalog* (**40**), and many libraries will use these two in conjunction as here recommended for meeting the needs of "precocious children." The selection provides for children from preschool through the sixth grade. The revision of the list and the addition of new titles were made in accordance with the usual practice in the series by an advisory committee of public librarians selected on a national basis, and was then submitted to a group of experienced children's librarians from dispersed geographic areas in the United States. The work is intended to be used not only as an aid in purchasing but also as a cataloging and reference aid, and for consultation in library schools. Part I, the classified catalog, arranged by the Abridged Dewey Decimal classification, lists the nonfiction, followed by sections of fiction, story collections, and "easy books." Each entry carries a descriptive annotation, frequently quoted from a review, and a recommended grade level in addition to bibliographic information. Part II consists of an index interfiling author, title, subject, and analytical entries, for a total of nearly 6,000 titles and over 11,000 analytics. The supplements each add over 500 entries. Paperbacks are included when there is no hardcover edition, and also when the same publisher offers both. Only the first book of a series receives full treatment in the entries. Editions listed are American, and publisher and distributor information is provided in Part III. As with its junior and senior high school equivalents, this thorough and careful compilation is impressive by its sheer size and inclusiveness. As with them, ease of use and the provision of criticism, as well as order information and detailed subject access, has made this a standard tool for public and school libraries. Its very merits constitute a danger that small libraries will utilize it as virtually a sole source of selection. However, lively collections must be prepared to look elsewhere for unusual, unconventional, and local books that they need. While it is a standby for American libraries, Canadian libraries, taking account of the different cultural setting and publishing scene, will find it more appropriate for occasional reference than for use as a *vade mecum*. A further annual supplement appeared in 1985, and a new edition is announced according to plan for 1986.

185. James, Philip Britton. *Children's Books of Yesterday.* **Detroit: Gale, 1976. 128p.**

This title is an unchanged facsimile reprint of the first edition of 1933, a "Special Autumn Number" of the influential art magazine, *The Studio*, edited by C. Geoffrey Holme. The selection was based on an exhibition of illustrated books for children at the Victoria and Albert Museum in London in 1932. James's brief but erudite introduction precedes a series of over 200 reproductions, some in color, of illustrations by noted British illustrators of the 19th and 20th centuries, such as Kate Greenaway, Richard Doyle, Walter Crane, and Randolph Caldecott. While this edition is a reproduction of the reproductions in the original, the quality still makes an attractive portfolio for reference by the historian and researcher of children's literature.

186. Johnson, Deidre. *Stratemeyer Pseudonyms and Series Books: An Annotated Checklist of Stratemeyer and Stratemeyer Syndicate Publications.* **Westport, CT: Greenwood, 1982. 343p.**

This annotated checklist gives a systematic and exhaustive treatment of the multifarious publications written and sponsored by this turn-of-the-century young people's author and editor, known better under a variety of pseudonyms, such as Horatio Alger, Jr. His syndicate of ghostwriters contributed to an extensive list of boys' series and over 40 separate volumes. The informative introduction precedes the bibliography, which is arranged by pseudonym and type of publication. The numerous appendices and full indexing identify almost every aspect of a complicated body of work. Collectors and rare-book librarians will be grateful for the detailed and excellent bibliographical documentation given to this significant facet of the history of American publishing for young people.

187. Johnson, Doris McNeeley. *Children's Toys and Books: Choosing the Best from Infancy to Adolescence.* **New York: Scribner, 1982. 196p.**

Parent-directed, the sage advice based on the author's own experience is a valuable addition to the confusing and inadequate literature about children's toys. But the books receive a minimal amount of attention, with a few condensed or core listings for different ages. These, though slight, may be of use to parents without access to more substantial sources, but hardly to educators and librarians who have an interest in "realia" such as toys—they will profit from the rest of the book.

188. Johnson, Ferne, ed. *Start Early for an Early Start: You and the Young Child.* **Chicago: American Library Association, 1976. 181p.**

A cooperative effort by the Preschool Services and Parent Education Committee of the American Library Association's Children's Services Division, with the cooperation of the Early Childhood Education Council, American

Association of School Librarians, this collection of articles was written for an audience of librarians, teachers, and parents "to provide tested effective methods, techniques and resources to help all those interested in the intellectual growth and development of young children." The contributors are all workers in the field. The book is divided into five parts: "The Preschool Child," "Parent/Child Interaction," "Experiencing Literature," "Parents in Search of Information," and "Opening More Doors." Most chapters are followed by a bibliography; e.g., "Poetry" has seven pages of an excellent list of titles for children's appreciation. The foreword by Anne R. Izard starts with a prophetic statement which is well recognized: "Beginnings are all important." This guide, while not completely comprehensive, is a very good beginning.

189. Jones, Dolores Blythe. *Children's Literature Awards and Winners: A Directory of Prizes, Authors, and Illustrators.* **New York: Neal-Schuman; Detroit: Gale, 1983. 495p. Supplement: 1984. 136p.**

This is the first edition of what can be regarded as the successor to *Children's Books: Awards and Prizes* (**79**), which terminated with its 1981 volume. The purpose is to provide a comprehensive reference source for awards granted in English-speaking countries for excellence in children's literature. Such international awards as can be given to a book written in English are also included. Both current and discontinued awards are listed. Part 1 arranges the awards alphabetically, with detailed information on each derived from the sponsoring agency, including purpose, history, selection criteria, and method of choice. The complete history of recipients of each award is supplemented by many titles in the runner-up and honor categories, all with full bibliographical data. Part 2 lists award-winning authors and illustrators alphabetically with all awards received by each. Part 3 is a selected bibliography of books, articles, and reports about children's book awards. With regular supplements, the volume will constitute a standard reference tool for those interested, such as librarians, teachers, researchers, publishers and booksellers, the general public, and parents.

190. Justen, Sue, ed. *Opening Doors for Preschool Children and Their Parents.* **2d ed. Chicago: American Library Association, 1981. 90p.**

Prepared by the Preschool Services and Parent Education Committee of the Association for Library Service to Children, this annotated bibliographical guide first appeared in 1976, edited by Ferne Johnson. Both editors also chaired the committee. The selection of titles was made by librarians working with preschool children to provide short working lists for parents, or adults who work with children, who need materials guaranteed to be successful with preschoolers. This edition is arranged in three sections: "Books and Non-Print Materials for Parents and Adults Working with Preschool Children," "Books for Preschool Children," and "Non-Print Materials for Preschool Children." Picture books are listed along with the other books, which are now cited by author, rather than by title as previously. Nonprint materials are arranged by format within categories. The lists are appropriate and useful.

191. Kamm, Antony. *Choosing Books for Younger Children.* **Gloucester, England: Thornhill, 1977. 32p.**

A brief guide to selecting from the children's books currently available in Great Britain. The introduction, "Children and Books," recognizes that "there has been quite simply a children's book revolution." Chapters discuss picture-story books, traditional fairy tales, poetry and rhyme, modern stories for reading aloud, reading on their own, and books of facts. A reference section is added. Selected titles are mentioned in the text. The book takes a very simple but sensitive approach, apparently directed primarily to parents, from a British point of view.

192. Kelly, R. Gordon. *Children's Periodicals of the United States.* **(Historical Guides to the World's Periodicals and Newspapers). Westport, CT: Greenwood, 1984. 591p.**

This bibliographical and historical survey of English-language periodicals intended specifically for American children extends over more than 200 years. Treatment is twofold: one hundred titles, selected as historically significant and as a broad sample of the field, receive an essay treatment from 49 contributors; others, up to a total of 432, are described bibliographically, being cited alphabetically, chronologically by starting date, and geographically by original place of publication in the appendices. The editor's preface and introduction provide a condensed but excellent summary of the genre and its significance. The lengthy essay entries give an analytical description of each title, describing its contents and providing full publication history. The account of the influential *St. Nicholas*, by Professor Fred Erisman, was regarded as a model by the other contributors, scholars in the fields of English studies, education, and librarianship. Regrettably, fullness and accuracy of indexing and provision of cross-referencing leave much to be desired. Barring this defect, there can be no question about the value of this very extensive piece of research, since these periodicals constitute an area of great sociological, historical, and literary interest, one where the previously available documentation had been very inadequate.

193. Kesterton, Anne. *We All Live Here: A Multicultural Booklist for Young Children.* **London: National Book League, 1983. 32p.**

This annotated selection includes 111 recently published books which feature children coming from cultures outside Great Britain. It emphasizes cultural variety, rather than assimilation, and aims to assist concerned parents and teachers in finding children's books which make a contribution to the better understanding of other races and cultures, both as part of the British multicultural society and abroad. Criteria for selection required that these cultures be featured in a positive light and that books be suitable for infants and children up to the age of eleven. Fiction and nonfiction for children are included, but not animal stories or folk or fairy tales. Annotations describe and comment on each title and give a rough guide to suitable age categories. For British libraries this guide will suggest a basic stock to cover a major problem area; for American libraries it mentions many titles to supplement those available in the United States.

194. Kimmel, Margaret Mary, and Segel, Elizabeth. *For Reading Out Loud: A Guide to Sharing Books with Children.* **New York: Delacorte, 1983. 230p.**

This guidebook by two university teachers of children's literature is intended to help adults who read to children. It had its genesis in conversations with librarian and educator Elizabeth Fast, and carries an introduction by Betsy Byars. The stated purpose is threefold: to point out the specific benefits of reading aloud to school-age children; to suggest ways of providing time to do this at home or in the classroom; and to describe outstanding books that are good choices for reading aloud to children from kindergarten age through eighth grade. The focus on children in elementary and middle school, rather than preschoolers, has reduced the scope of the list; picture books have been excluded as not representing the spoken word, and poetry has been confined to an appended short list of collections. Two of the initial chapters describe values and finding time, and the third explains how to read aloud effectively. Succeeding chapters present the 140 recommended books and then cross-list them by subject, length, and type, and by their settings and locations. Each title is provided with full descriptive and critical annotation. Specialists will find little to quarrel with in this well-selected personal choice, though practical experience may change occasionally the suggested age of listening level. The lists will be extremely helpful for professional programming.

195. Kimmitt, Marianne. *The World of Children's Books Showcase: A Selection of the Best Canadian, British, and American Children's Books.* **Edmonton, AB: World of Children's Books Magazine and Alberta Culture Library Services Branch, 1979. 31p.**

Made possible through grants by appropriate federal and provincial agencies in celebration of the International Year of the Child, this briefly annotated list divides fiction and nonfiction titles into three categories: preschool to grade three, grade three to grade six, and grade six to grade nine. Supplementary chapters list selection aids, magazines for children, and relevant books for adults. Chosen from lists submitted by children's literature specialists throughout the province, the selection was narrowed down to 200 titles. The choice of Canadian titles will still be of some service for collection building.

196. Kingman, Lee, ed. *The Illustrator's Notebook.* **Boston: Horn Book, 1978. 153p.**

This collection of essays, originally appearing in *The Horn Book* magazine, is intended to describe children's book illustrators' methods of work more than the books themselves. However, the latter receive frequent mention in comments on the illustrations they contain.

197. Kingman, Lee; Hogarth, Grace Allen; and Quimby, Harriet B. *Illustrators of Children's Books, 1967-1976.* **Boston: Horn Book, 1978. 290p.**

This succeeding volume to those covering 1744 to 1945, 1946 to 1956, and 1957 to 1968 (E/S 1945–75, p. 121) adds more to what has been termed an enormous treasury of information and graphic reproductions for lay people, artists, and librarians. The last two editors are new. The stated aim of the volume is to present a view of what has happened in the field of children's book illustration and to show how artists feel about themselves, their work, and their problems. This decade of illustration in children's books is illuminated by four assessments of the state of the art by acknowledged experts, followed by biographies and a bibliography of the illustrators, and a bibliography of the children's authors. The appendices give bibliographical support to the essays, a list of artists represented, and a cumulative index to the series of four volumes. The impressive new volume is a valuable asset, and altogether they constitute a standard reference work which is a delight and an inspiration to consult.

198. Kirkpatrick, D.L. *Twentieth-Century Children's Writers*. 2d ed. London. Macmillan; New York: St. Martin's, 1983. 1,024p.

First published in 1978, this is one of a succession of substantial and detailed reference books on branches of modern literature issued by these publishers, employing the same techniques of presentation. Over 700 entries cover English-language authors of fiction, poetry, and drama for children and young people, the selection of entrants being governed by a committee of 25 advisers, British, Canadian, and Australian. The entries were prepared by nearly 200 contributors in a standardized form of presentation which includes biographical notes on the authors, a bibliographic list of publications, a personal comment from the author concerned, and one or more extracts from signed critical appreciations. The preface by Naomi Lewis gives a lengthy, detailed, and often introspective account of the development and value of this "extraordinary literature." A supplementary reading list cites more than 100 critical works about children's literature. The impartiality of treatment of authors on both sides of the Atlantic, and the thorough coverage of those from other English-speaking countries, is as noteworthy here as in the companion volumes. The quality, scale, and coverage make this major reference source indispensable to librarians and to scholarly researchers, and to all branches of the book trade.

199. Kloet, Christine A. *After "Alice": A Hundred Years of Children's Reading in Britain. Material Selected and Catalogued...on Behalf of the Youth Libraries Group of the Library Association*. London: Library Association, 1977. 63p.

The centennial celebrations of the Library Association gave an opportunity for a significant exhibition of children's books, jointly organized at the Museum of Childhood in London by the Association and the Victoria and Albert Museum. This important catalog was compiled to accompany it. The choice of 189 titles of the later 19th century and the 20th century was designed to place the classics and the innovatory writing of the period alongside typical "more trendy and trashy fare." The compiler's selection is excellent and unusual. Full annotation of each item is touched with personal enthusiasm as well as scholarship and cumulatively presents a true survey of the children's literature of the period and an assessment of its significance. Many additional titles are referred to vis-à-vis those selected. Most are British, but American representation is substantial. The text is supported by numerous illustrations of high quality in color and black-and-white. This attractive publication joins the few major catalogs in the field which have permanent value for consultation by libraries and scholars.

200. ———. *Reading for Enjoyment for 12 Year Olds and Up*. 5th ed. Cranleigh, England: Baker Book Services, 1984. 32p.

This series of informal guides designed to help parents choose books for their children was initiated by the National Book League in 1970. Divided into age groups, and selected by children's literature specialists from current British publications, all editions maintain retrospective interest. Each was based on one of the League's traveling exhibitions. The selection for this senior group was compiled by Aidan Chambers in 1970 for eleven-year-olds and up, with a second edition in 1975 for twelve-year-olds and up (E/S 1945–75, p. 27). The same editor compiled the third edition in 1977 for eleven- to sixteen-year-olds, and the present editor took over for the completely new fourth edition in 1981 for twelve- to sixteen-year-olds. The annotated booklist cites 101 current British titles, 60 being retained from the 102 of the previous edition, with 41 fresh titles. The criteria for selection were that the works of imaginative literature should be enjoyable, well-written, and, if illustrated, well-illustrated. A wide variety of tastes and emotional and intellectual development was aimed at. Suitability for twelve- to sixteen-year-olds did not exclude some adult titles, though most were from British publishers' lists for children and young adults. Asterisks indicate books that "may require considerable maturity." Established classics were not included, and most titles were published during the preceding ten years. Well-written descriptive notes usually provide a résumé of the stories. The current editor, maintaining the reputation of her predecessor, has made a limited but quality choice. To North American libraries, this selection will suggest worthwhile overseas titles to supplement their collections. The companion selection for zero- to six-year-olds was made by Dorothy Butler (**58**), and for seven- to eleven-year-olds by Vivien Griffiths (**141**).

201. Kreider, Barbara K. *Index to Children's Plays in Collections*. 2d ed. Metuchen, NJ: Scarecrow, 1977. 244p.

First published in 1972, this index in its second edition substantially increases the collections covered with titles published from 1965 to 1974. Nine hundred fifty plays are added from 42 collections for a total of 1,450 indexed. A full bibliography is provided after the index entries; this bibliography suggests grade level of use. For librarians and educators who deal with elementary age children, the volume will form a valuable reference source. As a buying list, too, it will be useful to children's librarians who are aware of the convenience of having the collections in the library to which such a tool will lead inquirers.

202. Kusnetz, Len. *Your Child Can Be a Super Reader: At Last! A Fun and Easy Approach to Reading Improvement*. Roslyn Heights, NY: Learning House, 1980. 122p.

This guide for parents to "help their children discover the joy of reading" provides easy instructions for a reading program for children in grades three to nine. Its objective is to develop their reading skills to the highest level. Fiction and nonfiction books and magazines are listed with a recommended grade level and a sentence of annotation. A subjective view of what constitutes pleasurable reading appears to be the principal criterion for choice, and the titles make up an eclectic list of varied quality. An appendix provides a short bibliography of books for further reference by parents.

203. Lamme, Linda Leonard, ed. *Learning to Love Literature: Preschool through Grade Three.* **Urbana, IL: National Council of Teachers of English, 1981. 98p.**

Intended for teachers of preschool and primary school children and prepared by the Council's Committee on Literature in the Elementary Language Arts, this booklet contains materials and methods designed to help make literature the core of the early childhood curriculum. Chapters cover practical topics such as appropriate curricular areas, teaching strategies, methods of integrating books into the curriculum, and storytelling. The brief accompanying bibliographies suggest titles to school librarians that will support such a program, but are too slight for use in collection building.

204. ———. *Raising Readers: A Guide to Sharing Literature with Young Children.* **New York: Walker, 1980. 200p.**

This guide for parents to help them identify good literature for children and ways to share literature with their children was prepared by the Committee on Literature in the Elementary Language Arts of the National Council of Teachers of English, with Vivian Cox, Jane Matanzo, and Miken Olson. It presents "a variety of ideas for getting young children involved with literature from infancy until the beginning reading stages." Guidelines are indicated for choosing and frank advice is given such as "Don't push your child into it." Four age groups—infant, toddler, prereader, and beginning reader—are treated separately. Each chapter is accompanied by a very brief annotated booklist; however, involvement activities, rather than literary materials, are emphasized. With the current attention focused on the needs of the very young, the guide serves its purpose well.

205. Larrick, Nancy. *A Parent's Guide to Children's Reading.* **5th ed. Philadelphia: Westminster, 1983. 271p.**

First published in 1958, with succeeding editions in 1964, 1969, and 1975 (E/S 1945–75, p. 104), the text and accompanying bibliographical recommendations of this well-known work have been thoroughly revised in this edition and made more concise. A prefatory statement declares that "the continued plea for guidance in developing children's love of reading in today's scene has led to this fifth edition....It has been completely rewritten to include notes about the ways of children today, as well as the new print material which they find appealing." Four parts discuss: "How You Can Help Day In Day Out," "Getting the Materials They Need," "Children's Books and Magazines," and "Especially for Parents." There are references to individual titles throughout the text, and the third part provides an extensive annotated booklist arranged under developmental and topical themes. A useful author, title, and subject index is provided. As in previous editions, illustrations from children's books enhance the text. The new edition has maintained the appeal of this well-known and well-written guide to librarians as well as to the parents to whom it is directed. The new edition was also issued as a Bantam paperback in 1982, significantly increasing its availability.

206. Lass-Woodfin, Mary Jo, ed. *Books on American Indians and Eskimos: A Selection Guide for Children and Young Adults.* **Chicago: American Library Association, 1978. 237p.**

This critical bibliography of books suitable for young people about native peoples within the bounds of the continental United States and Hawaii is directed to librarians, parents, educators, and others concerned. A team of reviewers with special qualifications contributes systematic reviews which summarize content and outlook, comment on use, recommend grade level, and rate the titles as good, adequate, or poor buys. After an introduction that comments on the difficulties of identifying accurate information in the area, the children's and young adult literature on the topic are discussed. The annotated bibliographical entries number over 800 titles. The concluding subject index covers tribes, persons, and events. This thorough guide, which lists only books published before 1977, gives valuable insight into the character of ethnic literature, in addition to its careful recommendations for collection building.

207. Lassam, Christine. *Stories and Settings, Africa: A Handbook for Teachers and Librarians.* **London: National Book League, 1977. 20p.**

208. ———. *Stories and Settings, Americas, Caribbean, Arctic, and Antarctic: A Handbook for Teachers and Librarians.* **London: National Book League, 1978. 32p.**

209. ———. *Stories and Settings, Asia and Australasia: A Handbook for Teachers and Librarians.* **London: National Book League, 1978. 42p.**

210. ———. *Stories and Settings, England: A Handbook for Teachers and Librarians.* **London: National Book League, 1977. 48p.**

211. ———. *Stories and Settings, Europe and the U.S.S.R.: A Handbook for Teachers and Librarians.* **London: National Book League, 1979. 53p.**

212. ———. *Stories and Settings, Scotland, Wales, and Ireland: A Handbook for Teachers and Librarians.* **London: National Book League, 1978. 28p.**

This series was selected and annotated by the compiler. The purpose of these brief booklists is to assist teachers and librarians in finding stories relating to the geographical area, and to cater to the growing awareness of the important link between children's fiction and class projects. Titles, numbering about 400 or more in each of the booklists, were for the most part in print at the time of compilation. Arrangement is by country and then by subsidiary geographic location. A brief descriptive sentence or phrase of annotation is accompanied by a recommendation for approximate age range. Still helpful, the lists will need to be updated with subsequent titles and others published outside Great Britain.

213. Laughlin, Mildred, regional ed. *The Great Plains: North Dakota, South Dakota, Nebraska, Kansas.* (Reading for Young People). Chicago: American Library Association, 1979. 159p.

214. ———. *The Rocky Mountains: Montana, Wyoming, Nevada, Utah, Colorado.* (Reading for Young People). Chicago: American Library Assocation, 1980. 192p.

These two titles are part of a series of annotated bibliographies of fiction and nonfiction titles compiled for readers from the primary grades through the tenth grade, "designed to focus on the history and character of each region of these United States." Editors for each state within the area have chosen and annotated "approximately 100 of the very best books...available for each state." Criteria for choice were that books should "best portray the spirit, the vitality and diversity of each state of the region, while reflecting overall literary quality and informational accuracy." Out-of-print titles are included if still available in libraries. The annotated bibliography is divided into broad subject groups: fiction, folktales, poetry, drama and music, biography and personal accounts, and other informational books. Titles are arranged alphabetically within each group, and carry a brief quotation and a full paragraph of description. Grade ranges are suggested: P for primary, I for intermediate, J for junior high, and S for senior high. Supplementary annotated lists group the titles under each relevant state. The index combines authors, titles, and subjects, and information is given on regional publishers and suppliers. As with all volumes of this series, the selection and commentary are systematic and generous. Its availability is a boon to selectors in school and young people's libraries—indeed in all libraries with local interests—as well as to the region's young people.

215. Lawrence, Carol; Hutcherson, Jennabeth; and Thomas, James L. *Storytelling for Teachers and School Media Specialists.* Minneapolis, MN: Denison, 1981. 56p.

This collection of readings on storytelling was chosen for usefulness in a school setting as general background and how-to-get-started material. A short bibliography is provided of resources a school librarian or classroom teacher might find helpful. The reprinted articles, by such well-known practitioners as CharleMae Rollins, Lucille Thomas, and Barbara Baskin, are grouped under three headings: "Why Tell Stories in Schools?," "Using Storytelling to Promote School Objectives," and "Storytelling for Special Children." Further adult readings are cited in a final section. For an audience of teachers and school librarians untrained in storytelling, this slim activity book and listing is adequate, but it is only a beginning in a large and rich field.

216. Leonard, Charlotte. *Tied Together: Topics and Thoughts for Introducing Children's Books.* Metuchen, NJ: Scarecrow, 1980. 253p.

These informal essays are mostly adapted from the writer's column about children's books in the Dayton *Journal Herald*. The introduction is addressed to librarians who give book talks. Chapters are grouped into six sections on informal subject areas, such as outdoors, animals, and holidays, and most connect individual titles to a theme. Two short lists at the end give additional titles, some distinguished by the author with a star. Treatment is popular in tone, and low-key to the extent of appearing simplistic.

217. Lewis, Naomi. *Fantasy Books for Children.* **2d ed. London: National Book League, 1977. 55p.**

First published in 1975 (E/S 1945-75, p. 108), this entertaining guide in its new edition, again based on a National Book League exhibition, both adds to and subtracts from the previous listing. Recent titles are included, but out-of-print titles have been dropped, for a total of 185 annotated items. While these fantasies were published in Great Britain, their literary origin is not so confined; quite a few Continental books in translation are included. Because of the quality of the selection and the annotation, the previous edition will retain value for the omitted titles. The new edition will be valuable for all librarians with a clientele interested in this popular field.

218. Library Association Youth Libraries Group. *Storytelling: Practical Guides.* **Birmingham, England: The Group, 1979. 45p.**

Seven experienced storytellers, including Eileen Colwell and Grace Hallworth, contributed to this collection of papers on aspects of storytelling and reading. The introduction is by Margaret Marshall. A number of the articles give citations to titles in the text, in addition to a closing bibliography and list of references. There is also a final select bibliography of books on storytelling, each briefly annotated. This useful British symposium has a strongly practical emphasis.

219. LiBretto, Ellen V., ed. *High/Low Handbook: Books, Materials and Services for the Teenage Problem Reader.* **(Serving Special Populations Series). New York: Bowker, 1981. 210p.**

Prepared for teachers, librarians, and other individuals or institutions who must provide easy reading material for disabled and reluctant teenage readers, this guide to selection, evaluation, and use presents contributions by 11 experienced librarians, reading specialists, and book reviewers and provides complementary annotated bibliographies. The objectives are to promote understanding of high/low materials and to lay a foundation for collection development. The introduction by Lydia LaFleur, a young adult specialist at the New York Public Library, outlines the development of the high/low genre. The essays are arranged in two parts: "Identifying and Serving the High/Low Reader" and "Selecting and Evaluating High/Low Materials." Problem adolescent readers are categorized as "disabled"—those who score on the fourth grade level or below in reading tests—and "reluctant"—those scoring above that level, and who have some reading skills, but who lack motivation to read. The third part lists a core collection, of 175 recommended books and periodicals of first- to fourth-grade reading level, the majority published after 1975 and in print. Entries carry descriptive and critical annotations which show an interest level by grade and a reading level according to the Fry formula. A supplementary list gives 100 titles with briefer annotations from fourth- to eighth-grade reading level of interest to reluctant moderately skilled readers. A selection of relevant professional books, bibliographies, and reviewing journals is also provided. Titles chosen have proved their worth at low reading levels. The volume makes good its promise to be a practical guide and selection aid.

220. Lima, Carolyn W. *A to Zoo: Subject Access to Children's Picture Books.* **New York: Bowker, 1982. 464p.**

This extensive subject bibliography of more than 4,400 picture books for children is based on the collection in the San Diego Public Library. Included are fiction and nonfiction titles that are more picture than text and use a vocabulary suitable for preschool through grade two. The introduction discusses the genesis of English-language picture books and adds a select list of further reading. The arrangement in five sections provides systematic access. Subject headings are listed alphabetically referring to a unique, but Dewey-based, numerical classification; the subject guide lists titles alphabetically within these subject headings; and the bibliographical guide arranged by author and joint author provides bibliographical information about relevant subjects. The final sections give a title index and an illustrator index. Well laid out and clearly printed, the volume provides a fully adequate, practical, working tool for teachers and librarians. Although the compiler does not so claim, it will also function as a useful selection aid, and some titles listed will serve other age groups, such as older patrons unskilled in English. A second edition was published in 1985.

221. Lindskoog, John, and Lindskoog, Kay. *How to Grow a Young Reader.* **Elgin, IL: Cook, 1978. 166p.**

The philosophy of this publication, as stated in the preface, is "to promote and provide titles that adhere to a rigid interpretation of fundamental Christianity." Addressed to all interested persons, it takes a religious standpoint to explore general topics such as the history of children's book publishing, the effect of television on reading, and the encouragement of reading aloud. Twelve chapters on informal subject divisions and genres are accompanied by reading lists, some of medium length and some very brief. A proportion of the listed titles is annotated. The authors' emphasis on Christian nurture and values prompt them to discuss negatively current popular areas of publishing for young people such as realistic fiction. What they do recommend will be helpful to readers of similar persuasion.

222. Lochhead, Marion. *The Renaissance of Wonder in Children's Literature.* **Edinburgh: Canongate, 1977. 169p.**

A study of the development of the world of fantasy and fairy tales in children's literature from its renaissance in the 19th century to the great exponents of the 20th century. The author remarks that this is a very personal selection; she devotes three chapters to George MacDonald and the Scottish folk heritage and five chapters to C.S. Lewis and J.R.R. Tolkien. There are numerous plot descriptions of individual titles. The final chapter sums up developments in the post-World War II period. Within the author's own predilections, this is a valuable addition to the sociological history of fantasy and wonder literature.

223. Lukens, Rebecca J. *A Critical Handbook of Children's Literature.* **2d ed. Oxford, OH: Miami University Press; Glenview, IL: Scott, Foresman, 1982. 264p.**

First published in 1976, this textbook for librarians and students of librarianship and education seeks to develop critical thinking and increase understanding, and to provide a firm basis for discriminating between the good and the poor in children's books. Each of the chapters, on topics such as plot, character, and style, has a section on reading and evaluation, with assignment activities for students and a list of recommended books cited. The second edition expands the text and adds a chapter on genres; the titles listed have been increased by a quarter. These are of high literary quality and illustrate ably the evaluative emphasis of the text. Clearness of style makes this well-reviewed textbook a pleasure to read.

224. Lynn, Ruth Nadelman. *Fantasy for Children: An Annotated Checklist and Reference Guide.* **2d ed. New York: Bowker, 1983. 444p.**

First published in 1979, the updated and expanded edition of this bibliographical guide to fantasy literature recommended for children in grades three to eight increases the count of titles to over 2,000—1,500 being main entries and the balance sequels and related works. Inclusion now requires two recommendations from cited book-reviewing journals; the former edition required only a single recommendation. All titles are novels and story collections published in English in the United States, including translations, between 1900 and 1982, except for a few historically significant earlier works. Only half are still in print. Children's science fiction is excluded. Each entry carries one of three graded recommendation symbols and reference to review citations and awards gained. Those in print and a few outstanding out-of-print titles are given a brief descriptive annotation. Arrangement is alphabetical by author within topical chapters devoted to type or theme, the "Imaginary Beings" chapter having 23 subdivisions. The new edition also adds an introduction which surveys the critical literature about fantasy writing for children, and a second section which provides a bibliography of 1,725 critical and biographical works on the field. The "Guide to Use" consequently adds students of literature to the intended readership, along with librarians, teachers, and parents. All groups are well served by this comprehensive and valuable finding list for this perennially popular field.

225. Lystad, Mary H. *At Home in America: As Seen through its Books for Children.* **Cambridge, MA: Schenkman, 1984. 154p.**

Five chapters survey the field generally and cite usually familiar examples on a scale suitable for the beginning student. The more advanced reader will need to supplement this account with more detailed studies, including the author's own *From Dr. Mather to Dr. Seuss* (**226**).

226. ———. *From Dr. Mather to Dr. Seuss: 200 Years of American Books for Children.* **Boston: Hall, 1980. 264p.**

The research for this historical account of American children's literature from its beginnings to 1975 included a detailed sociopsychological analysis of 1,000 titles located in the rare books division of the Library of Congress.

The changes in book content over more than 200 years of development in publishing provide a framework for the study of contemporary beliefs about the nature of children and their place in society. Six chapters examine broad chronological periods up to the present, and two further chapters comment on changing social values and views on the socialization of children, including a tabular presentation of race and sex in children's books. Many individual authors and titles are mentioned in the text, often with lengthy quotations. Fifty well-chosen illustrations are presented in chronological sequence. This is a worthwhile addition to the histories of children's literature available to students.

227. MacCann, Donnarae, and Woodard, Gloria, eds. *Cultural Conformity in Books for Children: Further Readings in Racism*. Metuchen, NJ: Scarecrow, 1977. 205p.

The contributors to this collection of essays come from a variety of backgrounds, professions, and races; most are educators and librarians, but members of and workers with minority communities, and also literary critics, are included. The introduction notes that "children's librarians have a particular need to swim against the tide of cultural bias and misunderstanding." The essays, grouped into three divisions, address concerns such as multicultural goals, library policy implications, and the quality and authenticity of the literature. Part I, "The Case against Cultural Conformity," contains four essays. Part II, "Cultural Perspective; Its Application in Children's Literature," has 18 essays directed to Native American, Chicano, Puerto Rican, Asian American, and Black American groups. Part III, "Handling Racist Materials," has four essays relating to specific action by libraries. Some essays comment on individual titles such as *Mary Poppins* and *The Slave Dancer*. Appended is a list of selected additional readings in racism and multicultural education.

228. McCarr, Dorothy, and Wisser, Mary Wilkins. *Curriculum Materials Useful for the Hearing Impaired*. Beaverton, OR: Dormac, 1979. 197p.

Intended for teachers of the hearing impaired from primary to senior high levels, this bibliography does not attempt to be inclusive of all materials currently available. Omitted are basal series and adapted school district series. The compilers explicitly recommend using commercially produced materials rather than attempting to create your own in order to save time. The list is divided into subject areas appropriate to common school curricula, such as career education, driver education, family life and health, as well as academic subjects such as language and mathematics. Much of the material for students beyond primary age is of the high interest/low reading level type. Annotations for the entries are descriptive and evaluative, with recommended reading and interest levels. Material for teachers on the education of the hearing impaired is also included. This specialist, limited, tool, with its emphasis on teachers' needs, can also be helpful for librarians who deal with the same group of readers in the instructional setting.

229. McConnell, Anne. *Books from Other Countries, 1972–1976.* **Chicago: American Library Association, 1978. 95p.**

This volume extends the coverage of a similar title covering 1968 to 1971 (E/S 1945–75, p. 145) and is again sponsored by the American Association of School Librarians. Three objectives are now stated: to promote exposure to cultural interchange; to help the child who is an immigrant; and to identify titles for the researcher. The selection includes 195 books from 25 countries outside the U.S., both translations into English and works originally written in English, which were made available from 1972 through 1976. Books from Great Britain, Canada, and Australia are excluded. Arrangement is alphabetical by author within country divisions. Entries carry brief descriptive annotations. The list continues to provide a good selection of available international books. Well indexed, it constitutes a useful source for both teachers and librarians.

230. McCulloch, Lou W. *Children's Books of the 19th Century.* **Des Moines, IA: Wallace-Homestead, 1979. 152p.**

A labor of love by a local collector, this enjoyable informal account of various genres of 19th-century publications for children is preceded by an introduction from the collectors' viewpoint. Many titles are referred to in the text with comments on their relative scarcity and value. The treatment is not exclusively oriented to the scholarly and literary researchers; all readers will appreciate the lavish number of illustrations in black-and-white and color provided by Thomas R. McCulloch, which reproduce contemporary title pages and book illustrations.

231. McDonough, Irma, ed. *Canadian Books for Young People/Livres canadiens pour la jeunesse.* **3d ed. Toronto: University of Toronto, 1980. 205p.**

First published in 1976 as *Canadian Books for Children/Livres canadiens pour enfants*, the second edition of 1978 revised and expanded the coverage to include books for young people. All editions include publications in both official languages. The objective aimed for by the compiler and her collaborators Callie Israel and Ruth Osler (for English titles) and Micheline Persand and Danielle Ledoux (for French titles), all young people's librarians in Ontario, was to select the informative and excellent books for young people from among titles in print. Books primarily intended for adults have been included if they are relevant and relatively easy to read. The scope is intended to be inclusive rather than exclusive, and reflects growing Canadian publication in the field. The list of French titles follows the English titles. Each sequence is arranged in broad subject divisions, preceded by sections on picture books and folklore. Entries carry a paragraph of critical and descriptive annotation, and are marked as suitable for younger, middle, older, or mature readers. There are supplementary lists of publisher's series, award-winning books, and professional media. Each edition has established itself as a careful and reliable selection of Canadian young people's books and an excellent source for librarians, teachers, and the general public.

232. ——. *Profiles 2: Authors and Illustrators, Children's Literature in Canada.* **Ottawa: Canadian Library Association, 1982. 170p.**

The successor of *Profiles 1*, published in 1971 and revised and enlarged in 1975 (E/S 1945–75, p. 114), adds 44 sketches of Canadian authors and illustrators, which originally appeared as features in the periodical *In Review: Canadian Books for Children*, also edited by Irma McDonough, which regrettably ceased publication in 1982. Each sketch, contributed by a librarian, a writer, or an artist, includes a photograph and a bibliography. The series makes up a useful and attractively presented compendium of information about the current generation of creators of children's books in Canada.

233. McGovern, Edythe M. *They're Never Too Young for Books: Literature for Pre-Schoolers.* **Los Angeles: Mar Vista, 1980. 282p.**

Demonstrating belief in the positive results of reading to preschoolers, this bibliographical guide is addressed to parents as well as teachers and librarians, and is intended to assist the reader in establishing his or her own guidelines for wise selection. Priscilla Moxon, coordinator of children's services in the Los Angeles Public Library, contributed the preface. Three parts discuss "Meeting Immediate Needs," "Future Effects," and "Book Selection and Reading Aloud." In addition to the books discussed in the text, there are very extensive lists of recommended titles indicating the approximate age levels. Their comprehensiveness makes this an attractive selection aid for this age group.

234. MacLeod, Anne Scott. *A Moral Tale: Children's Fiction and American Culture, 1820–1860.* **Hamden, CT: Shoestring (Archon Books), 1975. 196p.**

This academic study focuses on what these books reveal about adult attitudes, rather than their appeal to children. Six chapters examine sociological issues and values chronologically, referring to relevant titles. The references, with the short select bibliography, provide a basic list of American juvenile literature of the period. The study is of interest to the student of social history and the literary historian.

235. ——, ed. *Children's Literature: Selected Essays and Bibliographies.* **(Student Contribution Series, No. 9). College Park, MD: University of Maryland, 1977. 153p.**

This collection of ten bibliographic essays on a sample of aspects of the field range from a critical bio-bibliography on Isaac Bashevis Singer to bibliographies for young readers on health and social problems. All are good and useful reading for children's literature specialists, librarians, students, and others.

236. McMullan, Kate Hall. *How to Choose Good Books for Kids.* **Reading, MA: Addison-Wesley, 1984. 80p.**

This brief guide with its annotated bibliography seems primarily directed to parents, and aims to offer sound advice in building a home library and encouraging reading. The compiler writes from the standpoint of a former elementary school teacher and a mother, and discusses matters arising with teachers and parents as well as with librarians, booksellers, and, "most importantly, kids." Following a brief but clear discussion of selection guidelines, four chapters relate to the age groups birth to two, beginning readers, six to eight, and nine to eleven. Briefly annotated booklists of about 30 titles follow each chapter. The selection is excellent and appropriate, though all too short. Slight though this presentation is, it does a good job of showing how parents can choose good books and encourage their use, and it presents a balance of suitable titles.

237. Mahoney, Ellen, and Wilcox, Leah. *Ready, Set, Read: Best Books to Prepare Preschoolers*. **Metuchen, NJ: Scarecrow, 1985. 384p.**

"This book has been written to give parents and other concerned adults help in selecting the best of literature and art...and to help them discover ways of involving children in the reading experience." The text is arranged in chapters which follow the development of the child, from the infant stage through toddlers and two- to three-year-olds up to four- to five-year-olds. Practical advice is interwoven with mention of many titles, usually with critical and descriptive comment and often with extracts. Each chapter is also followed by extensive booklists. Meticulous and detailed, this contribution by teachers of children's literature at the university level seems as well adapted to the needs of teachers and librarians and those training for those professions as for parents' use. Available for cataloging in publication in 1984, it subsequently appeared with a 1985 date.

238. Maloney, Margaret Crawford, ed. *English Illustrated Books for Children*. **Rev. ed. London and Toronto: Bodley Head, 1981. 88p.**

Originally published in Tokyo in 1979 in Japanese from a text prepared by five members of the Toronto Public Library, this English-language edition has been substantially revised, according to the preface. It was designed to accompany a magnificent series of color reproductions of volumes from the famous Osborne Collection of Early Children's Books, chosen for their literary or artistic importance. The introduction outlines the history of the collection, describes the development of the publishing venture, and provides scholarly sketches of the 26 works reproduced, with assessments of their importance in the development of the various genres of children's publications.

239. Manheimer, Ethel, and others. *Notable Children's Books, 1971-1975*. **Chicago: American Library Association, 1981. 36p.**

Prepared by the Notable Children's Books (1971-1975) Re-evaluation Committee, this is a successor to the volume covering 1940 to 1970 selected by Helen M. Mullen (**263**) and a previous committee. The seven members' function was to re-evaluate on the basis of established criteria titles originally chosen for the annual selection published in *Booklist* under the same name, to delete titles that have not stood the test of time, and to add titles if appropriate, in order to present a composite annotated list. Arrangement is alphabetical by author, and the brief descriptive annotations include a suggested age range. This checklist makes a superb selection tool, especially for those concerned with quality. The volume covering 1976-1980 was published in 1986.

240. Marshall, Margaret Richardson. *Children's Paperbacks, 5–11.* London: National Book League for the School Library Association, 1978. 24p.

This annotated selection of 132 children's paperbacks currently available in Great Britain has in mind children who are buying books for themselves. Many are standard titles also available in hard cover; some are books adults buy for children. Omitted are Enid Blyton, Dr. Who, and Mister books. Three groups comprise stories and picture books for five- to seven-year-olds, stories for eight- to twelve-year-olds, and a potpourri of information books. Each title carries a full paragraph of descriptive annotation, sometimes with critical comment.

241. ———. *An Introduction to the World of Children's Books.* (A Grafton Book). Aldershot, England: Gower, 1982. 189p.

This elementary introduction by a senior library school lecturer is not intended as a simple account of popular and classic children's literature, but tries to give a wider perspective on the complex structure of the children's book world. Chapters cover trends, what children's literature is, its development, the publishing scene, fiction and nonfiction, illustration, reading needs and interests of children, bibliographical aids, and promoting children's books in libraries. An international application is sought over and above the British references. The text, frequently answering questions raised in the paragraph headings, does not discuss many titles, but there are numerous tables, and further readings are recommended at the end of chapters. There are supplementary lists of titles referred to, books about children's books, and selected children's literature periodicals. As with many titles in this publisher's series, this can be regarded as a potential textbook for British library schools. Within the scope of the wide-ranging topics covered the treatment is minimal and the writing simplistic.

242. ———. *Seeing Clear: Books Suitable for the Partially Sighted Child.* Oxford: School Library Association, 1977. 24p.

Compiled for teachers of visually handicapped children in British special schools and primary schools as well as for parents and librarians, the potential audience for the books on this list comprises children who have difficulty in reading normal 10-point to 12-point type, from the nearly blind to those whose sight can be partially corrected with glasses. All titles have been personally seen and evaluated. Technical points taken into consideration included increased print size, generous leading, types, non-glare paper, and suitable illustration. The 160 titles and additional series are grouped in three parts: large-print books for children, divided into fiction and nonfiction; normal editions with the required features, divided into picture and storybooks and information books; and series with the required features, divided into teenage reading for backward readers and normal children's book series. Reading age and interest age are noted, and paperbacks and out-of-print titles are identified. There are only occasional annotations, usually technical ones. With some American titles and some classics, most selections are current British publications. A list of British publishers of large-print books is included as is a guide to print sizes. A new, expanded, edition appeared in 1985, set in large type.

243. Matthias, Margaret, and Thiessen, Diane. *Children's Mathematics Books: A Critical Bibliography.* **Chicago: American Library Association, 1979. 61p.**

This annotated bibliography of approximately 180 books suitable for children in kindergarten to grade six is designed for an audience of elementary school teachers, parents, and others concerned. The list is divided into six topics: counting, geometry, measurement, number concepts, time, and miscellaneous. For each entry there is a well-expressed annotation of a few short paragraphs, stressing the content, accuracy, illustrations, appropriateness, and style, and suggesting related activities. Notations are made indicating critical rating (as "recommended," "acceptable," or "not recommended"), the appropriate grade level, and whether the book is to develop single or multiple concepts. The cut-off date for inclusion was 1976, but publication of a number of titles was as late as 1975, making this a combination of good older titles and important newer ones. This sound bibliography constitutes a good buying list for school librarians, as well as being useful for teachers and parents.

244. Meacham, Mary. *Information Sources in Children's Literature. A Practical Reference Guide for Children's Librarians, Elementary School Teachers, and Students of Children's Literature.* **(Contributions in Librarianship and Information Science). Westport, CT: Greenwood 1978. 256p.**

This selected and annotated bibliography by a faculty member in a library school is specifically directed to the audience identified in the title, professionals catering to children from preschool through sixth grade, whether in the ordinary elementary school or in the children's section of a public library. It furnishes a key to the resources which refer to trade books and serial publications for children, and it provides critical analysis of the characteristics and use of relevant items. Omitted are books dealing with the history of children's literature and scholarly criticism, and publications outside the United States. The cut-off date for inclusion was 1976. Six chapters group entries by purpose: building the basic collection, science books and indexes, special fields, author and illustrator awards, using books with children, and technical processes. The lengthy annotations extending to two or more paragraphs are supplemented by reproductions of specimen pages. Three appendices cover organizing and running the school library and media center, criteria for evaluating a children's book, and further reading. An author-title index completes this comprehensive treatment of traditional types of tool, which serves well its stated purpose of providing a guide to the inexperienced, who will find it a valuable reference source.

245. ———, regional ed. *The Northwest: Alaska, Washington, Oregon, Idaho.* **(Reading for Young People). Chicago: American Library Association, 1981. 152p.**

One of a series of annotated bibliographies of fiction and nonfiction titles compiled for readers from the primary grades through the tenth grade, "designed to focus on the history and character of each region of these United States." Editors for each state within the area have chosen and annotated "approximately 100 of the very best books...available for each state." Criteria for choice were that books should "best portray the spirit, the vitality and diversity of each state of the region" while reflecting overall literary quality and informational accuracy". Out-of-print titles are included if still available in libraries. The annotated bibliography is divided into broad subject groups: fiction, folktales, poetry, drama and music, biography and personal accounts, and other informational books. Titles are arranged alphabetically within each group, and carry a brief quotation and a full paragraph of description. Grade ranges are suggested: P for primary, I for intermediate, J for junior high, and S for senior high. Supplementary unannotated lists group the titles under each relevant state. The index combines authors, titles, and subjects, and information is given on regional publishers and suppliers. As with all volumes of this series, the selection and commentary are systematic and generous. Its availability is a boon to selectors in school and young people's libraries—indeed in all libraries with local interests—as well as to the region's young people.

246. Meek, Margaret; Warlow, Aidan; and Barton, Griselda, eds. *The Cool Web: The Pattern of Children's Reading*. London: Bodley Head, 1977. 427p.

A substantial collection of 50 essays by distinguished authors, critics, and others, mostly of the present generation, but some of a previous one, seen as having a common concern for the needs and growth of children's literature. Contributors include C.S. Lewis, W.H. Auden, William Golding, Mordecai Richler, Elaine Moss, Geoffrey Trease, Maurice Sendak, and Edward Blishen. The editors' choice is designed to illustrate the truth of the argument that stories are central to a child's experience and "a basic instrument for making sense of his own as well as other people's lives." The essays are linked together by the editors' own critical commentary and arranged in five divisions to demonstrate particular themes. "The Reader" defines the experiences undergone when reading apropos of the outside world and the inner world of personality. "What the Authors Tell Us" demonstrates how authors see their role. "Approaches to Criticism" shows the application of critical ideas to children's literature. "Ways Forward" points out the relevant fields of study. The "Bibliography" lists surveys and specialist studies on certain aspects of the reading experience which deepen and extend the ideas raised; each of these carries a paragraph of annotation. Editorial concern for the storytelling and narrative in the art of fiction has resulted in a great deal being included about how to write books. Numerous titles are mentioned throughout the text, usually criticized and frequently quoted. And there is much more in this collection of significant articles that is of importance, not only to librarians, teachers, and researchers, but also to critics and authors themselves. It was published in New York by Athenaeum in 1978.

247. Meyer, Susan E. *A Treasury of the Great Children's Book Illustrators*. New York: Abrams, 1983. 272p.

The scope of this lavishly illustrated volume is limited to 13 classic illustrators of children's books in the 19th century. Admittedly the author's favorites, the biographees selected range in date from Edward Lear to W.W. Denslow. Their work for adults receives no comment. After a general introduction on the field and the period, individual essays present a study of each along with a generous selection of reproductions of their work. The full-color, full-page frontispiece by Edmund Dulac is a typical specimen. A short bibliography of important references is included. A "coffee table" volume that is a joy to look at, this production by a well-known firm of art-book publishers also provides excellent reading for the specialist as well as the amateur. Both pictures and text will be useful for reference librarians of historical collections.

248. Mills, Joyce White. *The Black World in Literature for Children: A Bibliography of Print and Non-Print Materials.* **Vol. 2. Atlanta, GA: Atlanta University School of Library Service, 1976. 45p.**

The first volume of this annotated bibliography appeared in 1975 (E/S 1945–75 pp. 121–22) covering up to 1974. This volume includes 111 new titles issued in 1975 and 1976. Its purpose as stated is to give today's public information about the availability of juvenile materials by and about Black people in the U.S. and Africa, as well as to make a historical notation of such material. The basic arrangement remains the same, alphabetical, with book and audiovisual titles interfiled, within groups for younger children (three to eight) and older children (nine to thirteen). A group for adults lists reference sources, with the books arranged by publisher and the audiovisual material arranged by distributor. Although much material relevant to the field has been published subsequently, the critical evaluations and ratings make this still a useful aid within its limits.

249. Modern Language Association. Division on Children's Literature and the Children's Literature Association. *Children's Literature.* **Philadelphia: Temple University Press; New Haven, CT: Yale University Press, 1973– . Annual.**

This academic journal, sponsored by the Children's Literature Foundation, with Francelia Butler as editor-in-chief, has contained about 20 articles a year on themes, authors, and books in the area of children's literature.

250. Monson, Dianne L., and McClenathan, DayAnn K., eds. *Developing Active Readers: Ideas for Parents, Teachers, and Librarians.* **Newark, DE: International Reading Association, 1979. 104p.**

This collection of articles developed for the Association's Library Resources and Reading Committee is planned as a guide to the theory and technique required to advance the teaching of reading through literature. The objective is to "produce readers who respond actively to literature—who enjoy it, value it, and will make reading a lifetime habit." It is organized in two parts: Part I, "The Right Book for Each Child," has six essays on book selection and library use; Part 2, "Involving Children with Literature," has five essays with comment on children's titles in the text. There is also a short annotated list of reference sources. The volume, unindexed, is primarily valuable for the ideas presented; the bibliographical element may be informative for parents and teachers, but is too unsophisticated to serve librarians for collection building.

251. Monson, Dianne L., and Peltola, Bette J. *Research in Children's Literature: An Annotated Bibliography.* **Newark, DE: International Reading Association, 1976. 96p.**

This comprehensive compilation of studies which appeared from 1960 to 1974 includes 332 entries for unpublished doctoral dissertations and masters' theses, as well as published works, relating to literature for children and adolescents. It is organized in three sections: dissertations and ERIC documents, journal articles, and related studies. There is a detailed index. The researcher will find numerous entries relating to children's authors and types of literature for young people which include bibliographical components.

252. Moon, Marjorie. *John Harris' Books for Youth, 1801 to 1843: Being a Checklist of Books for Children and Young People Published for Their Amusement and Instruction by John Harris and His Son, Successors to Elizabeth Newbery, Including a List of Games and Teaching Toys.* **Cambridge, England: The Compiler and M.J.B. Spielman, 1976. 185p.**

A bibliographical checklist of over 1,000 children's titles put out by the business successors of the famous John Newbery. The first part gives an alphabetical list of the books; the second part covers games, toys, and teaching aids. Full bibliographical details are provided and title pages and illustrations are reproduced in the text and in a section of half-tone plates. Appendices include a chronological index of the earliest known editions and references to contemporary reviews. The compiler published an 18-page supplement in 1983 with a further 45 newly identified titles.

253. Moransee, Jess R., ed. *Children's Prize Books: An International Listing of 193 Children's Literature Prizes/Preisgekronte Kinderbücher: ein internationales Verzeichnis von 193 Kinderbuch Preise.* **2d rev. ed. Munich: Sauer, 1983. 620p.**

The first "revised and enlarged" edition appeared in 1979, preceded by other editions of 1959, 1964, and 1969 (E/S 1945–75, pp. 156, 157). In a country-by-country arrangement, this latest edition lists 187 awards from 38 countries, with six international awards. As before, citations and other contents are bilingual. Each entry carries a brief annotation. About 50 noteworthy illustrations are reproduced from the books. An introduction by the former editor, Walter Scherf, and a preface by the current editor give a background for the book awards and set the prevailing international scene. Now substantially more inclusive than were the earlier editions, this valuable tool will immediately commend itself to librarians as a source for collection building, as well as for reference. Constituting, as it were, a refereed list of the "best of the best," the selections will also be useful to teachers, publishers, booksellers, and the general public.

254. Morgan, Frederick Charles. *Children's Books Published before 1830: Exhibited at Malvern Public Library in 1911.* **Hereford, England: Hereford Book Services, 1976. 33p.**

The checklist of an early exhibition of children's books made a pioneer contribution to bibliophile collecting in the field. Entries have a few bibliographical notes, and some half-tone plates reproduce items. The compiler was librarian of this English public library from 1910 to 1925.

255. ———. *Stratford-upon-Avon, A 19th Century Library and My Reading from the Age of 4 to 20 Years.* Hereford, England: The Author, 1977. 22p.

Many of these reminiscences of a former public librarian in his 99th year are concerned with a boy's reading from 1882 to 1900, with mentions of classic titles and standard fare in Victorian literature for young people. Those familiar with historical collections in the field will find this an interesting reading experience.

256. Mortimer, Sheila M. *What Shall I Read?: A Select List of Quality Books for Children.* **2d ed. London: Library Association, 1978. 168p.**

First published in 1973 (E/S 1945–75, p. 124), the aims and principles of this officially sponsored selection remain unchanged. However, besides new authors and new titles, this edition includes some very useful out-of-print titles, and the representation of acknowledged classics has been strengthened where they still have relevance to and bring pleasure to children of today. This booklist remains a basic and sound guide for smaller British libraries and a useful way of accessing good British children's books for small North American libraries.

257. Mortimore, Arthur Dennis. *Index to Characters in Children's Literature.* **Bristol, England: The Author, 1977. 191p.;** *Children's Literary Characters Index 1981: The First Supplement.* **Bristol, England: The Author, 1981. 78p.**

Based on nearly 4,000 books available in British libraries written by British, American, Australian, Canadian, French, and other international authors, this alphabetical index of the memorable characters appearing in them, including many minor ones, is intended to help librarians, teachers, and parents to locate books that children ask for. References are made from character to author and title, and often an identificatory phrase is provided. A select list of books in series is appended. The supplement adds five years' further coverage to the basic index which covered up to 1975–76 and incorporates suggested additions to it supplied by librarians. Becoming a standard staff tool in British libraries, the index is not without applicability to North American collections.

258. Moss, Elaine. *Picture Books for Young People 9–13.* **(A Signal Bookguide). Stroud, England: Thimble Press, 1981. 46p.**

This annotated list, put out by the publishers of the children's literature periodical *Signal*, is concerned with the recent publishing phenomenon of the picture book for the not so young, partly visual and at the same time a real book. The preface examines the educational opportunities offered by the new-style picture book for older children, in spite of some educational reluctance to accept it. The 84 titles chosen examine aspects of life openly and controversially, often humorously. Four sections illustrate "A Wry Look at Ourselves," "A Deep Look at Ourselves," "Keep Moving: Ourselves in Picture Strip," and "Cosmorama: A Relative Look at Ourselves in Time and Place." The entertaining annotations are a blend of criticism and description. Titles are British publications, but not necessarily British in origin.

This is an original selection of original books. A revised edition appeared in 1985.

259. Moss, Elaine, and others. *Children's Books of the Year.* **London: Hamish Hamilton, 1970–1982. Annual.**

This outstanding annual selection and review of current children's books published in Great Britain (E/S 1945–75, p. 125) commenced with the year 1970 and carried on through the year 1982. Elaine Moss, sole editor until 1978, was joined by Barbara Sherrard Smith as coeditor for nonfiction in 1979, and the latter became sole editor in 1980, when Julia Macrae Books replaced Hamish Hamilton as the publisher in association with the National Book League. The NBL's annual traveling exhibitions continued to be the basis for the booklists. Books, 300 a year until 1981, and 250 in 1982, were chosen "to give an overall picture of the year's good publishing for children, bearing in mind the different needs of English-speaking children the world over which parents, teachers, and libraries are trying to meet." A new introduction each year highlighted the year's developments. Regrettably the economics of publishing terminated the series with the volume for 1982. For its 13-year span, it came to be regarded as an authoritative choice of the best in Great Britain's children's books, though overseas publications were not neglected, useful for librarians and individuals alike. For smaller British libraries, it was an invaluable buying guide, for American libraries a ready means of keeping up with quality children's literature from across the Atlantic. The backfile remains a valuable retrospective tool.

260. Moss, Joy F. *Focus Units in Literature: A Handbook for Elementary School Teachers.* **Urbana, IL: National Council of Teachers of English, 1984. 238p.**

This manual for kindergarten to sixth-grade teachers seeks to present an instructional model rather than just a method for teaching reading. Comment and listing of individual titles make up a considerable portion of the text. Each of the 13 chapters follows a similar pattern for the six grades and provides descriptive annotations for about 15 books appropriate for group sessions, followed by much more extensive citation of books suitable for independent reading. These superior choices, mainly of current vintage, will aid teachers to introduce literature in a sophisticated way. School and public librarians with their greater access to titles may still find these an interesting selection.

261. Muir, Marcie. *A Bibliography of Australian Children's Books.* **Vol. 2. London: Deutsch, 1976. 554p.**

The first volume of this standard bibliography appeared in 1970 (E/S 1945–75, pp. 126–27). The second extends coverage from the end of 1967 to the end of 1972; a further extension is not planned. The compiler has been far more selective for the additional years, due to the proliferation of publication, particularly of educational books. The previous arrangement is followed whereby authors are listed alphabetically and titles chronologically under their author. As before, there is a supplementary bibliography covering the southwest Pacific area. There are 26 more illustrations and corrigenda for the first volume.

262. ———. *A History of Australian Children's Book Illustration*. Melbourne, Australia: Oxford University Press, 1982. 160p.

This pioneer account by the bibliographer of Australian children's literature includes not only Australian artists and publications but also the absentee artists who illustrated foreign publications featuring Australian themes. Together they reveal a vigorous and varied tradition which is lavishly documented here with numerous color and black-and-white reproductions. The text explores the field chronologically from nineteenth-century beginnings and analyzes the various genres, such as books for the nursery, books for boys and for girls, and the stories of fairies and bush creatures with uniquely Australian characteristics. The conclusion brings the story up-to-date. This will rank as the standard account of a hitherto neglected field.

263. Mullen, Helen M., and others. *Notable Children's Books 1940-70*. Chicago: American Library Association, 1977. 84p.

Prepared by the 1940–1970 Notable Children's Book Committee of the American Library Association's Children's Services Division, this list replaces and extends its predecessor published in 1966, which covered books from 1940 to 1959 (E/S 1945–75, p. 110). It re-appraises, after they have been "critically and continuously judged," the books which had been chosen by the Book Evaluation Committee of the Division on an annual basis and published in *Booklist*. This wider perspective has added and eliminated titles to and from the list. The Committee's criteria for the concept of "notable" are explained. The list is arranged alphabetically by author and each entry carries a brief but carefully phrased descriptive annotation. A title index is provided. The succeeding volume covering 1971–1975 appeared in 1981 and was selected by Ethel Manheimer (**239**) with a succeeding committee. All volumes form an excellent selection aid for American libraries, and—as representing the best from America—for libraries in other English-speaking countries.

264. National Association of Independent Schools. Library Committee. *Books for Secondary School Libraries*. 6th ed. New York: Bowker, 1981. 844p.

First published in 1955, with expanded editions appearing in 1955, 1961, 1968, and 1971 (E/S 1945–75, p. 130), this extensive unannotated listing reached its fifth edition in 1976. The present edition was again updated and greatly expanded by an ad hoc committee of many members coordinated by Pauline Anderson as editor. The committee aimed to select books representing high standards of scholarship in traditional academic disciplines, as well as books that reflect current interests and concerns. It now lists more than 9,000 nonfiction titles and series, an increase of more than 3,000 entries. Expansion was most evident in the arts, history, philosophy, and religion. Entries remained arranged by Dewey Decimal classification with Library of Congress subject headings supplied, a considerable cataloging convenience for school libraries. In this edition, the subject index has been separated from the author-title index. The objectives of the Association and its committees have continued to ensure that titles chosen are especially useful for the academically talented. But because of the high quality and wide range of the selection, this list can be a valuable tool when collecting nonfiction for other ages and educational levels.

265. New York Public Library. Committee on Books for Young Adults. *Books for the Teen Age.* **New York: The Library, 1955– . Annual.**

This time-honored list was selected and published in the library's *Bulletin* as far back as 1929 (E/S 1945–75, pp. 134–35). Members of the committee drawn from the library staff working with this age group all over the city's jurisdiction annually revise a list of books "constantly tried and tested with teenage readers" on subjects of special interest and appeal to teenagers. Presentation that is clear, vivid, appealing, and imaginative remains a criterion for selection. The majority of titles, now some 1,250 a year, are adult publications, juvenile titles included having value for all ages. Current-year publications and other new additions to the selection, averaging a quarter of the total count, are indicated with an asterisk. Arrangement is in five broad areas subdivided into over 70 subject areas, and entries are alphabetical by author within those. Annotation is limited to a short, expressively worded phrase. A subject index precedes and a title index follows the entries. This outstanding annual selection continues to be an indispensable acquisition tool for all libraries and professionals concerned with young adult reading, in addition to its value for parents and young people themselves. Many of the hard-cover editions listed are also available in their favorite paperback format. Libraries outside the United States will find the selection convenient for indicating new arrivals and trends in American publications for young adults.

266. ———. Office of Children's Services. *Children's Books: One Hundred Titles for Reading and Sharing.* **New York: The Library, 1911– . Annual and Biennial.**

This selection of children's books, chosen by children's librarians from throughout the city's system, has appeared since 1911 (E/S 1945–75, pp. 133–34) with variations of title and irregularities of publishing schedule in recent years. Since 1976 biennial appearance has been the norm, with a fold-out pamphlet replacing it in some alternate years. Titles are arranged in genre categories, and since 1983 software has been added to the records (listed since 1972) and the books. In all formats it remains a high-quality, professional selection and constitutes a valuable source, not only for purchase by parents and others concerned, but also for checking and collecting in all libraries, whether public or school. For libraries outside the United States, it conveniently presents a short list of the "best of the best" in current American publication for children.

267. Newman, Janet. *Sex Education: A Critical Evaluation of Materials.* **Birmingham, England: Library Association Youth Libraries Group; Oxford: School Library Association, 1978. 54p.**

This annotated book list designed for parents, teachers, and young people themselves has as its objective the critical evaluation of materials for young people available in Great Britain, including multimedia but not films. Criteria for choice include style and method of presentation, vocabulary, age and reading levels, illustration, accuracy, coverage, and—since items represent a wide range of viewpoints—attitudes, bias, and sexism, for which some titles included are criticized. Contents are divided into five sections, each separately introduced: "Guides for Parents and Teachers," "Pre-School and Infants," "The Junior Years," "Puberty and Young Adolescents," and

"Young Adults." The lively and personal annotations on each item extend from one to three paragraphs. Publications are British, but a number of translations are included.

268. Nicholson, Margaret E. *People in Books; First Supplement: A Selective Guide to Biographical Literature Arranged by Vocation and Other Fields of Reader Interest.* **New York: Wilson, 1977. 792p.**

As in the original volume which appeared in 1969 (E/S 1945–75, p. 136), this reference guide classifies biographees by vocations, activities, or other characteristics which made them famous. This extensive supplement can be regarded as essentially an independent work; since it indexes biographies that are contained in bibliographical lists—such as the *Public Library Catalog*—that were published between 1967 and 1971, it consequently includes books earlier than 1967 which were recommended by those lists, thus largely superseding its predecessor. The number of vocational and other headings has been increased from 249 to 344. Annotations for the entries indicate reading levels. Appendices include indexes to "people" by country and century, a list of the collective biographies indexed that were selected as containing biographical material of particular interest to schools and public libraries, autobiographies, and those individuals mentioned in the main section. Most useful perhaps at the secondary school level, it remains an indispensable tool for all types of libraries requiring biographical information of this kind.

269. Norton, Donna E. *Through the Eyes of a Child: An Introduction to Children's Literature.* **Columbus, OH: Merrill, 1983. 664p.**

Written by a university professor of education, this substantial textbook is intended for any adult who is interested in evaluating, selecting, and sharing children's literature, but it is also identified, more appropriately, as being designed for children's literature classes taught in departments of English, Education, and Library Science. Three introductory articles on providing a historical background, proposing guidelines for selection, and examining the place of illustration precede a chapter-by-chapter treatment of traditional genres. Each concludes with suggestive discussions of relevant issues which emphasize use and developmental tendencies. Only the final chapter deals with nonfiction rather than imaginative literature where poetry is stressed along with fiction. Titles that receive comment are appropriate for prekindergarten through grade eight, and it is claimed that 25% were published subsequent to 1981. The author offers a future update to the present bibliographical selection, listed alphabetically by author at the end of each chapter. Brief annotations, rather uneven in character but usually descriptive, include an interest level and a reading level derived from the Fry formula, which is explained in an appendix. Artistic considerations are featured, with personal statements by illustrators and a section of excellent color reproductions. This is one aspect of the quite lavish format, wider than it is high, which uses methods such as boxed features, charts, and graphs to aid visualization by the reader. This attention to graphic detail by the publisher assists the author's organization of the genre material and genre-related activities, and makes the volume a serious contender among curricularly oriented textbooks dealing with children's literature. But beginning professional students will still require other treatments of the field as learning aids to supplement this particular approach.

270. O'Dell, Felicity Ann. *Socialisation through Children's Literature: The Soviet Example.* **(Soviet and East European Studies). Cambridge, England: Cambridge University Press, 1978. 278p.**

This scholarly analysis deals essentially with the reading matter available to Soviet children in the early 1970s, and demonstrates how official concern for character education results in reading for children being centrally controlled and planned to the greatest possible extent. The introductory first part examines children's literature and social control in the Soviet context. The second part looks at the production and dissemination of Soviet children's literature, particularly primary school readers and the most popular children's magazine *Murzilka*. The third part considers the impact of Soviet children's literature in the development of specific character traits, secular morality, and secular myths. Somewhat regrettably, mention of individual children's books is minimal.

271. Opie, Iona, and Opie, Peter. *Three Centuries of Nursery Rhymes and Poetry for Children.* **2d ed. Oxford: Oxford University Press, 1977. 116p.**

First published in 1973 (E/S 1945–75, p. 138) as the catalog to an exhibition at the National Book League, the revised and expanded edition, limited to 500 copies, contains 24 full-page plates and line block illustrations in the text. Though textual changes were not extensive, this edition provides a more permanent form for this valuable reference work by the outstanding scholars of the English nursery rhyme. The new edition was sponsored by Justin G. Schiller of New York.

272. Ovens, Walter. *Recent Adult Fiction for School and College Libraries: Fifty Novels First Published 1965–82, A Personal Selection.* **Oxford: The School Library Association, 1984. 31p.**

This selection intended, for British secondary schools of all kinds is stated to be a successor to Norman Culpan's similar list published by the Association in 1967 (E/S 1945–75, p. 39). The compiler has included "all sorts of books here, historical, love, war, humour, fantasy, etc." He does note that "the outspokenness permitted today means that one cannot always recommend unreservedly." Titles such as *The Collector* and *Changing Places* were recognized as "good" but omitted as "not for a school library." A few out-of-print books are included and special attention has been paid to paperbacks. The annotations, personal in tone, usually extend to two or three paragraphs and are both descriptive and critical. In spite of the hint of censorship, this selection includes books of a high level of appeal to the demanding and quite mature audience for which it is intended. As a short list of recent novels published in England, it may also be of interest to other types of libraries.

273. Paulin, Mary Ann. *Creative Uses of Children's Literature.* **(Library Professional Publication). Hamden, CT: Shoestring Press, 1982. 730p.**

Described in the foreword by Marilyn Miller as a rich resource of titles, ideas, techniques, and sources for reading guidance, this combination of an instructional manual and an extensive annotated bibliography is addressed to all who want to know about good books to suggest to children, to select audiovisual materials appropriately, to plan reading guidance activities, and to enrich the curriculum. The initial chapter deals with introducing books in different ways, and succeeding chapters examine types of publication or activity: picture books, music, poetry, playing stories with live action and puppets, and riddles, magic, jokes, and folk themes. Each is preceded by lists of chapter objectives and techniques for use. Interwoven in the text are mentions of and comments on a large number of titles, and at the end of each chapter a numerical coding refers these to the bibliographical indexes of books and nonprint multimedia. A comprehensive title index with nearly 6,000 entries and a subject index with references to more than 2,000 subjects, including ages, grades, and curricular relationships, are also provided. The bibliographical element combines up-to-date titles with those found successful in the long term in teaching units. The professional objectives of this substantial guide are amply fulfilled; it also makes an excellent acquisition list for the elementary school in all the media covered.

274. Paulin, Mary Ann, and Berlin, Susan. *Outstanding Books for the College Bound.* **Chicago: American Library Association, Young Adult Services Division, 1984. 92p.**

The antecedents of this collected edition of earlier reading lists for upwardly mobile high school students go back to 1959, when the National Education Association asked the American Library Association to prepare a list of outstanding fiction. This was selected by members of the Young Adult Services Division and published in the *NEA Journal*, followed by similar lists of nonfiction, biography, theater, and the performing arts. Twenty-four editions, totaling almost half a million copies, were distributed in pamphlet format to students, teachers, parents, and librarians over a five-year period. Requests by librarians to have the lists revised and combined for reference resulted in this volume, intended to be used for readers' advisory work with young adults and as a basic selection list for any collection aimed at teenagers. Some 600 titles were selected from all of the previous lists. The criterion for the choice of fiction was that the books should represent significant contributions to literature that sharpen the reader's perception and are part of a broad cultural heritage. A similar standard for books representing current thought, interpretation, and historical background applied to the nonfiction, and works selected in the performing arts demonstrated central themes and major developments. Arrangement is alphabetical within the groups. Annotations, though brief, are carefully written and well expressed. Both the original and the latest editions of titles are cited. Some books are out of print; classic works and other earlier titles, a number previous to World War II, are well represented. The list fulfills its claim to be appropriate for library and home reference use. Useful for the students themselves as well as for librarians and teachers, it takes its place with the limited number of booklists designed for personal use by intelligent young people, and can be helpful to professionals when selecting books for them and other age groups.

275. Pearl, Patricia. *Religious Books for Children: An Annotated Bibliography.* **(A CSLA Bibliography). Bryn Mawr, PA: Church and Synagogue Library Association, 1983. 36p.**

Primarily directed to church and synagogue libraries, the purpose of this booklist is to provide a guide for selecting children's religious books and evaluating present library collections. Titles were selected for use from preschool through sixth grade. Only books dealing principally with religion or having a strong overt religious theme are listed, and the compiler stresses that some excellent children's literature with implicit religious themes is not included, nor is religious curriculum material. Particularly important and exceptional books are noted with an asterisk. Arrangement is by broad subject area, each being divided into two age groups: preschool through elementary, and middle elementary and up. Entries carry a brief descriptive annotation and a grade recommendation. The bibliography is claimed to be extensive, critical, and as current as possible, though the selection is necessarily limited for such a wide subject range. School and public libraries as well as small religious libraries will find its solid recommendations useful for collection building in an area where it is not easy to select.

276. Pellowski, Anne. *The World of Storytelling.* **New York: Bowker, 1977. 296p.**

Written for all who are interested in storytelling and who wish to know more about the historical traditions of this art, this handsome volume presents in print the skills and knowledge of a famous international storyteller. Five parts include the history and definition of storytelling, the types of storytelling, past and present, the format and style of storytelling, the training of storytellers, and a multilingual dictionary of storytelling terms. The author emphasizes the use of creative dramatics at their best, bringing to attention traditional sources and materials from all over the world. Over 30 illustrations show ancient and modern storytellers and their equipment. The concluding notes and bibliography provide a brief but fundamental list of storytelling resources, including books, periodicals, and nonprint material. For all who consult this entertaining and informative account, there will be a better understanding of the scope, the methods, and the history of the storytellers' art.

277. Pennypacker, Arabelle, regional ed. *The Middle Atlantic: New York, Pennsylvania, New Jersey, Maryland, Delaware.* **(Reading for Young People). Chicago: American Library Association, 1980. 164p.**

One of a series of annotated bibliographies of fiction and nonfiction titles compiled for readers from the primary grades through the tenth grade, "designed to focus on the history and character of each region of these United States." Editors for each state within the area have chosen and annotated "approximately 100 of the very best books...available for each state." Criteria for choice were that books should "best portray the spirit, the vitality and diversity of each state of the region" while reflecting overall literary quality and informational accuracy. Out-of-print titles are included if still available in libraries. The annotated bibliography is divided into broad subject groups: fiction, folktales, poetry, drama and music, biography and personal accounts, and other informational books. Titles are arranged alphabetically within each group, and carry a brief quotation and a full paragraph of description. Grade ranges are suggested: P for primary, I for intermediate, J for junior high, and S for senior high. Supplementary unannotated lists group the titles under each relevant state. The index combines author, titles, and subjects, and information is given on regional publishers and suppliers. As with all volumes of this series, the selection and commentary are systematic and generous. Its availability is a boon to selectors in school and young people's libraries—indeed in all libraries with local interests—as well as to the region's young people.

278. Peterson, Carolyn Sue, and Fenton, Ann. *Reference Books for Children.* **3d ed. Metuchen, NJ: Scarecrow, 1981. 265p.**

First published in 1970, with a second edition in 1975 (E/S 1945–75, pp. 141–42), the work's new edition, which adds a coauthor, is planned to begin a series of five yearly revisions. The title has been changed to reflect its appropriateness for both school and public libraries which cater to the same age range as elementary and junior high schools. Nearly 900 entries with descriptive annotations indicating contents and use are grouped within broad fields of knowledge—general reference, humanities, recreation, science, and social science—each of which is subdivided into specific subject topics. Scope was planned to be deliberately broad, covering a wide span of interests, curriculum needs, and levels of difficulty. Its claim to be a compilation of sound, usable titles is amply justified, and the compilers' comments that the size is deliberately restrained and the selection is merely a guide are perhaps overly modest. For school and public librarians this substantial list of carefully chosen titles forms a valuable tool for reader guidance as well as for acquisition purposes. With continued editions, it will maintain its position as one of the few guides to reference material specifically addressed to young people's requirements.

279. Peterson, Carolyn Sue, and Hall, Brenny. *Story Programs: A Source Book of Materials.* **Metuchen, NJ: Scarecrow, 1980. 294p.**

This handbook of information designed for librarians and teachers is a practical manual which contains sample story programs for three age groups: toddlers, preschoolers, and those in primary school. The bibliographical element is limited: there is an annotated bibliography of picture books for the story program, a concluding list of additional sources of material, and mentions of titles in the text, which are accessible through the author-and-title index.

280. Peterson, Linda Kauffman, and Solt, Marilyn Leathers. *Newbery and Caldecott Medal and Honor Books: An Annotated Bibliography.* **Boston: Hall, 1982. 427p.**

Intended as a reference tool for all those who work with children's literature, this volume is basically a chronological annotated listing, with a terminal date of 1981, of books that have gained honorable mention or won these prestigious awards for children's writing and its illustration. The authors, both university teachers, have divided the field, Peterson being responsible for the Caldecott and Solt for the Newbery, each providing introductory essays on characteristics and trends. Annotations, first for the medal books and then for the honor books within the year-by-year sequence, usually extend to a full page, and provide a description with a plot summary and critical comment which has a decidedly literary approach. Appendices include the terms, definition, and criteria for the awards and a distribution list of titles by type of literature. There is an author-illustrator-title index and a subject index. This is a fine guide, perhaps more slanted toward practitioners of literature and education rather than librarianship. It joins a plethora of books about these awards; however, because of its use of typescript typography its visual appeal will not compare with the attractive presentation of the *Horn Book* series.

281. Pflieger, Pat. *A Reference Guide to Modern Fantasy for Children.* **Westport, CT: Greenwood, 1984. 690p.**

Intended to form an introduction to the work of 36 British and American authors of the 19th and 20th centuries who have among them written over 100 works of fantasy for children, this dictionary provides related entries for authors, titles, characters, places, and magical objects, adding up to an in-depth study of the genre for over a century. However, the author's parameters for the concept of fantasy are carefully limited according to a definition of J.R.R. Tolkien's. For the purposes of this work, the "marvelous" excludes science fiction and also books based on illusions and dreams. Short works of under 100 pages and very well known titles such as *Alice in Wonderland* are also excluded. Entries for authors include biographies with bibliographical lists of their juvenile fantasy and nonfantasy, their adult books, and related secondary works. Title entries give a descriptive summary of approximately two pages. Appendices provide a select list of books about fantasy, a chronology of publications and of authors' dates, and a list of illustrators. The whole amounts to a significant contribution to literary research. For the enthusiast who can accept the author's limitations of what fantasy means, the book is a treasure trove. Librarians, too, will find it rewarding as a source of information and as a bibliographical checklist for a fictional genre very popular with children and young adults.

282. *Phaedrus: An International Annual of Children's Literature Research.* **New York: Columbia University, 1973– . Annual.**

Commencing as the *Newsletter of Children's Literature Research*, from 1981 on the title incorporated the word "International" to reflect the principal direction of its articles. These scholarly contributions usually address the state of the art of children's literature in various countries worldwide. There are frequent mentions of individual titles in the articles, sometimes with bibliographic lists subjoined. This invitational journal of high quality offers to researchers and librarians a valuable opportunity to become acquainted with overseas publications in the field, and often with information not easily obtained.

283. Pickering, Samuel Francis. *John Locke and Children's Books in Eighteenth Century England.* **Knoxville, TN: University of Tennessee Press, 1981. 286p.**

Based on the examination of 18th-century children's titles in the British Library, the author's researches establish the pervasive influence of the philosopher as a theoretical umbrella for much of the writing for children in the period. Various genres are examined, but fairy tales and nursery rhymes are not emphasized. There are many mentions of contemporary titles, and full notes with bibliographical references.

284. Pillon, Nancy Bach. *Reaching Young People through Media.* **Littleton, CO: Libraries Unlimited, 1983. 279p.**

Specified as a textbook for college courses in adolescent literature, this gathering of original articles by 14 recognized specialists, a number of them university faculty, has four related objectives: to teach something about the adolescent's world, to consider the role of a variety of materials, to establish criteria for evaluation and selection, and to develop techniques for sharing material. Part I covers selection of materials, and Part II programming and promotion, with seven or eight chapters in each part. While not systematic, coverage of fundamental topics is wide and conversant with current trends. Many of the essays are book-oriented, though other media are examined, with mentions of titles in the text and notes and supplementary unannotated lists of suggested reading. This is a collection of merit with interesting and authoritative articles supported by up-to-date bibliographical recommendations. Because of this it is as suitable for the practitioner as for the student audience for which it is intended.

285. Polette, Nancy. *Books and Real Life: A Guide for Gifted Students and Teachers.* **Jefferson, NC: McFarland, 1984. 117p.**

This teaching tool for classroom activities, intended for students, teachers, and also librarians and others concerned with young people, aims, as the introduction states, "not to deal with a child's personal problem, but to examine the losses of life" by treating such topics as adoption, divorce, and death. A selected booklist cites 130 titles alphabetically by author within two age sections: preschool and primary, and junior novels. As with previous volumes by this author, titles were chosen with gifted children particularly in mind. Annotations for each entry relate the theme of the book to the subject topic and list questions which may be used in discussion. A subject index connects some 15 topics to the titles. In addition to classroom use, the citations may serve school media specialists and librarians as a checklist.

286. ——. *E is for Everybody: A Manual for Bringing Fine Picture Books into the Hands and Hearts of Children.* **Metuchen, NJ: Scarecrow, 1976. 147p.**

Described as a manual for teachers and librarians, this volume is introduced by Marjorie Hamlin. Patricia Gilmore acted as art consultant. The 147 picture books were selected as appropriate for use with children in the elementary grades through junior high school. Part I, "The Books and the Activities," combines descriptive summaries of the books with suggestions for activities connected with them. Part II, "Children Interpret Literature through Art and Media," advocates an integration of the art and literature experiences. The overall emphasis is on the classroom, but librarians can use the selection as a checklist, especially in schools where classroom teachers are using this manual.

287. ———. *Picture Books for Gifted Programs*. Metuchen, NJ: Scarecrow, 1981. 220p.

This volume, intended for those who take part in programs for gifted children, provides an annotated bibliography of suitable books for developing the thinking process. In the first part, titles are arranged in five categories with separate introductions and cover about 20 books each: books to enhance cognitive development in early childhood, books to promote visual literacy, books to stimulate language development, books to promote productive thinking, and books to stimulate critical thinking. Each entry receives a detailed descriptive annotation with reference to how it can aid the process. In the second part, teaching techniques are described, including discussion questions and creative activities. A list of resource citations for teachers and parents and an author-title index complete the volume. Many good picture books have been selected and related thoughtfully to the skills in a very specific way that has in mind the involved professional. The book represents current concern in America both with early education and the education of the gifted.

288. Polette, Nancy, and Hamlin, Marjorie. *Celebrating with Books*. **Metuchen, NJ: Scarecrow, 1977. 175p.**

This annotated bibliography about ten major holidays, including United Nations Day, that are familiar to the Judeo-Christian tradition is intended for teachers to promote holiday activities in the classroom through the use of books. Some 150 titles were selected for their familiarity and easy availability and grouped according to holiday, with a brief introductory essay preceding each group and suggested activities included. Annotations indicate grade levels. Because holidays form a curricular subject in most elementary schools, the list will be helpful, but it is a slim volume compared with alternative sources, and its exclusion of religious holidays for other groups is regrettable. Its emphasis on activities, however, is important for the classroom and useful for children's services elsewhere. The author-and-title index assists use in libraries for bibliographical checking.

289. ———. *Exploring Books with Gifted Children*. Littleton, CO: Libraries Unlimited, 1980. 214p.

Intended as a guide to teachers and librarians, this teaching methodology suggests strategies to build excitement and anticipation for the reading experience, so that young readers will become sensitive to the personal and social, as well as the technical, problems of humankind. It attempts to help educators provide those conditions in which the child can act upon what he or she has read. Eleven chapters give models for instruction, often by giving a long and detailed plot summary of a work by a well-known children's author, with mentions of the author's other titles. Two appendices list selection aids to develop study unit models and suggest topics and titles. These range from books for preschoolers to junior novels for eleven- to fifteen-year-olds. This book for classroom activities with gifted children is a valuable source of suggestions for educators, and gives sound recommendations for appropriate titles.

290. Polkingharn, Anne T., and Toohey, Catherine. *Creative Encounters: Activities to Expand Children's Responses to Literature.* **Littleton, CO: Libraries Unlimited, 1983. 138p.**

Fifty books are prescribed here as 50 creative ideas for teachers, librarians, reading specialists, and others who work with children from kindergarten to grade six, with the objective of extending children's literature beyond the story hour and the curriculum. Each book is given descriptive annotation from the point of view of the child reader; this is followed by three paragraphs entitled "Purpose," "Materials," and "Let's Begin," which lead to ideas for suggested activities and displays. Besides the 50 titles treated in detail, an appendix lists a further 250 titles by a wide range of children's authors. Well illustrated with drawings and diagrams, this volume is primarily a practical handbook for teachers, but media specialists can use the appropriate choices in both text and appendix as a bibliographical checklist.

291. Posner, Marcia. *Selected Jewish Children's Books.* **New York: JWB Jewish Book Council, 1982. 28p.**

Sponsored in cooperation with the National Foundation for Jewish Culture, this annotated list of current books was compiled in response to many requests to the Council for recommended titles for Jewish children. It caters to ages four through fourteen, though a few appropriate adult titles have been included. Age levels are recommended and entries carry a one-sentence annotation which emphasizes the Jewish relevance. Titles that have won Jewish book awards have been specially noted. Chosen by a librarian, this excellent but slim selection may reflect a lack of children's publication in the field. Its selectivity, however, adds to its usefulness for school and public libraries as a checklist for quality titles on this theme, as well as for the audience intended.

292. Potvin, Claude. *Le Canada français et sa littérature de jeunesse: Bref historique, sources bibliographiques, repertoire des livres.* **Moncton, NB: CRP, 1981. 185p.**

Essentially a new edition of the author's 1972 title, *La littérature de jeunesse au Canada français* (E/S 1945–75, p. 143), this provides an enlarged historical sketch of Canadian children's literature in French, an annotated list of bibliographical sources, and a catalog of children's titles as complete as possible, up to 1979, arranged alphabetically by author-title entry within chronological groups. For inclusion, works were required to be published in French Canada by Canadian authors who wrote in French. A list of pseudonyms, an author index, and a title index complete this carefully researched and indispensable reference to this significant area of children's literature, about which information is hard to obtain.

293. Probst, Robert E. *Adolescent Literature: Response and Analysis.* **Columbus, OH: Merrill, 1984. 260p.**

This book, aimed at high school teachers, especially teachers of English, "teaches that literature is experience, not information, and that the student must be invited to participate." Three parts discuss "The Logic of Response-Based Teaching," "The Literature," and "The Literature Program." Primarily a teaching tool for the classroom, its bibliographical element is in the second part, the first and third being concerned with literary analysis and the curriculum, with specific suggestions and procedures for implementing response in the classroom. Unannotated lists cover recommended adolescent and popular adult literature, recommended books on media, and a number of lists of books for young adults on topics, themes, and genres, such as "Violence," "Friendship," "Love, Romance, and Sexuality," and "Science Fiction." Overall, these titles were mainly written in the 1970s, have a wide range of interest and reading levels, and are currently popular with young adults. School media specialists and others will find them useful as a bibliographical checklist. There is an author, title, and subject index to the volume.

294. Purves, Alan C., and Monson, Dianne L. *Experiencing Children's Literature*. Glenview, IL: Scott, Foresman, 1984. 216p.

Two professors of education have written this textbook "because we sense a need for a book that would be useful to our students—prospective and actual teachers....we have chosen a theory of literature that seems to make the most pedagogical sense—the transactional theory of Louis Rosenblatt." Chapters discuss the transactional approach, folktales, prose, and evaluating and designing literature programs. Children's titles receive comment in the text and unannotated lists are provided at the end of chapters, mainly of well-known popular and classic books. There are also references to professional works and a few bibliographies, and an author, title, and subject index. For prospective and beginning elementary teachers, this volume can fulfill one of its aims, "to help...connect practice with theory," but it will be of little use to librarians.

295. Quayle, Eric. *Early Children's Books: A Collector's Guide*. Newton Abbott, England: David and Charles, 1983. 256p.

This is a successor, rather than a new edition, of the author's 1971 title, *The Collector's Book of Children's Books* (E/S 1945–75, p. 144). Written by a lifelong bibliophile and collector of children's books, this general account for collectors contains much information for other students of early children's literature. After an introductory discourse on the practice of book collecting in the field, the text blends bibliography and literary history, incorporating numerous extracts from the books themselves. Chapters cover the earliest periods from the 16th to the 18th century, fairy and folktales, books that were inducements to learning, verse and rhyme, tales for youth, boys' adventure stories, toy books, periodicals, annuals, and "penny dreadfuls." The terminal date is about 1910. Prominence is given to late 19th- and early 20th-century developments, supplementing the systematic account of the better known earlier books. An impressive selection of illustrations, chosen from the author's own collection, reproduce pages from the books themselves. A final select bibliography lists reference works which the collector needs to consult. The author has been criticized for bibliographical inaccuracies, and the researcher should double-check facts in other accounts of the field; however, this valuable narrative will be useful constantly to collectors and rare book libraries. An American issue was published by Barnes and Noble in the same year.

296. Quigly, Isabel. *The Heirs of Tom Brown: The English School Story.* **London: Chatto and Windus, 1982. 296p.**

This book studies in an entertaining fashion a genre of young people's literature which had a long life and important sociological influence. The social climate and the social attitudes of the authors are given prominence. Chapters examine the schools behind the school stories, the head master of fact and fiction, the central school story of Talbot Baines Reed and others, girls' school stories (briefly), "pop" school stories (Greyfriars and Company), and the decline of the school story. Careful analysis is made of the 20th-century authors whose books were not school stories in the traditional sense but who used a school environment, including P.G. Wodehouse, Hugh Walpole, and Alec Waugh. Many authors and titles are referred to or quoted in the text. The bibliography refers to the social and literary background, not to the stories themselves. This is a readable and scholarly account of a field now receiving renewed attention.

297. Quimby, Harriett B., ed. *Let's Read Together: Books for Family Enjoyment.* **4th ed. Chicago: American Library Association, 1981. 111p.**

First published in 1960, with succeeding editions appearing in 1964 and 1969 (E/S 1945–75, p. 131), this fourth edition with a foreword by Francis Smardo, is sponsored only by ALA's Association for Library Service to Children. Previous editions were under the joint sponsorship of the National Congress of Parents and Teachers and ALA's Children's Service Division. The editor is here assisted by the five members of The Let's Read Together Revision Committee, chaired by Barbara Rollock. The preface identifies a similar audience as before: "parents seeking just the right books for family sharing," and other adults seeking books to read aloud to children in classrooms, libraries, and other locations. The revision has given equal attention "to retain[ing] those timeless books, favorites of generations" as to updating with "contemporary books well on their way to becoming classics"; many were held over from previous editions, and many were selected from publications of the previous decade. Selection for various age groups range from picture books to be shared with the prereading child to books for older children that reflect our changing society, and respect the differences in ethnic diversity. Entries are arranged alphabetically by title within 22 genre, subject, and purpose-oriented categories, some with subdivisions; for instance, "Books for Family Sharing" has 11 sections on different issues. Some categories have been changed from previous editions and some are new. The descriptive annotations of a couple of sentences include a final critical phrase, and broad age and grade recommendations are designated by letters. Paperbacks are indicated. There is an appendix of series books, and an author-title index concludes. This list continues to reflect the skill of experienced librarians in selecting, and is excellent for school and public librarians to use with teachers as well as parents, and as a checklist for their own collections.

298. Quimby, Harriett B., and Kimmel, Margaret Mary. *Building a Children's Literature Collection: A Suggested Basic Reference Collection* *for Academic Libraries and a Suggested Basic Collection of Children's Books.* 3d ed. (Choice Bibliographical Essay Series). Middleton, CT: Choice, 1983. 48p.

First appearing in *Choice* in 1974 and separately published in the following year (E/S 1945–75, p. 144), this booklist appeared in a revised edition in 1978. The current edition, with a new joint compiler, has the same main purpose as previously, to support the teaching of a basic course in children's literature, and the revision is designed as a guide to remodel and update the collection. The two divisions specified in the subtitle are compiled respectively by the two authors, who contribute a bibliographical essay to precede each booklist. The first section by Harriett Quimby lists about 1,000 citations which, as in the previous edition, represent materials supportive of almost all aspects of children's literature. The second section, representing about 1,000 children's titles arranged within broad genre and subject groups, has been thoroughly revised by Margaret Kimmel according to selection criteria which rely less than previously on other lists and texts. The choice is a fine attempt to delimit the essential in this hard-to-define field. It emphasizes tradition and quality while taking note of fresh evaluations. While no such selection can ever be accepted as perfect, the objective of specifying a basic body of titles needed by the student and researcher has been worthily met. Both parts of this now standard bibliography are indispensable checklists, not only for academic collections.

299. Raban, Bridie, and Moon, Cliff. *Books and Learning to Read.* (Books in the Primary School). Oxford: School Library Association, 1978. 34p.

This bibliographical essay, directed to the first level of the British school system, is intended to help teachers determine purposes and develop criteria for the selection of books which can constitute a primary school reading program. The first part looks at the reading process and examines reasons for including "real" books in the school program. The second presents a select list of books in a narrative commentary arranged in three developmental stages: "Beginning Reading," with about 60 titles; "Learning to Read," with about 75 titles; and "Children and Books," with almost 60 nonfiction titles. The third part presents a tabular checklist for assessing children's attitudes to reading and their level of attainment. An appendix lists and annotates some recent books on reading. This is a careful selection and exposition of appropriate British publications by two experienced instructors in and writers about the teaching of reading skills.

300. Rathbone, Nicky. *Mirth without Mischief: An Introduction to the Parker Collection of Early Children's Books and Games.* Birmingham, England: Library Association West Midland Branch, 1982. 42p.

This description of books in a special collection in the Birmingham Reference Library mentions the major items and puts them in their social and literary perspective. There are numerous small black-and-white illustrations. A selected list of books and catalogs relating to the history of English children's books is appended.

301. Rauter, Rosemarie, ed. *Printed for Children: World Children's Book Exhibition.* Munich and London: Sauer, 1978. 448p.

This substantial catalog of international children's books brings together publications from 70 countries. The exhibition on which it was based was installed at the Frankfurt Book Fair of 1978 in connection with its special focus on "The Child and the Book" and the forthcoming "International Year of the Child" of 1979. The foreword by the director-general of UNESCO refers to the impressive global panorama of children's literature presented. Each country contributed sample publications printed for children. Arrangement is by country, each section having a preface which relates to the local book trade and its children's publications. The subsequent bibliography of selected titles is unannotated. The catalog provides a mine of material for libraries seeking fuller representation of children's books from other lands, particularly from Third World countries.

302. Ray, Colin. *Background to Children's Books.* **New ed. London: National Book League, 1977. 20p.**

Previously published in 1971, 1974, and 1975 (E/S 1945–75, p. 146), the fourth edition of this annotated short list of the most useful books—not in general the highly specialized works—on children's books and reading has been brought up-to-date, but still includes relevant out-of-print titles. It remains a well-selected and convenient tool for the teachers, researchers, and parents for whom it is intended.

303. Rees, David. *The Marble in the Water: Essays on Contemporary Writers of Fiction for Children and Young Adults.* **Boston: The Hornbook, 1980. 212p.**

These bibliographic essays discuss the work of eight British and ten American authors, exploring some of the likenesses and the major differences in fiction for children and young adults. The author intends "to call attention to certain good writers whose work is being unjustifiably ignored, and also to point out that some of our more famous authors do not always match up to the praise that is lavished upon them." The range of their writing extends from childhood up to adulthood and all are of a recent generation, including Philippa Pearce, Alan Garner, E.B. White, Robert Cormier, Judy Blume, Paula Fox, and Beverly Cleary. Rees "calls the shots" critically as he sees them, which makes stimulating reading. Many titles are discussed in the text and cited in appended lists, and the author-title index assists use as a selection source. The appeal of the book is not only to librarians but also to critics, reviewers, and to other interested readers of this literature.

304. Rees, John; Pike, Pam; and Wild, Meg. *Knowing and Doing: Information Books.* **(Books in the Primary School). Oxford: School Library Association, 1983. 34p.**

Compiled by a primary school teacher and two librarians with the assistance of many individuals and bodies, the aim of this selection is to help British primary school children get acquainted with good information books on which they can rely. The introduction poses the question "Why information books?" and the first part discusses sources relating to subject topics and areas of interest, commenting on relevant titles. The second part lists more titles, unannotated, arranged broadly according to Dewey in 22 sections, each prefaced by an introduction. Readability levels are indicated as 1, 2, or 3, books of special value being designated with T, and books for browsing with B. Teachers are provided with eight criteria to use in book selection. Text and lists together make up a valuable bibliographical source for teachers and librarians in the British school system.

305. Richardson, Selma K. *Magazines for Children: A Guide for Parents, Teachers, and Librarians.* **Chicago: American Library Association, 1983. 147p.**

Developed from the compiler's *Periodicals for School Media Programs,* 1978, this publication resulted from a decision to extract from that work those magazines intended primarily for children. It has been especially designed to fulfill the needs of librarians serving children in school and public libraries to develop magazine collections, besides serving the interests of teachers and parents. Criteria for inclusion of the approximately 90 selected were suitability and interest for children through age fourteen or eighth grade, as well as quality of content and format. Excluded categories were periodicals for adults and readers of fifteen and above, professional journals, student productions, religious periodicals, local and state publications, and comic books. Arrangement is alphabetical by title. New, descriptive annotations are lengthier and more detailed to assist in evaluating the magazines. These run up to a whole page and include full publishing information. Appendices provide a classification of age and grade levels as recommended by publishers and suggestions about some adult and teenage periodicals enjoyed by children. The subject index classes titles under broad subject headings. Both the high level of selectivity and the full information provided make this an excellent tool to use in all children's libraries.

306. ———. *Magazines for Young Adults: Selections for School and Public Libraries.* **Chicago: American Library Association, 1984. 329p.**

Developed from the compiler's *Periodicals for School Media Programs,* 1978, this annotated listing of nearly 600 titles, 150 of which are newly included, is intended to be an aid in the selection and acquisition of magazines, indexes, and newspapers that can be used by young adults. Magazines primarily for children are not included, being described in the compiler's complementary *Magazines for Children,* 1983. Introductory material describes criteria and methodology for the choice and discusses the use of periodicals in school library programs. Arrangement of the entries is alphabetical by title. Annotations, many rewritten since the previous work, extend to a substantial paragraph of description and evaluation, often with suggestions for curricular use. Full publishing information is provided, with references to periodical indexes, which are listed in an appendix, as are age and grade levels suggested by publishers. The subject index classes titles under about 60 subject headings. The balanced coverage of this extensive and careful selection and the excellent annotations make it an exceptionally useful tool for all libraries catering to young adults. It is also of considerable interest to teachers and others concerned with adolescents. It was up-to-date in this volatile field of publication as of time of compilation.

307. ———. *Periodicals for School Media Programs.* **Chicago: American Library Association, 1978. 397p.**

This guide revises and updates *Periodicals for School Libraries,* 1973, by Marian H. Scott (E/S 1945–75, p. 159). The objective of the compilation is "to give assistance to those who must carefully and judiciously determine which periodicals would be most appropriate for their schools." With the same coverage, features, and criteria for selection as its predecessor, this annotated selective list contains over 500 titles of magazines, newspapers, and periodical indexes, a slight increase. Other periodicals useful to school media centers have been added and defunct titles have been dropped. All the annotations are newly written. A subject guide to the magazines is provided in an appendix. When published, this edition formed an invaluable selection aid for school and other libraries. Two later titles by the compiler serve to update parts of its coverage, *Magazines for Children* (**305**), 1983, and *Magazines for Young Adults* (**306**), 1984.

308. ——, ed. *Research about Nineteenth-Century Children and Books: Portrait Studies.* Urbana, IL: University of Illinois Graduate School of Library Science, 1980. 145p.

This volume collects papers presented on April 27 and 28, 1979 at a symposium sponsored by the school in association with the ALA's Committee on National Planning for Special Collections of the Association for Library Service to Children. The meeting was planned to bring together portraitists, from novice to experienced, who are interested in depicting 19th-century children. The papers, well illustrated, comment on various aspects of children's literature during the period, and are both scholarly and readable. There is, regrettably, no index to titles mentioned in the text.

309. Richter, Bernice, and Wenzel, Duane. *Children's Science Books: A Bibliography of Books Shown at the Museum of Science and Industries Children's Science Book Fair.* Chicago: Museum of Science and Industry, 1973– . Annual.

This annotated catalog was originally designed to provide visitors with a record of the book exhibits. Of recent years, it has come to serve a much wider audience as a source of information for teachers, librarians, and others about current science books for children. Its value as an annual selection made from science review sources is increased by the brief critical and descriptive annotations, and the inclusion of recommended grade levels and recommendation ratings, varying from AA ("strongly recommended") to D ("rejected"). The materials, including nonprint, are arranged alphabetically by title within subject groups. Its usefulness as a selection tool for children from kindergarten through grade twelve was enhanced by the publication in 1985 of a retrospective edition which collected all the reviews from 1973 to 1984.

310. Roginski, Jim W. *Little Truths Better than Great Fables: A Collection of Old and Rare Books for Children in the Fort Worth Public Library.* Fort Worth, TX: Branch-Smith, 1976. 125p.

This catalog of a representative collection of early children's books, presented to Fort Worth Public Library by Mrs. Charles Reimers, was a contribution to the Bicentennial. It is strong in British and American books from the late 19th and early 20th centuries. Over 100 titles receive scholarly annotation and full indexing. It includes a substantial number of illustrations in black-and-white and color, which add to its interest for collectors, scholars, and rare book librarians.

311. ――――. *Newbery and Caldecott Medalists and Honor Book Winners: Bibliographies and Resource Material through 1977*. Littleton, CO: Libraries Unlimited, 1982. 332p.

Among the number of works available on both awards, this can be singled out as the work of a librarian who is an enthusiastic expert on these books. It provides an inclusive listing of publications and related materials from the beginning of the careers of 266 authors and illustrators who have been recipients. Entries itemize awards, bibliographical details, nonbook media, special collections in libraries, and background reading. Appendices give yearly listings of the Newbery from 1922 and the Caldecott from 1938. As there is much important related and peripheral material to be found here which is not available elsewhere, the volume will be very useful to public librarians, and also to others, such as teachers, researchers, and booksellers. The serious limitation of this valuable reference source is the terminal date of 1977.

312. Rollock, Barbara. *The Black Experience in Children's Books*. New York: New York Public Library, 1979. 113p.

The publishing history of this booklist, with several editions under a different title, goes back to 1949. The immediate predecessor of this edition was published in 1974, when Barbara Rollock replaced Augusta Baker as compiler (E/S 1945–75, p. 149). Prefaces by both are included in this updated edition, which commemorates the International Year of the Child. The same criteria for choice were used with the objective of presenting the best interpretations of the Black experience in children's books. The over 300 titles are organized in informal subject groups with brief descriptive annotations. A new feature lists Black authors and illustrators in an appendix. It remains a valuable source in which librarians and teachers can check and select significant books for children from kindergarten to twelve years of age. A companion volume, *The Black Experience in Children's Audio-Visual Materials*, originally published in 1973, was also revised in 1979, and complements the book list.

313. Rosenberg, Betty. *Genreflecting: A Guide to Reading Interests in Genre Fiction*. Littleton, CO: Libraries Unlimited, 1982. 254p.

Many of the types of formula fiction discussed here are eagerly devoured by young people, often as much as by adults. The genesis of this critical account of popular societal forms of reading material was in a course on reading interests given by the author. Each genre and subgenre is defined and discussed, the potential clientele identified, leading authors noted, and many titles listed. Original, stimulating, and amusing, the focus on reader's interests and preferences makes it significant for librarians, not least for those serving young adults. As a bibliography it is not exhaustive, though there are plenty of titles to serve as a checklist for public and school libraries, and it is well indexed for reference.

314. Rosenberg, Judith K. *Young People's Literature in Series: Fiction, Non-Fiction, and Publishers' Series, 1973–1975.* **Littleton, CO: Libraries Unlimited, 1977. 234p.**

This supplements both of the compiler's two previous bibliographies, *Young People's Literature in Series, Fiction,* 1972, and *Young People's Literature in Series, Publisher's and Non-Fiction,* 1973 (E/S 1945–75, pp. 151–52). Information supplied remains similar, but annotation of both fiction and nonfiction series has been expanded. The potential readership for fiction is grades three to nine; for nonfiction, grades three to twelve. A designation has been added to series for reluctant readers. Indexes are supplied for fiction series, authors, and titles. Series constitute a large part of young people's reading, so this compilation is a valuable selection tool for school and public libraries, both for its listing element and for the quality of its critical annotations.

315. Rossi, Mary Jane Mangini. *Read to Me! Teach Me! A Guide to Books.* **Wauwatosa, WI: American Baby Books, 1982. 75p.**

This "complete reference guide to books for fun and early learning" is compiled for parents of children from birth to age five or six. Ninety-nine titles are arranged alphabetically by title within six chapters corresponding to age, with brief descriptive annotations. Most are well recognized, and the selection, along with the large-print text and simple style, will make this elementary tool helpful to parents, and of some use to others dealing with young children, if not to librarians and teachers.

316. Rudman, Masha Kabakow. *Children's Literature: An Issues Approach.* **2d ed. New York: Longman, 1984. 476p.**

First published in 1976, this survey of children's literature "is designed for use as a reference and a guide to the selection of children's books, with regard to their appropriateness for the purpose of bibliography, as well as a consideration of how issues of a societal and developmental nature are treated." The ten chapters introduce and discuss issues such as family, racial heritage, various special needs, old age, and war. Each includes suggested activities, relevant reference sources for adults, and an annotated list of appropriate children's titles. Grade levels are recommended. There are indexes for authors and illustrators, as well as indexes for titles and subjects. In addition to demonstrating a currently popular approach to children's literature, the selection of children's books, overhauled in this edition to include recent publications, makes up a sound checklist of significant titles for librarians and teachers.

317. Sadker, Myra Pollack, and Sadker, David Millar. *Now upon a Time: A Contemporary View of Children's Literature.* **New York: Harper, 1977. 475p.**

Directed to teachers, this "focused manageable text" is identified by the authors as something of a departure from the traditional children's literature text. Concerned with current social issues, it "maps a journey through literature to...reduce the trauma of present and future shock." Four parts examine "Life's Cycle," with chapters on family, sex, old age, and death; "The American Mosaic," with chapters on racial groups and women; "Save

Our Planet, Save Ourselves," with chapters on ecology and war and peace; and "Approaches to Working with Children and Books," with discussions on censorship and creative teaching. There are quotations in the text and extensive booklists following each chapter. An appendix provides an annotated bibliography of books describing the handicapped. For educators using an "issues" approach, this volume makes many suggestions for bibliographical support.

318. Sale, Roger. *Fairy Tales and After: From Snow White to E.B. White.* Cambridge, MA: Harvard University Press, 1978. 280p.

This contribution to the literary history of children's books emphasizes the real importance of fairy tales for later children's literature. Using the point of view of a constructive and appreciative critic, the author looks at the "very good books" and the "classic successes." Chapters examine traditional and authored fairy tales and a succession of 19th- and 20th-century authors writing in the same spirit. These form an original and thoughtful series of essays representing academic criticism of the field as pure literature.

319. Salway, Lance. *Humorous Books for Children.* 2d ed. (A Signal Booklist). Stroud, England: Thimble Press, 1980. 47p.

This annotated selection of over 100 humorous books for children was compiled by a writer and translator of children's books and edited by Nancy Chambers, the coeditor of *Signal*, the British children's literature magazine. It fully revises the first edition, published in 1978, also based on a National Book League exhibition. Described as "a personal choice, a private ramble through the forest," it ranges from picture books for the very young through to teenage novels. Sections cover picture books, comic strip books, learning to read books, stories to read aloud, stories for six- to nine-year-olds and for ten- to twelve-year-olds, novels for young adults, poetry, jokes and riddles, and humorous prose. Each title carries a full paragraph of descriptive and critical annotation. Titles were currently available in Great Britain; this edition comments that it omits some good out-of-print titles.

320. ——, ed. *A Peculiar Gift: Nineteenth Century Writings on Books for Children.* Harmondsworth, England: Kestrel, 1976. 573p.

This selection of 19th-century writing about children's books gives an indication of the remarkable extent of the serious consideration given to them at the time. Articles, many reprinted from contemporary journals, were chosen to illustrate trends and developments. A number are interesting, unusual, and entertaining examples by familiar and sometimes unexpected authors, including Dickens, Thackeray, Ruskin, Conan Doyle, and Conrad. The essays are grouped to provide relevant comparisons in seven parts with evocative titles: "A Century of Children's Books," a preliminary discussion of development in the whole period; "The Fairy Tale Never Dies"; "The Magic of Rhyme"; "To Entertain with Grace"; "What Boys and Girls Should Read"; "Awful Fun"; and "Rare and Peculiar Faculties." Over 30 illustrations from early editions of the books mentioned are reproduced. Short biographical and bibliographical notes are made for each contributor, and there are a number of bibliographical notes to the text. A select bibliography is added of about 120 titles useful for further investigation, and an appendix reprints a 1902 article on children's book illustrations.

This substantial and valuable collection brings together important material for researchers.

321. Sarkissian, Adele, ed. *Children's Authors and Illustrators: An Index to Biographical Dictionaries.* **3d ed. (Gale Biographical Index Series). Detroit: Gale, 1981. 667p.**

This originally appeared in 1976 compiled by Dennis LaBeau, with a second edition compiled in 1978 by the present editor. This third edition now cites from 275 biographical dictionaries and other sources, providing some 20,000 entries for authors and illustrators of children's books. The primary aim was to be as comprehensive as possible, furnishing quick and easy access to biographical information. Two types of entry refer to the sources: main entries for real names with dates, and pseudonyms or variant entries for pen names, etc., which refer to the main entries. The format permits additions to be entered by reference librarians. Now much expanded, it is a worthwhile reference tool for all types of libraries, and particularly for librarians in school libraries and for teachers, since biographical material figures largely in many school assignments.

322. ———. *Writers for Young Adults: Biographies Master Index: An Index to Sources of Biographical Information.* **2d ed. (Gale Biographical Index Series). Detroit: Gale, 1984. 354p.**

The subtitle of this work, which first appeared in 1979, specifies that the index covers novelists, poets, playwrights, nonfiction writers, songwriters and lyricists, and television and screen writers; its intended audience is high school students and teachers, librarians, and researchers interested in high school reading materials. Within these parameters, the age range of the authors' appeal is deliberately broad, from children's authors to adult authors. The present edition, intended to simplify research, includes 15,000 authors drawn from 500 sources. While it is a useful reference tool for libraries, entries do not cite the authors' works, so bibliographical information can only be sought indirectly through the sources quoted.

323. Schaaf, William L. *The High School Mathematics Library.* **7th ed. Reston, VA: National Council of Teachers of Mathematics, 1982. 84p.**

First published in 1960, with enlarged and updated editions in 1963, 1967, 1970, and 1973 (E/S 1945–75, p. 154), this selective subject bibliography, prepared under the auspices of a prestigious educational body, has been a guide for high school librarians and has also served teachers, students, and parents. The 1976 edition and the present one were substantially revised to reflect new fields and changing emphases of mathematical study in schools. Increased attention has been given to computers and calculators, programming, automation and computer recreations, and other topics, as well as to professional books for teachers. The scope of the list is not limited exclusively to the interests of high school students. Slightly over 1,000 titles are cited in 15 chapters, each covering a division of mathematics, and three others covering professional books (almost a quarter of the total), dictionaries and handbooks, and NCTM publications. A brief sentence of annotation summarizes each entry. For libraries with small budgets, significant titles are starred. This substantial, if not comprehensive, list is a reliable and invaluable tool for school libraries, and the quality of the selection maintained through the series of editions makes it useful for other types of libraries as well.

324. Scherf, Walter. *The Best of the Best: Picture, Children's, and Youth Books from 110 Countries or Languages.* 2d ed. **New York and London: Bowker, 1976. 342p.**

As with the first edition of 1971 (E/S 1945–75, p. 156) this bilingual publication carries a German title page with the imprint of Verlag Dokumentation in Munich. Subtitles identify it as a catalog of the International Youth Library. The staff members there collected examples of quality children's titles from almost double the previous number of countries, though some gaps in coverage are still admitted. Entries are arranged alphabetically by author within national divisions, and many are accompanied by small illustrations. The introduction by the editor comments on international children's book publishing and its value for world understanding. One of his remarks, that "children of minority groups should be able to find in their school library...the best children's books in their mother tongue," indicates a use for this impressive list in North American libraries. Though many titles are not available in English translations, some are, and would be excellent additions to school and public library collections for English-speaking children. This is an increasingly valuable guide for fostering international understanding. It states that the International Youth Library will make supplements available, including annual selected lists of books for larger language groups and of titles recommended to the publishing industry for translation.

325. Schmidt, Nancy J. *Children's Books on Africa and their Authors. Supplement.* **(African Bibliography Series). New York: Africana, 1979. 273p.**

This supplement adds nearly 1,500 titles to the compiler's original title of 1975 (E/S 1945–75, p. 157). Half of the volumes included are fiction. The cut-off date for the supplement was the summer of 1977. The annotations, as previously, describe the African content of the entries, not their literary quality. The author's experience as an anthropologist and a librarian is an assurance of accuracy. Thoroughly indexed, this is a significant contribution to an area underresearched bibliographically and currently of keen interest to young people.

326. ———. *Children's Literature and Audio-Visual Materials in Africa.* **Owerri, Nigeria: Conch Magazine, 1977. 109p.**

Edited by the librarian of the Peabody Museum of Archaeology and Ethnography at Harvard, and originally appearing as an issue of *Conch* in 1975, this collection presents a series of signed reviews from different perspectives, originally appearing elsewhere. Compiled in response to the great need for evaluating children's material about Africa, it identifies children's books that realistically and accurately represent the diversity of African life. Included are *Bibliographies of Children's Literature about Africa, 1970–1975* by Hans Panofsky, and *Locating Resources about African Children and Children's Books on Africa* by Judi Lutsky. Other chapters cover audio visual, picture books, books on history, society, politics, art, folklore, fiction,

African wildlife, and recent books for South African children by African writers. The volume was printed in the United States.

327. Schon, Isabel. *A Bicultural Heritage: Themes for the Exploration of Mexican and Mexican-American Culture in Books for Children and Adolescents.* **Metuchen, NJ: Scarecrow, 1978. 158p.**

This annotated bibliography is designed to expose students to the customs and history of Mexican and Mexican-American cultures, and is intended for librarians, teachers, and students in training for library service and education. Arrangement and supplementary material have mainly the school system in mind and the need to instill social recognition and understanding of these groups. Chapters examine theme categories, such as lifestyles and folklore, and divide these into sections by grade level: kindergarten to grade three, grades three to six, and grade seven to high school. Each section features divisions on "Outcomes" or objectives; "Books," some carrying a starred recommendation "Discussions," which summarize criticism and highlight; "Evaluation" and "Follow-up Activities." About 35 titles, published between 1930 and 1974, are fully treated in each section. Appendixes include a discussion on selecting Spanish-language and bilingual material, a list of further relevant reading for adults, and notes on books for young people from Spain. Although this list is not extensive, detailed and thorough treatment makes it a valuable tool for educators.

328. ———. *Books in Spanish for Children and Young Adults: An Annotated Guide. Series I* **and** *Series II.* **Metuchen, NJ: Scarecrow, 1978, 1983. 153p., 162p.**

These annotated booklists are intended to serve as a guide for any adult (teacher, librarian, counselor, layperson, or parent) interested in selecting books in Spanish written by Hispanic authors for children of preschool through high school age. There is a variant title in Spanish; the citations for the books are in Spanish and the annotations in English. Annotations extend to one or two paragraphs and are descriptive and evaluative. Recommendations, from "outstanding" to "not recommended" are coded, and tentative grade levels are assigned. The primary arrangement is by geographical area; this is subdivided into subject categories, and arrangement within these is alphabetical by author. Translations and textbooks are excluded. Dates of coverage for the first series is from approximately 1973 to 1977, and for the second series from 1978 to late 1982. Books were still in print at the time of publication, and most are stated to be readily available in Hispanic countries. Two appendices list book dealers in Hispanic countries and in the United States. Indexes cover authors, titles, and subjects. This is a thorough listing, carefully annotated by a specialist, and will be a useful tool for all libraries with a youthful Spanish-speaking clientele, as well as for educators.

329. ———. *A Hispanic Heritage: A Guide to Juvenile Books about Hispanic People and Cultures.* **Metuchen, NJ: Scarecrow, 1980. 168p.**

This annotated bibliography of titles in the English language is designed as an aid for librarians and teachers who are interested in exposing students to the cultures of Hispanic peoples through books for children and adolescents. Titles are grouped under specific countries or cultures in alphabetical order by author, noteworthy books being starred. Suggested grade levels are supplied. Not all titles are recommended. A paragraph of evaluative annotation is given for each entry. Indexes include subjects, titles, and authors. This substantial booklist by a recognized authority is useful for selection by smaller libraries and as a checklist for larger library systems. A second volume appeared in 1985.

330. The School Librarian. *Seven Studies of Contemporary Authors: Reprinted from the School Librarian with Revised Bibliographies.* **Oxford: School Library Association, 1982. 42p.**

The collected reprint makes more conveniently accessible some critical articles from this British periodical about recent writers of children's and adolescent fiction. Authors included are Bernard Ashley, Lucy Boston, Jill Chaney, Roald Dahl, Mollie Hunter, Jan Mark, and K.M. Peyton. A booklist on each, revised to date, cites both books by and articles about them.

331. Schwartz, Sheila. *Teaching Adolescent Literature: A Humanistic Approach.* **Rochelle Park, NJ: Hayden, 1979. 216p.**

This methods book for secondary school English teachers stresses the use of the rapidly growing adolescent literature genre, with its focus on adolescent problems and behavior, to provide the student with "a jumping off place for his examination of self and world." Seven chapters examine social and literary topics such as teenagers and sex, violence, family life, lifestyles, and "Science Fiction as Prophecy." About 20 books are discussed in each chapter, some very critically, and short lists are appended. Teachers sympathetic to this approach will find the book rewarding, and should be aware of titles listed, which are commonly available in school and public libraries. Librarians, however, will not find the selection current.

332. Scott, Dorothea Hayward. *Chinese Popular Literature and the Child.* **Chicago: American Library Association, 1980. 181p.**

This is a scholarly account of a vast traditional literature little known or appreciated in the West. It covers popular legends and tales told by storytellers to adults and children alike over a long course of history. Chapters include: myths, legends, and symbolism; storytellers, puppets, and theaters; folk epics from the 15th century; popular novels; 20th-century developments; and folklore and nursery rhymes. The emphasis on older tales is brought out by entertainingly presented synopses of original plots. The account is not planned to review the new children's literature but to indicate how the seeds of it were sown. Bibliographies of further reading for researchers and librarians are provided. This well-written and charming study opens up a rich new field for Western children's writers, storytellers, and educators to cultivate.

333. Senick, Gerard J. *Children's Literature Review: Excerpts from Reviews, Criticism, and Commentary on Books for Children and Young People.* **Detroit: Gale, 1976– . Biennial, annual, and biannual.**

Volumes in this continuous series have appeared irregularly, with frequency tending to increase. The first volume had Ann Block and Carolyn Riley as editors, the second Carolyn Riley alone, and the succeeding volumes the present editor. Each volume presents excerpts from published criticism on the literary works of authors who create books for children from preschool to junior high age. The number of authors varies from approximately 15 to 40 per volume. Coverage aims to be international in scope. No time limits are applied to the selection of authors; established and recently prominent writers may figure in each volume, though earlier volumes emphasized criticism published after 1960. From 1982, young adult authors were excluded. The pattern for each entry consists of a portrait, a summary introduction, and three sections of criticism, the author's own comment, and other comment on individual titles. Included are bibliographical citations, numerous extracts, and reproductions of illustrations. All volumes carry cumulative indexes to authors, nationalities, and titles; authors to appear in forthcoming volumes are also listed. The criterion for the selection of all material was "Will today's student, teacher, or critic find this pertinent to today's needs?" As a reference source, its strength is accumulative, rather than selective; the researcher is likely to find much information here that is not available in slimmer and more formal aids. It provides a current source of popular titles and an overview of criticism that constitutes a valuable checklist for librarians and others. Volumes 8 and 9 appeared in 1985; volumes 10 and 11 appeared in 1986.

334. Shannon, George W.B. *Folk Literature and Children: An Annotated Bibliography of Secondary Materials.* **Westport, CT: Greenwood, 1982. 124p.**

The scope of this annotated bibliography is restricted to folk literature and its effects on children. Four hundred sixty-five entries cite and briefly describe monographs, theses, articles, and extracts. The informative introduction summarizes the pros and cons of three centuries of controversy. Author, title, and subject indexes aid access by the researcher. Since the point is still moot as to the values and consequences of this ancient genre, educators, storytellers, librarians, and library historians will find this documentation of interest.

335. Shapiro, Jon E., ed. *Using Literature and Poetry Affectively.* **Newark, DE: International Reading Association, 1979. 126p.**

These articles were collected for the benefit of teachers, librarians, and parents "to present methods designed to develop a greater awareness of the affective domain, and to examine the way children's literature and poetry is used at school and at home." Twelve contributions by specialists on relevant topics are grouped in three parts: "Examining Attitudes," "Using Literature," and "Using Poetry." Many of the articles make references to children's titles, but regrettably these are not made accessible through an index. Consequently, the volume cannot be used as a selection tool, but the text does provide thoughtful ideas on young people's reading to professional members of the Association and to others.

336. Shapiro, Lillian L. *Fiction for Youth: A Guide to Recommended Books.* **New York: Neal-Schuman, 1980. 252p.**

This annotated bibliography of 20th-century fiction that appeals to thirteen-to eighteen-year-olds is "intended for the capable reader, often college-oriented, who would read more and better books if motivated or encouraged to do so." The majority are adult titles; the others, juvenile titles with "more than passing value." Criteria for choice included literary quality, relevance to subjects of interest to adolescents, and attention to themes of universal import. Entries are arranged alphabetically by author with descriptive annotation. Titles are included as late as 1978 and were available at the time of compilation; out-of-print titles are listed in an appendix. A title index and a subject index are provided. This is a well-selected list that is an excellent source for librarians, teachers, and parents. It also forms an excellent checklist for collection building in school libraries and public libraries that cater to this age group.

337. Sharp, Peggy Agostino. *An ABC of Children's Book Activities.* **Hagerstown, MD: Alleyside, 1983. 57p.**

This activities workbook is addressed to library media specialists, teachers, and parents of children from three to twelve years of age. Follow-up activities are provided "for 91 popular children's picture books and poems..to enhance the book read, to motivate greater interest in books, and to encourage development of the life-long habit of reading." Arranged alphabetically by title, entries receive up to a page of description with appropriate follow-ups. The selection is eclectic, favorite traditional titles being accompanied by more recent ones well received by librarians. It serves as a useful checklist for collections with picture books.

338. Sherrard-Smith, Barbara. *Read and Find Out: Information Books, 9–13.* **2d ed. London: National Book League, 1979. 39p.**

First published in 1976, this revised edition omits many out-of-print titles and lists new publications. The selection goes beyond conventional reference tools to include useful informational books, ranging from those to "entice and intrigue" beginners to more detailed and specialist titles for advanced levels. Selected titles, however, share the criteria of informational accuracy, originality in subject or presentation, and visual attractiveness. Most are current British publications. Arrangement is within broad subject groups: the arts, hobbies and sports, people and places, science, national history, and technology. The quite full descriptive and critical annotation for each title is enthusiastically written. It generally indicates the level of appeal, but there is no specific coding for age suitability. This useful guide is complementary to the compiler's similar title for six- to nine-year-olds, and was also based on a National Book League exhibition.

339. ——. *Read and Find Out: Information Books, 6–9.* **3d ed. London: National Book League, 1979. 30p.**

First published in 1975 (E/S 1945–75, p. 162) and revised in 1976, this further revision omits out-of-print titles listed previously and adds new publications. It, too, was based on a National Book League exhibition. The objectives remain, "to open new horizons, to provide new interests, and above all give great pleasure." Dictionaries, encyclopedias, and textbooks are omitted. The 143 nonfiction titles are arranged in subject groupings, with brief descriptive and critical annotations. Catering to a wide range of children's needs, this is a stimulating selection of British publications, which complements the compiler's similar list for nine- to thirteen-year-olds.

340. Siegel, Mary-Ellen Kulkin. *Her Way: A Guide to Biographies of Women for Young People.* **2d ed. Chicago: American Library Association, 1984. 415p.**

This enlarged revision of the first edition of 1981, appearing under the name of Kulkin, now identifies 1,700 biographies of more than 1,100 women appropriate for use by children from kindergarten through grade twelve. Arrangement is in two sections: individual and collective. Entries are alphabetized by title with a brief annotation and a recommended reading level. Books were rated according to specific criteria, but in this edition unacceptable, superseded, and unavailable titles have been omitted. The preface points out that new, better biographies of women, now added, have been a feature of recent publishing. This has increased the value of this list for young people, the libraries that serve them, and teachers who are strengthening feminist recognition in the curriculum.

341. Silverman, Judith. *Index to Collective Biographies for Young Readers: Elementary and Junior High School Level.* **3d ed. New York: Bowker, 1979. 405p.**

First published in 1970, with a second edition in 1975 (E/S 1945–75, p. 163), this edition, which makes a slight variation in the title, retains all previous material and adds 1,412 names from 22 more volumes, for a total of almost 7,250 biographees. They are listed alphabetically and also in a subject section arranged by occupation and nationality. Detailed indexing covers all features of the volume. This standard tool continues to be indispensable for librarians working with children and invaluable for reading guidance, class work, and individual study.

342. Simmons, Beatrice T., and Carter, Yvonne B. *Aids to Media Selection for Students and Teachers.* **7th ed. Indianapolis, IN: National Association of State Educational Media Professionals, 1982. 144p.**

First appearing under a different title in 1966, supplemented in 1967, and with succeeding editions under this title in 1971, 1973 (E/S 1945–75, p. 25), 1976, and 1979, this federally initiated selection tool for educators is no longer published by the U.S. Government Printing Office for the Office of Education in the Department of Health, Education, and Welfare. This first edition by the Association remains a guide to bibliographies and journals that review books, periodicals, audiovisual materials, and microcomputer hardware and software useful for instructional purposes, listing only tools appearing since the previous edition. The emphasis is on selection aids for curriculum-oriented materials in elementary and secondary schools. Minor changes include a new section on sources of computer technology and the reorganization of multiethnic material within the general subject sections. The list remains of proven usefulness to educators and to school librarians as a basic selection source.

343. Small, Robert C., and others. *Books for You: A Booklist for Senior High Students*. **7th ed. Urbana, IL: National Council of Teachers of English, 1982. 323p.**

The prestigious educational association the National Council of Teachers of English sponsored these lists in 1945, 1951, 1954, and 1964 (E/S 1945–75, p. 191); the sixth edition, edited by a committee with Kenneth L. Donelson as chair, appeared in 1976. The present edition was prepared by the current Committee on the Senior High School Booklist, with Robert C. Small as editorial chairman. The nearly 1,400 titles represent only new publications or reprints since the last edition, with a deadline of the beginning of 1982. Entries are arranged alphabetically within 35 informal subject groups which are also in alphabetical order. The paragraphs of annotation for each are descriptive and carefully written to interest the reader. The introduction, addressed to the the the student, states, "*Books for You* was written to help you find the books you want to read when you want them." One of the criteria for choice was that the books would be enjoyable to read. The approach reinforces the current educational interest in personal reading, especially at the high school level. However, its currency and the quality of selection make this still an authoritative checklist for librarians and teachers, as well as for their students. Since the holdings of the two editions are exclusive, the previous version is worth retention.

344. Smith, Dorothy B. Frizzell, and Andrews, Eva L. *Subject Index to Poetry for Children and Young People, 1957–1975*. **Chicago: American Library Association, 1977. 1,035p.**

Compiled after seven years of work with the assistance of consultants, this successor to the 1957 volume (E/S 1945–75, p. 161) indexes 263 anthologies and other collective volumes of poetry, none previously represented. It is intended primarily for librarians to use with children and young adults from kindergarten through high school. The subject headings that provide the basic arrangement are mostly from the tenth edition of the Sears list; added entries derived from other reference works reflect topics of current interest and contemporary significance or the growing attention to ethnic, cultural, and national origins. Grade or interest levels are indicated in the listing of the volumes indexed. This supplement renews the index's usefulness as a standard reference tool to young people's libraries and will also be useful to teachers and other interested readers.

345. Smith, Elva Sophronia. *Elva S. Smith's The History of Children's Literature: A Syllabus with Selected Bibliographies*. **Rev. ed. Chicago: American Library Association, 1980. 290p.**

Margaret Hodges and Susan Steinfirst have enlarged and thoroughly revised this acknowledged classic first published in 1937, which had its origin in a syllabus for course work in children's literature. "The intention of this edition is to be useful to the researcher preparing a dissertation or scholarly article, to the teacher on either the undergraduate or the graduate level, to the student who wishes to read widely in specific phases of the history of children's literature, and to the librarian who sees a need to expand a collection in this field or to examine a current collection for important out-of-print titles.... The selection for this edition includes most of Elva Smith's sources, and adds many new ones that throw light on historic backgrounds, issues, and persons in the history of children's literature." Sixteen chapters treat general bibliography, folklore, and historic periods from Anglo-Saxon times to the late 19th century, with each annotated booklist being preceded by an introductory essay. An author-title index is included. The editors, recognized specialists, have ably resuscitated this important earlier source with their own contributions.

346. Smith, James A., and Park, Dorothy M. *Word Music and Word Magic: Children's Literature Methods.* Boston: Allyn, 1977. 564p.

This text is concerned with developing an understanding of children's literature for the student in training and for the classroom teacher. The authors' philosophy is that "literature must be experienced as well as 'heard' in order to be enjoyed." They believe that "appreciation and taste can be developed through adventuring" with books. Sixteen chapters, each with appropriate booklists appended, are grouped in four parts: "Introduction to Books and Children," "People Who Create Children's Literature," "Adventures with Literature," and "Resources for Teaching Children's Literature." Appendices include references to various media and genres. Most of the books cited in the work are publications of the 1960s and 1970s, and represent a traditional type of selection that will be helpful to teachers. Libraries can check their holdings against titles cited.

347. Smith, Lillian Helena. *The Unreluctant Years: A Critical Approach to Children's Literature.* Harmondsworth, England: Penguin, 1976. 193p.

This paperback reprint makes available the text of the 1953 edition (E/S 1945–75, p. 166), but there is no updating of that inspirational and charming account, with its traditional and literary treatment of the field.

348. Smyth, Margaret. *Count Me In: Books for and about Disabled Children.* Birmingham, England: The Library Association Youth Libraries Group, 1981. 28p.

This YLG pamphlet is a selective list of 84 titles about handicapped young people, concentrating on books readily available in Great Britain; most were less than ten years old at the time of publication. The objective was to help librarians, teachers, parents, and others to find books that can lead to a greater understanding of handicaps in young people. Criteria for choice included realism, credibility, and the exclusion of indulgent attitudes. Historical fiction was largely rejected. A wide age range is catered to; there are many books "about" disabled children in addition to books "for" disabled children. Three sections cover fiction, biography, and handicapped adults. A paragraph of descriptive annotation for each title identifies the appropriate group and the disability or illness concerned. Besides a title index, there is an index of types of disability.

349. Southall, Ivan. *A Journey of Discovery: On Writing for Children.* New York: Macmillan, 1976. 101p.

This first American edition is a textually unchanged reprint of the 1975 English edition (E/S 1945–75, p. 167) of lectures by this British children's author.

350. Sowell, Judith Baldwin, and May, Ruth Graham. *Yes, Johnny Can Read: Matching Young Readers with Books.* **Dubuque, IA: Kendall-Hunt, 1983. 102p.**

The objective of this manual "is to promote reading for enjoyment with as little frustration as possible for young children." Addressed to teachers, reading specialists, children's librarians, parents, and other interested persons, it deals mainly with motivation and readability for children from prekindergarten through grade four. After foreword, preface, and introduction, the text is presented in five chapters: "Factors in Matching Children with Books," which discusses motivation and readability in general; "A Guide to Using this Book," which explains the book's organization; "The Book Matchmaker," which provides a booklist of titles "precisely graded and annotated"; "Readability and its Uses by the Professional," which gives a reasoned explanation of the many formulas; and "To Parents...the Ultimate Teachers," which defines parents' role and suggests ideas. The 452 entries in the booklist, ranging in date from the 1950s to the early 1980s, are arranged by title within 22 interest categories, briefly annotated, and rated for readability by the Harris-Jacobson formulas, accurate to the sixth grade. A glossary, title index, author index, and readability level index conclude. This is a helpful book, especially for beginning professionals and parents. The statement that the booklist "will also be extremely useful for children's Librarians interested in matching children with books" is justified, and the selection can be used to check holdings, though the experienced professional will rarely need the grading and interest-level categorizations.

351. Spache, George Daniel. *Good Reading for Poor Readers.* **10th ed. Champaign, IL: Garrard, 1978. 284p.**

This standard booklist for high interest/low vocabulary books has a long publication history, its present title dating back to 1954, with successors in 1960, 1964, 1966, 1968, 1970, 1972, and 1974 (E/S 1945–75, p. 167). The tenth edition has been partially rewritten with a renamed first chapter and new references. An appendix explains revisions to the Spache readability formula. This selection aid by the distinguished specialist remains an important source and a favorite with educators in an area where titles are still hard to locate. Librarians should be able to supplement its recommendations, particularly with titles that deal with developmental and current issues at the high interest end of the "high/low" area.

352. Spirt, Diana L. *Introducing More Books: A Guide to the Middle Grades.* **New York: Bowker, 1978. 240p.**

This further volume to *Introducing Books* (E/S 1945–75, p. 67) presents 72 entirely new titles, selected as "an amalgam of the most popular books of the finest literary quality, as well as a sample of different levels, in children's literature since the early 1970s. The introduction by the editor of *School Library Journal*, Lillian Gerhardt, describes the author's "carefully organized approach to introducing children to books." The range of age levels has been extended a year each way, from eight to fifteen; the formula of presentation remains. Titles receive a long plot summary written as an aid in the presentation of book talks, a short thematic discussion, and a listing of related materials and media, almost 500 titles in all, to use or to be suggested with the books. Arrangement is under nine developmental themes, such as "Developing Values" and "Respecting Living Creatures." Indexes cover titles, authors, illustrators, and subjects. The updating of the range of titles enhances the usefulness of these manuals for book talking, discussion, and reading guidance. The listing of titles also serves as a checklist for holdings in both school and public library collections.

353. Stanford, Barbara Dodds, and Amin, Karima. *Black Literature for High School Students.* **2d ed. Urbana, IL: National Council of Teachers of English, 1978. 271p.**

This textbook for teachers is a revision of *Negro Literature for High School Students* written by Barbara Dodds alone and published in 1968 (E/S 1945–75, p. 46). The addition of a Black joint author helped to meet some criticism of the first edition; Stanford questions here whether her reaction to the books is necessarily the same as that of a Black person. The ten chapters discuss many titles in the text, as well as providing booklists. In the present edition those cited are predominantly of the 1960s and 1970s, reflecting the growth and change of focus of Black literature publishing over the previous decade. These constitute an excellent basic bibliography that, with current updating, will serve small and medium-size public and school libraries as a valuable source for book selection in the area. Educators, too, will find the choices useful.

354. Stensland, Anna Lee. *Literature by and about the American Indian: An Annotated Bibliography.* **2d ed. Urbana, IL: National Council of Teachers of English, 1979. 382p.**

First published in 1973 (E/S 1945–75, p. 170), this booklist in its second edition is greatly increased in size and scope. The title of the first edition specified its use to be for junior and senior high school students; now it caters to young people from age six up to adult. The 775 items include a substantial list of works for the elementary grade level, contributed by Anne M. Fadum. Geographical coverage has been extended to Alaska, Canada, and Mexico. An introductory section on "Teaching the Literature of the American Indian," is supplemented by a list of references, which enhances its value for teachers. The principal sequence of entries is arranged alphabetically by author within seven topical groups, such as "Traditional Life and Culture." Reading levels are identified as one to three, four to six, elementary, junior high, senior high, and adult. The annotations are descriptive and sometimes critical. Author and title indexes are provided. The updating and enlargement of this widely accepted bibliography has improved its high value as a source for selection by all types of libraries.

355. Stewig, John Warren. *Children and Literature.* **(Rand McNally Education Series). Chicago: Rand McNally, 1980. 562p.**

Directed primarily to teachers, this text aims to provide a balanced, comprehensive, and analytical view of a field of study, to make a literary analysis of available children's books, and to indicate ways to use literature with children through the eighth grade. The author also seeks "to convey my own joy in children's books." Chapters evaluate books according to genre, each appending a list of about 100 relevant titles. Other chapters deal with organizing reading and related programs and curricula. The importance of illustration is emphasized and media are discussed. As a textbook for teachers and professional students this volume can be commended. Titles noted are up-to-date and of good quality and are well annotated, so librarians can be advised to check their holdings to provide for teacher and student demand.

356. Stone, Karen, and others. *A Bibliography of Non-Sexist Supplementary Books, K–12: Developed by the Northwest Regional Educational Laboratory Center for Sex Equity.* **Phoenix, AZ: Oryx, 1984. 108p.**

First published by the Center in 1982 as *BIAS: Building Instruction Around Sex Equity*, and compiled by a team of seven including the director, Barbara Hutchinson, this annotated list of books for students from kindergarten to grade twelve aims to provide teachers with materials to offset the influence of sex-biased texts and to provide a balanced reading experience for students. It was made possible by a grant from the U.S. Education Department's Women's Educational Equity Act Program. Criteria for choice were that the books should promote sex equity and present a wide range of careers and interests for both girls and boys. Titles are organized by reading level on a scale from 1 to 12. A paragraph of annotation for each gives a brief description of content and the gender, ethnicity, or nationality of the major characters, with "qualitative information" from the nonsexist viewpoint. Titles have been chosen with great care to provide classroom teachers and librarians with a full range of books for use in promoting equitable education for all students, but the slimness in quantity, especially for the early and final grades, makes this laudable aim seem somewhat grandiose. Nevertheless, the fiction and nonfiction titles described are a useful beginning, and should be checked by book-selection librarians.

357. Stones, Rosemary, and Mann, Andrew. *"Spare Rib" List of Non-Sexist Children's Books.* **London: Spare Rib, 1979. 23p.**

The authors, members of the Children's Rights Workshop, have made a "roundup" of nonsexist children's books from those reviewed in *Spare Rib* magazine over a five-year period. Four age groups cover picture books and storybooks for the under-sixes, books for younger readers from six to eight years old, including stories to read to children and books they can read themselves, books for older readers from eight to twelve years old, and young adult books for thirteen-year-olds and upward. Signals identify those considered exceptionally important contributions to nonsexist literature and winners of the "Other Award" British prize. A short descriptive annotation on each title indicates nonsexist strengths. There are a number of half-tone illustrations in the text. A short list of background reading on nonsexist children's literature is appended. For a more extensive retrospective bibliography, the compilers refer to *Little Miss Muffet Fights Back*, 1974 (E/S 1945–75, p. 23).

358. Stott, Jon C. *Children's Literature from A to Z: A Guide for Parents and Teachers.* **New York: McGraw-Hill, 1984. 318p.**

This broad overview of children's literature covering the writers, illustrators, and books of the 19th century and the 20th century up to the present was prepared by a professor of English with a readership in mind of both adults who work with children and adults who enjoy reading and studying children's books, including parents and grandparents. The text is presented as an alphabetical series of entries which principally consist of biographical essays covering an extensive list of authors and illustrators, but which are interfiled with articles on types of literature, folktales, and awards. Major authors and genres receive a lengthier treatment than the "representative sampling" of authors and illustrators of the post–World War II era. The material for each subject is not only informational and descriptive in character, it also provides critical assessments and ideas for use, many entries carrying a concluding paragraph termed "Tips for Parents and Teachers." Extensive though the coverage is, 1,400 titles receiving mention, the content is not comparable to those massive surveys of the field familiar to students, and practicing librarians may question why some currently popular writers are included and others omitted. It is not a tool to be used as a checklist for collections. Though the claim that it is "unique, and comprehensive" can be discounted, it does meet the author's stated objectives for his audience and warrants careful reading by professionals in training, as well as parents. It is best regarded as a wide-ranging personal commentary from a literary point of view. As such, it presents excellent criticism and "a good read." Concluding the volume is a bibliographical essay citing works for further study, which is too slight to cover the field adequately, and a title index which is an asset to the book's usefulness.

359. Stratford, Brian, and Stratford, Maureen. *Fiction for the Slow Reader.* **London: National Book League, 1977. 29p.**

Believing that it is no easy task for teachers to find fiction for slow learners, the compilers aim to give examples of the kind of books available in Great Britain which will appeal to these pupils beyond the first school or primary level, whether specially written for others or not. The needs of young teachers and parents are particularly considered. The introduction discusses the nature of fiction for the slow learner. Criteria for choice were instant eye appeal, relatively short length or slim bulk, and plentiful illustrations or a good blend of illustration with text, though some titles are unillustrated. The 200 items include a number of series. All items carry a short descriptive annotation with a final sentence on suitability and a coding for reading age and interest age. An inevitable overlap is pointed out with the publishers' *Help in Reading* (E/S 1945–75, p. 160). This is a useful source for British teachers, librarians, and others who help children in this category.

360. Summerfield, Geoffrey. *Fantasy and Reason: Children's Literature in the Eighteenth Century.* **London: Methuen, 1984. 315p.**

This study of ideas found in the works of some 18th-century authors combines a literary and philosophical viewpoint without following a strictly chronological pattern. Locke, Addison, Watts, Rousseau, Blake, Lamb, Godwin, and others receive attention apropos of the "rehabilitation of the imagination" and the changing adult attitudes of the period. Some full-page reproductions from contemporary books illustrate the text.

361. Sunderlin, Silvia, ed. *Bibliography of Books for Children.* **Wheaton, MD: Association for Childhood Education International, 1984. 112p.**

This new edition, for 1983, of an important selection tool for librarians, teachers, parents, and community workers represents an increasingly professional approach. The publication, edited by special committees of the influential educational association, has a long history and has made a triennial appearance since 1965 (E/S 1945–75, p. 186). The chairperson for the 1977 edition was Lois B. Watt, Silvia Sunderlin resuming the chair in 1980. In the current edition, she is assisted by three contributory committees, chaired by Katherine R. Roedder for books for children, Phyllis G. Sidorsky for reference books, and Barbara Hatcher for periodicals. The last section is a valuable new feature represented by ten pages of annotated titles of magazines and newspapers arranged alphabetically. "Selected References for an Elementary School Library" forms an ideal collection, financially speaking, of good current material, arranged alphabetically by title under broad subject areas and genres. The "Bibliography of Books for Children" covers picture books, easy reading, wordless books, fiction, story collections, and nonfiction arranged by Dewey; within these groups and the classification, arrangement is alphabetical by author. Annotation is descriptive and extends to a couple of sentences with an age recommendation suggested. Title and author indexes are provided. This guide is a serious attempt to recommend quality titles for elementary age children. Its careful selectivity represents a blend of good older titles with worthwhile new ones. The change of emphasis to children and the professionals who serve them has reduced some of its previous luster as a classic source for parents, and it is now best regarded as a secondary tool for librarians.

362. Sutherland, Zena. *The Best in Children's Books: The University of Chicago Guide to Children's Literature, 1973–1978.* **Chicago: University of Chicago Press, 1980. 547p.**

This supplement to the compiler's volume, *The Best in Children's Books: The University of Chicago Guide to Children's Literature, 1966-1972,* again draws on staff reviews originally published in the *Bulletin of the Center for Children's Books* to make up an annotated booklist of about 1,400 of the best books published for children in the years 1973 to 1978. The scope of the selection includes books for children and young people of all ages, including occasional adult books of particular interest to adolescent readers, but it is not numerically balanced for the various age groups. The introduction stresses that choice has been made primarily on the basis of literary quality with representation of subject as a secondary consideration. It reflects the strengths rather than the weaknesses of the books considered in terms of use and appeal. All inclusions are regarded as being "recommended," except a few titles marked "additional" or for the "special reader"; titles originally reviewed after September 1975 are marked with asterisks if of "special distinction." Arrangement is alphabetical by author in a numbered sequence. Each entry receives a long paragraph of descriptive annotation which includes a plot outline. The full indexing is very helpful, comprising indexes for titles, developmental values, curricular uses, reading levels, subjects, and types of literature. This is a distinguished selection which fulfills its purpose of describing "the best in American children's literature and some of the best in British children's literature." For those requiring recommendations based on quality supported by clear and full annotation it is an invaluable resource.

363. Sutherland, Zena; Monson, Dianne L.; and Arbuthnot, Mary Hill. *Children and Books.* **6th ed. Glenview, IL: Scott, Foresman, 1981. 678p.**

This well-established textbook for teachers and librarians in professional training was first published in 1947 under the authorship of May Hill Arbuthnot. It was revised in 1957 and 1964, and then in 1972 with Zena Sutherland as coauthor (E/S 1945–75, p. 6). Sutherland was principal author when the book went into its fifth edition in 1977. In this edition, Part 1, "Knowing Children and Books," adds chapters surveying "The State of Children's Literature Today," "The Basic Needs of Children," and "Aspects of Major Developmental Theories." Part 2, "Discovering Books with Children," now includes a chapter on "Books for the Very Young." Part 5, "Areas and Issues," presents significant material. The text, the extensive list of references, and the annotated bibliographies have been systematically updated. The listing of "Book Selection Aids" in the appendix, however, is not free of errors. Overall, this deservedly standard work gets better with each revision and maintains its appeal to a wide circle of readers far beyond a narrow professional group. The seventh edition appeared in 1985.

364. Tarbert, Gary C. *Children's Book Review Index: Master Cumulation, 1969–1981.* **4 Vols. Detroit: Gale, 1982. 2,059p.**

This multivolume cumulation brings into a single alphabet the entries in the series of annual volumes from 1975 to 1981 and in addition those in the thrice-annual issues of the periodical from 1969 to 1974. A single title index is also provided. Useful in saving time, cumulation has other research applications; for instance, an author's publications can be examined over a considerable period. This set is now completely superseded by the latest edition, published in 1985 which covers all issues since the beginning of 1965 through 1984 and accesses over 50,000 titles.

365. ――――, ed. *Children's Book Review Index.* **Detroit: Gale, 1975– . Annual.**

These annual cumulations incorporate the entries of the thrice-annual issues which are the basic form of publication for the *Children's Book Review Index.* This cites reviews of books identified as books for children of preschool to junior high age that appear in the periodicals listed on the flyleaves. This list derives from the same publisher's *Book Review Index,* and in 1984 included more that 450 serials, an increase from 230 in 1975. Arrangement of entries is in a single alphabet by author, giving reference to titles and the citations to reviewing journals; this is complemented by a complete title index referring to the main entry. As a current and a retrospective aid for all libraries selecting or holding young people's books, this index is a necessary tool.

366. Taylor, Bing, and Braithwaite, Peter, eds. *The Good Book Guide to Children's Books.* **2d ed. Harmondsworth, England: Penguin, 1984. 79p.**

First published in 1983, this lavish and colorful paperback was prepared by the editors of the British periodical *The Good Book Guide* for parents and children to use separately or together. The objective is to help build up a really good selection of books for home use. The revised edition includes 600 books independently chosen and reviewed, with Elaine Moss as editorial adviser, from the whole range of British publishers, and the selection covers all types of books that children read as they grow up except textbooks. A "Look Me Up Chart" is provided which relates the books to stages in a child's reading development and supplies a rough guide to reading ages. The first part describes the different types of book and the roles they play and gives advice on how to choose the right book for any particular age. The second part provides a recommended selection of books, 50% of them paperbacks. Lively descriptive annotations vary in length from a sentence to a paragraph, and every item is illustrated with a color photograph of the cover. Twenty-seven sections blend types of publication with subject groupings, the last one, "What Next," listing novels and stories for twelve-to fifteen-year-olds with a suggested list of adult paperbacks. The final part gives advice on buying children's books in Great Britain. Titles, authors, and illustrators are indexed. This is a stimulating and helpful guide for British readers. Distribution as a Penguin paperback and its attractive presentation have helped it gain considerable attention outside Great Britain.

367. Taylor, Maureen and Hurwitz, Kay. *Books for Under-Fives in a Multi-Cultural Society.* **London: Islington Libraries, 1979. 26p.**

Originating in the exhibition *Come Over to My House* at this English public library in 1978, this annotated selection of 169 titles is geared to the particular needs of under-fives in nurseries and playgrounds in the multiracial society to be found in many London boroughs. The introduction discusses the need for such a list. The books chosen include information books, folk and animal stories, stories about children and their family relationships, and rhyme and simple reading books. The list is divided into picture books with a multiracial setting, published in England and in North America, elementary science books, simple readers, and a geographical breakdown covering Africa, the Caribbean, China, the Indian subcontinent, and Cyprus. Titles about each area are subdivided into background books, books about children, and folk and animal stories. A supplementary section lists paperback picture books available from Indian publishers. Annotations are quite lengthy, clearly descriptive, and critical. Books believed offensive or too long have been omitted. Because of its citations of relevant overseas publications, this carefully selected British list can suggest titles in other areas where these minorities exist.

368. Thomas, Carol H., ed. *Merlin's Magic: A Reading Activities Idea Book for Use with Children.* **(A Fun with Reading Book). Phoenix, AZ: Oryx, 1984. 86p.**

Directed primarily to teachers, librarians, and interested people in the community, this organizational manual seeks to provide numerous ideas for events, projects, and activities which involve reading. It was developed from materials generated at a summer library program sponsored by the State of Wisconsin Department of Public Instruction's Division of Library Service. Extensive bibliographical support is provided by seven annotated lists of print and nonprint material relevant to the themes developed in the text, and two further lists of additional resources and audiovisual materials are also appended. Annotations are usually condensed from reviews in *Booklist* and the titles are graded for prekindergarten to grade twelve. Though the books date from the late 1950s into the 1980s, most are publications of the 1960s and 1970s and represent a traditionally oriented selection. All of the books will be useful, especially to teachers in elementary and junior high schools.

369. Thomas, James L., ed. *Death and Dying in the Classroom: Readings for Reference.* Phoenix, AZ: Oryx, 1984. 100p.

This collection of 18 articles by educators cites a number of young people's titles which are relevant to death education and which might be read or discussed apropos of the teaching environment. Some of the articles discuss books in the text, and an appendix lists five pages of print and nonprint media for children and young adults, which include principally fiction, but also some nonfiction and audiovisual material. Appropriate use for preschool, primary, intermediate, middle, high, or a combination of levels is indicated. The list is current to 1984, though most titles are of the late 1970s. School librarians and other professionals will find this a useful resource when dealing with this topic.

370. Thomas, James L., and Loring, Ruth M., eds. *Motivating Children and Young Adults to Read.* 2 vols. Phoenix, AZ: Oryx, 1979, 1983. 189p., 100p.

This collection of essays examines the motivational factors that stimulate participation in the reading process from early childhood through the young adult years. The second volume represents material collected by the editors after the publication of the first; both group six to nine articles into major sections covering "Attitudes and Interests," "Methodologies," "Programs," and "Activities." Most articles append a brief annotated bibliography of appropriate books, besides discussing individual titles in the text. This is a useful source for bibliographical checking by librarians, because titles included have proved effective. The volume achieves its aim in being helpful to educationists.

371. Tiedt, Iris M. *Exploring Books with Children.* Boston: Houghton Mifflin, 1979. 560p.

This textbook prepared for teachers, librarians, and parents has multiple but related objectives: to provide an overview of children's literature and its development; to recognize current trends in education; to encourage the reading of books, not just reading about them; and to present strategies and develop skills for teaching children's literature. The ten chapters on topics such as "The Universal and Traditional in Literature" and "Realistic Perspectives of Life for Children" relate together to provide the sought-after coverage. Each discusses many appropriate titles and supplies ideas for activities. The focus is on using contemporary books in the elementary school. A section of color reproductions selects illustrations from new and old books. The comprehensive index allows the reader to locate the titles, authors, and subjects described in the text. This delightful volume ranks with the limited number of excellent survey-type texts about children's literature. It is especially suitable as a source for librarians who wish to bring books to the attention of elementary school teachers, as well as to check their own collections.

372. Townsend, John Rowe. *A Sounding of Storytellers: New and Revised Essays on Contemporary Writers for Children.* **Harmondsworth, England: Kestrel, 1979. 218p.**

This set of essays on leading contemporary children's writers by an author who is one himself had its genesis in his similar collection, *A Sense of Story* (E/S 1945–75, p. 175), the introduction to which is reprinted here. The new collection reflects the changed atmosphere since 1971. In particular, the author takes issue with the growing assumption that children's books are tools for shaping attitudes and should be assessed in reference to their social context. The choice of 14 authors is balanced between British and Americans, with the addition of an Australian. The new essays about authors not previously discussed are limited in number, but those remaining from the earlier volume have been reassessed after they had written more books and often moved on to new ground. Each critical sketch is preceded by a brief biographical and bibliographical note, and also by a statement by the author concerning his or her aims and objectives as a writer. As usual with this author, these essays repay reading and considering. An American edition was published by Lippincott in the same year.

373. ———. *Twenty-five Years of British Children's Books.* **London: National Book League, 1977. 60p.**

One reason for the significance of the National Book League exhibition of which this is the catalog is that the choice and the annotation were made by a notable children's author and critic, who is in effect assessing the whole generation of his contemporaries. The 221 titles represented comprise original creative work for children in fiction, poetry, and picture books by British and Commonwealth writers and published during the first 25 years of Elizabeth II's reign. Excluded are information books, American books, translations, and books first appearing before 1952. The compiler states that his selection was personal but not eccentric, and used the general criterion of literary and artistic merit: "My yardstick has been my own experience and judgement, rather than a shopping list of qualities." Choice has been made in the belief that children's books exist to give pleasure, and that indirect benefits are only bonuses. The arrangement is alphabetical by author. Each entry carries a long paragraph of annotation which elegantly blends criticism with description. This often cites other titles by the author and indicates possible age ranges, assigned "with some misgiving": A for up to six, B from seven to ten, and C for eleven to sixteen, with overlaps being indicated. There are a number of black-and-white illustrations in the text. Regrettably there is no title index. Because the included titles have been evaluated by the author's announced subjective criteria, there will be extensive debate about the pamphlet's appropriateness as a selection aid. Given this honest proviso, however, overall the books cited are worthy of inclusion. Additionally, if one measures circulation, they serve readers well.

374. ———. *Written for Children: An Outline of English-Language Children's Literature.* 2d rev. ed. Harmondsworth, England: Kestrel, 1983. 384p.

This survey was first published in 1965 and revised in 1974 (E/S 1945–75, p. 175) with a Penguin paperback reprint of the latter in 1976. In this edition the main body of the text has been unchanged, but it has been updated to late 1982 by the addition of two chapters. "Since 1973 (i)" covers fiction for older children, and "Since 1973 (ii)" covers fiction for younger children, picture books and poetry. The objectives and the age parameters remain the same. As in the original edition, there is some attention given to international titles, but British books occupy the preeminent position. The author acknowledges that due to pressure of space, some writers' works since 1973 have not been noted. This personal but authoritative treatment of the field by the well-known British children's author retains its value. An American publication by Lippincott and an English Pelican paperback also appeared in 1983.

375. Tucker, Alan. *Poetry Books for Children.* 2d ed. (A Signal Booklist). Stroud, England: Thimble Press, 1979. 33p.

First published in 1976, this complete revision notes more than 100 poetry titles for children from the earliest years to the midteens. The entries form a more or less continuous narrative in reading-age order, with everything itemized, indexed, and cross-referenced. The informative and personal annotations are quite full, and usually comment on the books' format and appearance. While most are British publications, some titles from America and elsewhere have been included. The compiler, a poet and lecturer, has made a stimulating and original selection.

376. Tucker, Nicholas. *The Child and the Book: A Psychological and Literary Exploration.* Cambridge, England: Cambridge University Press, 1981. 259p.

This discussion of children's literature in its developmental aspects from the combined viewpoint of a student of literature and of educational psychology is concerned mainly with 20th-century British writers, and assesses particular books and authors for their potential psychological appeal. The introduction poses the question "Why are certain themes and approaches in children's literature so popular?," with special reference to the literary presentation acceptable to the young and the recurrent and predictable patterns in children's imaginative needs and interests. Chapters examine: first books, from zero to three years; story and picture books, from three to seven; fairy stories, myths, and legends; early fiction, from seven to eleven; juvenile comics, from seven to eleven; literature for older children from eleven to fourteen; selection, censorship, and control; and "Who Reads Children's Books?" The author constructs a fine balance between the literary and psychological aspects in this stylish presentation. The net result is that it will not be sufficiently avant-garde for some on both sides of the Atlantic, and it will also seem insufficiently traditional for others. Fortunately, however, there is a sizable population of professionals who will find it just right.

377. ———, ed. *Suitable for Children?: Controversies in Children's Literature.* London: Chatto, for Sussex University Press, 1976. 224p.

A collection of 25 articles and extracts, mainly from British authors, some from the 19th century and others more recent and current, which often reflect the conventional, but varying, viewpoint of their authors' time and place. Five parts, each with an editorial introduction, discuss fairy stories, comics, children's books and fear, children's classics and controversies about them, and the value of children's literature. A short select bibliography of books about the subject is appended. The author, who is well known as a critic on the young people's literature scene, has collected a stimulating group of articles that provides interesting reading, whether one agrees with the conclusions or not. As they say in the methodology of research, if you don't agree with the assumptions, you can't be expected to agree with the research.

378. Turner, Ernest Sackville. *Boys Will Be Boys: The Story of Sweeney Todd, Deadwood Dick, Sexton Blake, Billy Bunter, Dick Barton, et al.* 3d ed. Harmondsworth, England: Penguin, 1976. 304p.

This paperback printing makes available unchanged the text of the hardbound edition of 1975 (E/S 1945–75, p. 177).

379. Tway, Eileen, ed. *Reading Ladders for Human Relations.* 6th ed. Washington, DC: American Council on Education; Urbana, IL: National Council of Teachers of English, 1981. 398p.

This annotated bibliography is meant to be a catalyst to help parents, teachers, and librarians bring books and young readers together in the quest for better human relations. First appearing in 1947, revised and enlarged editions were published in 1949, 1955, 1962, and 1972 (E/S 1945–75, pp. 147–48). This new edition "consists mainly of books printed since the last edition, with the exception of outstanding books that are pertinent...for each group of children." Each of the five age groups (one to five, five to eight, eight to eleven, eleven to fourteen, and fourteen up) has a ladder of books within the basic arrangement of themes: "Growing into Self"; "Relating to Wide Individual Differences" (new to this edition); "Interacting in Groups"; "Appreciating Different Cultures"; and "Coping in a Changing World." With the same objectives and based on the same plan as previous editions, the updating continues to make this influential guide an important selection source for all concerned.

380. *University Press Books for Secondary School Libraries.* New York: American University Press Services, 1967– . Annual.

This sequence of annotated booklists (E/S 1945–75, p. 179) changed frequency from biennial back to the original annual with the 1981 edition, but the objectives and arrangement remain unchanged. Titles from the lists of this group of academic publishers are chosen by a selection committee of the American Association of School Librarians, to reflect the needs of the gifted student and the student requiring material on particular, specialized areas. Titles amounting to about one-fifth of the total annual output of publications are selected, arranged in order by the Dewey Decimal classification, and annotated with extracts from reviewing journals or publisher's descriptions. The quality of the original publications, complied with the practical examination and choice by professional librarians who work with secondary level students and teachers, make this valuable tool a discriminating source of titles for all libraries dealing with young adults of high school age, and even college students. The series continues, and the seventeenth edition appeared in 1985.

381. Urfer, Pamela. *Risky Reading: A Look at Today's Children's Books.* **(The Christian in the Arts). Soquel, CA: Creative Arts Development, 1983. 84p.**

The aim of this discussion of issues and bibliographical guide is demonstrated by the author's advice to parents that "the best thing we can do for our children, at any age, is to teach them discernment—how to critically evaluate what they read and then how to separate the good from the bad, the false from the true, the helpful from the harmful." Part One assesses the situation as it is; Part Two describes some examples. The opening chapters discuss "a few unpleasant surprises" and "alternatives to censorship," the author maintaining that "I would much prefer that my children read a controversial book at a time when I am available to answer their questions and help them discover the biblical approach to these matters." Examples are discussed in chapters about the occult, homosexuality, eastern religion, "God-words," mythology for today, situational ethics, and in conclusion, good relationships with God, and "A Look at What We've Found." Thirty-two titles, listed at the beginning of the book, are discussed in Christian biblical terms on a basis of "Absolutism" versus "Humanitarianism." The more current titles are those generally read by junior and senior high age individuals, the "encouraging" examples being of older publication vintage, generally read by elementary age children. Readers' beliefs and values will obviously come into play when assessing this author's advocacy of parental discretion joined with discussion, in opposition to censorship. Nonetheless, the appearance of this guide will extend the controversiality of some of the titles listed.

382. Van Vliet, Virginia, and others. *Bibliography on Disabled Children: A Guide to Materials for Young People Aged Three to Seventeen Years.* **Ottawa: Canadian Library Association, 1981. 50p.**

Edited by the convenor-chairperson and members of the Committee on Library Service to Disabled Children of the Canadian Association of Children's Librarians, this guide is directed to librarians, teachers, and parents "to promote...empathy." It was issued in recognition of the 1980 International Year of Disabled Persons. Arrangement is in six main sections on major topics, such as visual impairment and emotional disorders, which are further subdivided by type of material—fiction and nonfiction—and by age level: "Young Child" (three to seven), "Middle Child" (eight to twelve), and "Young Adult" (thirteen to seventeen). Brief annotations are provided which relate to the disability concerned. The materials analyzed and methodology used make this list a valuable tool. Although the quantity of titles is limited, the careful selection guarantees their usefulness.

383. Vandergrift, Kay E. *Child and Story: The Literary Connection.* **(Diversity and Directions in Children's Literature). New York: Neal-Schuman, 1980. 340p.**

This study focuses on both the literary and the psychological aspects of story as they relate to the developing child. Prefaces by the series editor, Jane Ann Hannigan, and by the author, an experienced teacher and librarian, and a foreword by the noted educator Leland B. Jacobs indicate that it is directed to a professional audience in education and librarianship. The bibliographical element consists of footnote references and a list of children's titles cited at the end of each of the ten chapters; a selected booklist of books about children's literature is appended. Practitioners and students will find this an interesting approach which merits thoughtful reading. As a selection aid, however, its usefulness is limited.

384. Varlejs, Jana, ed. *Young Adult Literature in the Seventies: A Selection of Readings.* **Metuchen, NJ: Scarecrow, 1978. 452p.**

This collection of articles reprinted from periodicals is intended to serve as an introduction to the field of young adult reading for professionals and parents "in getting kids 'hooked on books'." The contributors, practitioners, authors, and professors of library science, include many well-known names. A number of the titles that receive comment are popular ones familiar to librarians who deal with young adults. Discussions are critical in the best sense, and will be useful in a research setting to highlight sociological trends in the literature of the decade. This book makes a helpful contribution to the introductory study and discussion of librarianship for young people.

385. Walker, Elinor. *Book Bait: Detailed Notes on Adult Books Popular with Young People.* **3d ed. Chicago: American Library Association, 1979. 164p.**

First published in 1957, with a second edition in 1969 (E/S 1945–75, p. 183), the third edition of this well-tried title continues the approach and the organization of its predecessors. It provides young people and others concerned with lengthy descriptive accounts of easier adult books, along with critical notes indicating how they can be used by professionals. Out of the 100 books listed, 68 are newly added. Librarians across the country as well as teenage reading clubs were consulted as to the choices. All the titles included in the new edition have been tried out with young people and have their approval. A subject index to the titles discussed has been added to this edition. The book continues to be a standard and useful aid for book talkers, and the titles cited should be checked in collections for teenagers.

386. ———. *Doors to More Mature Reading: Detailed Notes on Adult Books for Use with Young People.* **2d ed. Chicago: American Library Association, 1981. 233p.**

First compiled in 1964 as an outgrowth of the publication *Book Bait* by Elinor Walker, Donald W. Allyn, Alice E. Johnson, and Helen Lutton, all members of ALA's Book Bait Sequel Committee of the Young Adult Services Division, this volume included titles intended for more mature readers. This second edition has been compiled for librarians, teachers, and parents and other adults who are enthusiastic about introducing the good readers among teenagers to books that are "worth the time spent in reading them." Of the books chosen, many are long adult books that bring challenges and open new vistas. Choice has been based on value, and no effort has been made to make this a balanced list; it includes many fields of information as well as adventure, ideals, and romance. "Titles which give the impression that the seamy side of life is attractive have been avoided." The same formula of presentation as in *Book Bait* has been adopted. The long annotations have lucidity and style. This is a successful companion to the author's volume for younger readers, and professionals concerned will find it helpful in a similar fashion.

387. Ward, Martha E., and Marquardt, Dorothy A. *Authors of Books for Young People. Supplement to the Second Edition.* **Metuchen, NJ: Scarecrow, 1979. 302p.**

First published in 1964, with a supplement in 1967 and a second edition in 1971 (E/S 1945–75, p. 185) the current supplement to this reference tool adds 1,250 new names of authors with biographical and bibliographical annotations which are longer and more critical than in previous parts. The compilers state that an attempt has been made to include authors whose books have received children's book awards, including the American Library Association's "Notable Books" and *Horn Book's* "Fanfare" listings, in addition to Newbery and Caldecott award winners from 1970 to 1978. As previously, however, its value as a reference source for public and school libraries is demonstrated by its inclusion of many minor authors, rather than the more famous figures that can be traced elsewhere.

388. Warren, Dorothea. *Fiction, Verse and Legend: An Annotated Guide to a Selection of Imaginative Literature for Middle and Secondary Schools.* **2d ed. Oxford: School Library Association, 1978. 58p.**

First published in 1972 (E/S 1945–75, pp. 186–87) this extensively revised edition no longer has Griselda Barton as a collaborator. It retains most in-print books listed in its predecessor, and books published between 1972 and 1976 are "fairly represented." This annotated selection by the librarian of a London girls' school does not claim to be definitive, since imaginative literature must be a matter of personal choice. The introduction explaining her guidelines deplores the censorship of Billy Bunter, but Enid Blyton has been eliminated, as have been abridged editions of the classics. The enjoyment of a good story provides the general yardstick for inclusion, including readable fiction on the theme of understanding people, but the compiler has not thought it fair to overburden children with a disproportionate number of books on social and psychological problems, such as drug addiction, homosexuality, and abortion. Careful descriptive annotation, with critical recommendations for use by age and sex groups, is provided. Dates of original publication have been noted in parentheses. Over 900 titles are arranged alphabetically by author within nine sections: general stories and adventure; stories with historical settings; family relationships; stories with a school background; stories with animal interest; science fiction; fantasy, including ghost stories; myths, legend, and fairy tales; and poetry. Besides an author index, there is an index of historical settings and a regional index to myths and legends. This thoughtful selection of predominantly in-print British publications will offer some good alternative titles to young people's librarians outside Great Britain.

389. Wehmeyer, Lillian Biermann. *Images in a Crystal Ball: World Futures in Novels for Young People.* **Littleton, CO: Libraries Unlimited, 1981. 211p.**

This annotated bibliography and guide was designed to assist teachers and librarians who are considering novels as a vehicle to explore with young people the future of the human species in this universe. Potential readership ranges from grades three through eight and up. Two beginning parts discuss "Working with Futuristic Fiction: Why and How" and "Futuristics and Futuristic Novels." The third part is the heart of the book for teachers and librarians, the bibliography that describes 150 novels arranged alphabetically by author. Annotations identify topics and themes and provide a plot summary with a range of interesting interpretations. Suggested grade levels according to the Fry formula are provided. The final part indexes topics and themes occurring in the novels described. Many well-known science fiction writers read by juveniles are represented, for example, H.M. Hoover and John Christopher, though surprisingly, not Ursula LeGuin. This outstanding book explores a trend that has recently surfaced in young adult reading, and can serve in several ways: for book talks and discussions, as a buying list or checklist, as a teaching tool, or for other projects worth investigating.

390. Weiss, Jacqueline Schachter. *Prizewinning Books for Children: Themes and Stereotypes in U.S. Prizewinning Prose Fiction for Children.* **Lexington, MA: Heath, 1983. 455p.**

Intended for children's librarians, as well as parents and the general public, "this book emphasizes primary themes of readily obtainable children's literature that have won U.S. prizes." Seven hundred seventeen winners of 42 awards and prizes are grouped into four parts by grade divisions: preschool, primary, middle elementary, and upper elementary. Chapters within each treat the various literary genres, which in turn are subdivided by primary theme, such as family, friendship, or freedom. This arrangement is designed to provide a "simple and clear" framework for quick reference by elementary teachers and children's librarians rather than for "extensive literary criticism." Brief descriptive annotations on the entries center on treatment of theme and stereotyping, analyzed from a traditional rather than a psychological viewpoint. The criticism is detailed rather than incisive. Appendices provide statistical analysis on titles and prizes, and there are title, subject, and author indexes. As the author contends, this is the only comprehensive analysis available on themes and stereotypes in these influential children's books, and the references will be suggestive for collection building as well as informative to teachers and parents.

391. Weiss, M. Jerry, ed. *From Writers to Students: The Pleasures and Pains of Writing.* **Newark, DE: International Reading Association, 1979. 113p.**

This publication of the Association's Literature for Adolescents Committee contains interviews with 17 well-known authors of titles popular with young people from sixth grade up, such as Paul Zindel, Judy Blume, and Mollie Hunter. The introduction on adolescent books and writers is by Ken Donelson. The interviews follow a question-and-answer format. They are also available in cassette form. Interesting for its biographical and bibliographical contributions, teachers will find its use encouraging for inspirational and motivational purposes.

392. Wheeler, Margariete Montague, and Hardgrove, Clarence Ethel. *Mathematics Library: Elementary and Junior High School.* **Reston, VA: National Council of Teachers of Mathematics, 1978. 43p.**

First published in 1960, with a second edition in 1968 and a third in 1973 (E/S 1945–75, pp. 77–78), this annotated bibliography, again thoroughly updated, is intended "to enrich the mathematics program by providing sources of recreational and informational reading" for students from preschool through grade nine. It is a companion volume to the sixth edition of William L. Schaaf's *The High School Mathematics Library* (**323**) published in 1976. Entries are arranged in alphabetical order with descriptive annotations summarizing content and recommending grade placement. This list, backed by an educational association active and responsible in its field, remains a standard source for teachers and school librarians.

393. Whitaker, Muriel A. *Children's Literature: A Guide to Criticism.* **Edmonton, AB: Athabascan Publishing, 1976. 65p.**

This brief guide by a professor of English aims to assist parents, teachers, librarians, and students in acquiring a set of standards by which books may be judged and to suggest sources of information. Focus is on British and American works, with some emphasis on Canadian and Australian titles, mainly of the last ten years. Chapters discuss bibliographies and reference works, the history of children's literature, criticism, myth and folklore, individual authors, and periodicals. Each has a paragraph of introduction followed by a list of titles with the author's comments. Not intended to be exhaustive, these make up a slight but helpful introduction to the field.

394. White, Marian, ed. *High Interest-Easy Reading for Junior and Senior High Schools.* **3d ed. Urbana, IL: National Council of Teachers of English, 1979. 98p.**

First published in 1965 with a second edition in 1972 (E/S 1945–75, p. 189), the new edition was again prepared by a special committee with Marian White as editorial chair. The same easy reading criteria were used, with emphasis placed on books of high literary quality that deal with topics of interest to the average adolescent. With more nonfiction than in previous editions, the total reaches 400 titles. The annotations are vivid summaries which can easily be enjoyed by young people. This substantial booklist maintains its high reputation for successful use by teachers and librarians, as well as by young people themselves.

395. White, Mary Lou. *Children's Literature: Criticism and Response.* **Columbus, OH: Merrill, 1976. 252p.**

The author's overview of the field is intended not solely to support children's literature as an area of literature worthy of analysis but to examine the implications for teaching stemming from this body of criticism. Along with her own contribution, critical articles, both historical and current, by different authors are collected and arranged in five parts. Four treat various aspects of criticism: psychological, sociological, archetypical, and structural.

For each, the theory is discussed, relevant articles selected, and a short list of titles mentioned is appended. The final part gives advice on helping children respond to literature. Author-editor and title indexes are provided. There are interesting interpretations to be found here by teachers, librarians, and students.

396. ———, ed. *Adventuring with Books: A Booklist for Pre-K to Grade 6*. 5th ed. Urbana, IL: National Council of Teachers of English, 1981. 472p.

Edited by committees of the influential national association of educators, editions of this well-established bibliography were published in 1950, 1966, 1973 (E/S 1945–75, p. 150), and in 1977, when it was prepared by the Committee on the Elementary School Booklist, chaired by Patricia Cianciolo. The committee for the fifth edition reduced the top age level from the eighth to the sixth grade, although otherwise the purpose and the plan remain similar. The stated objective is to inform teachers of recently published good books to share with children. In addition to using the criteria of quality and enjoyment previously employed, Mary Lou White's committee chose titles which demonstrated equitable treatment of minorities and recognized quality books of the past. Twenty-five hundred titles, published from 1977 to 1980 inclusive, are recommended and briefly annotated. Titles are arranged in broad subject and genre groups. A category for "wordless" books has been added, and picture books have been integrated into the fiction area. A list of professional books about children's literature is included. The updating has maintained the helpfulness of the booklist to teachers and its usefulness for checking collections in libraries. The previous edition retains value because of the date limitations of the present version.

397. White, Virginia L., and Schulte, Emerita S. *Books about Children's Books: An Annotated Bibliography*. (Annotated Bibliography Series). Newark, DE: International Reading Association, 1979. 48p.

Entries were selected from partial bibliographies in textbooks, recommended lists in professional journals, and advertisements in catalogs, brochures, and journals, items prior to 1967 being excluded. Arrangement is in eight categories: bibliographies, biographies, criticism, histories, indexes, teaching methodology, research, and textbooks. Although an assemblage rather than a professional selection, this substantial booklist is useful and a good source of material difficult to find elsewhere.

398. Wilkin, Binnie Tate. *Survival Themes in Fiction for Children and Young People*. Metuchen, NJ: Scarecrow, 1978. 256p.

This annotated bibliography seeks to present selected materials that reflect sensitivity to the individual and to societal issues. The foreword is contributed by Jerome Cushman. A preliminary historical outline, which shows how social elements have affected the development of children's literature, covers six eras, ranging from the 14th to the 20th century. Three parts of the booklist group entries under the headings "The Individual," "Pairings and Groupings," and "Views of the World." Each of these has an introduction with educational, sociological, and psychological interpretation and comment on prevailing attitudes, followed by topical subdivisions containing the titles, some of which receive lengthy annotation and some brief annotation. The fourth part, "Sources and Notes," includes a title listing of 117 easy-to-read books, further readings for adults, and an author-subject index. The interpretative commentary makes this selection interesting reading, and bibliographically it will be useful to book selectors.

399. Wilkinson, Donald. *Information Books for the Slow Reader.* **2d ed. London: National Book League, 1979. 19p.**

First published in 1976 with both editions prepared in conjunction with National Book League exhibitions, this annotated booklist for slow readers takes account of different levels of reading ability. The objective is to stimulate interest and the motivation to read. After consultation with teachers and school librarians, titles were chosen as suitable for use at home and in school, particularly for topic and project work. Pictorial and typographical appeal were considered. A number of British publishers' series are cited. Arrangement is sectional under broad headings: nature, science, social and environmental studies, and activities, which is subdivided into making things, doing things, and thinking. The annotations are quite fully descriptive and indicate usefulness, code numbers from 1 to 3 indicating stages in learning to read.

400. Williams, Helen Elizabeth. *The High-Low Consensus.* **Williamsport, PA: Bro-Dart, 1980. 259p.**

This annotated bibliography was prepared for librarians and reading teachers. It includes books determined to be appropriate for use by junior and senior high school students, or other young adults, who need high-interest/low-reading-level materials. High-low books are defined as those books which are designed for or are useful to reluctant, retarded, or problem readers among older students, who need books with reading levels below their interest levels. The accepted two-year divergence between the two levels has been taken into account. Eleven hundred titles were professionally chosen from those listed in a number of cited recommending sources, many of them well-known aids. These are arranged in ten reading level bibliographies, a title being repeated if appropriate for more than one level. Each title is briefly annotated and accompanied by notations for scholastic grade interest level and readability level, according to the Dale-Chall, Fry, or Spache formulas, as derived from the recommending source. Subject entries are also specified, a valuable feature which connects with the subject index. An author-title index is provided. The whole makes up a useful, substantial, and current selection tool for librarians and all concerned with the large population of reluctant readers.

401. Williams, Helen Elizabeth, and Gloden, Katherine Mary. *Independent Reading, K–3.* **Williamsport, PA: Bro-Dart, 1980. 120p.**

The successor to a 1975 volume compiled by Gale Sypher Jacob for grades one through three (E/S 1945–75, pp. 94–95), the revised and expanded version of this annotated booklist retains its in-print titles and adds others taken from professional recommending sources. Besides adding coverage for kindergarten, 12 additional subjects have been included. Twelve hundred seventy-four titles have been grouped by subjects appropriate to grade and age levels. The brief annotations and references to Spache reading levels are unchanged features. For younger reluctant readers in grades three to six, it is possible to use this volume in conjunction with the first editor's *The High-Low Consensus*, published in the same year. This successful volume provides a helpful current selection tool for librarians and others serving the age group.

402. Wilson, Jane B. *The Story Experience*. Metuchen, NJ: Scarecrow, 1979. 163p.

Written primarily for librarians, teachers, and other educators, this guide offers practical suggestions for storytelling. It is introduced by a well-respected figure in American librarianship, Robert B. Downs. Chapters cover aspects of the field, such as planning, execution, story programs, and promotion. An extensive bibliography of books, articles, and films to use for storytelling and for further study and an author-subject index are also provided. Although only a partial contribution to a very wide topic, the book is rewarding reading and will be especially helpful to the student practitioner.

403. Winkel, Lois, ed. *The Elementary School Library Collection: A Guide to Books and Other Media. Phases 1-2-3*. 14th ed. Williamsport, PA: Bro-Dart, 1984. 1,055p.

The continuing series of editions of this major selection aid for school libraries serving preschoolers through sixth-grade children commenced in 1965 and continued on an annual basis until the 1976 edition, edited by Lois Winkel (E/S 1945-75, p. 181). From 1977, biennial editions have been the pattern, with the same editor, who was assisted in this fourteenth edition by ten collaborators, including Mary Virginia Gaver, the original editor. Like earlier editions, it represents a complete reevaluation of titles and makes several significant changes to take note of new trends in elementary education. New titles published from 1981 to 1983 are combined with titles formerly listed that were re-evaluated and judged useful. Out-of-print, outdated, and superseded older titles were dropped. Primarily designed to serve as a resource to assist in the continuous maintenance and development of existing collections or for the establishment of new library media centers in the United States and Canada, the list of materials was selected to meet two purposes: to implement elementary school curricula and to be of interest and appeal to elementary school children. The total of over 13,000 items, including nearly 9,000 books, 160 periodicals, and over 4,000 audiovisual pieces, were available for purchase at the time of publication. Section I forms the catalog classified by the eleventh abridged edition of Dewey, and divided into reference, nonfiction, fiction, easy reading, periodicals, and the professional collection. Entries receive a concise paragraph of annotation, primarily descriptive, with critical points and audience use noted. Code notations are made which indicate "Phases," that is, priorities of acquisition (Phase 1 being for all libraries, Phase 2 for continuing development, and Phase 3 for specialized significance); Interest Level, indicated by a letter code; and Readability Level Estimate, according to either the Spache or the Fry formula depending on grade. Section II provides author, title, and subject indexes, and Section III the appendices, which list media for preschool children. The whole volume reflects a high grade of professional selection, careful assessment, and sophisticated organization. It is well entrenched as a standard selection tool, deservedly so.

Reservations as to its use in the practical library situation could stem from its very good qualities. In the current financial climate, it would be a prosperous school system that could afford even a majority of titles in its first phase of choice. Using it as a principal guide to selection in a school library might adversely affect an independent response to the local situation and its own particular needs.

404. Wise, Bernice Kemler. *Teaching Materials for the Learning Disabled: A Selected List for Grades 6–12.* **Chicago: American Library Association, 1980. 64p.**

This annotated list was compiled as a key to available materials that can be used by teachers and librarians in working with learning-disabled students in grades six through twelve for reading remediation, as an aid for academic subjects, and for recreational reading. Criteria for selection were relationship of material to the curriculum, topicality, quality, and format. Three sections cover professional materials, reading programs, and curriculum/noncurriculum materials. Each section has a list of annotated titles, the first two directed primarily to teachers and librarians. The third section arranges material for students by subject with annotations that describe the theme and indicate reading and interest levels. This list of current materials can be regarded as a fundamental selection aid for this category of reader.

405. Wittig, Alice J. *U.S. Government Publications for the School Media Center.* **Littleton, CO: Libraries Unlimited, 1979. 121p.**

This selected and annotated list aims "to provide a quick introduction for those people working in school libraries to whom this is a largely unexplored subject, and to be a time-conserving source of reference and a checklist for librarians who feel that they may be overlooking and/or underutilizing some areas in this rich field of information." The over 300 documents included were chosen on the basis of their potential usefulness to patrons of school libraries and media centers. Part I supplies information on depository libraries, indexes and selection aids, and ordering information. Part II arranges the documents alphabetically by title within 41 general topics. Entries are briefly annotated and supplied with bibliographical information which includes the Superintendent of Documents classification number and the Government Printer stock number. Allowing for the out-of-print problem that rapidly affects many U.S. government publications, the information supplied in this small curricularly oriented list is still useful for practitioners and researchers as a convenient finding aid. When published it was helpful for selection purposes in small public libraries as well as media centers.

406. Wolff, Kathryn; Fritsche, Joellen M.; Gross, Elma N.; and Todd, Gary T. *The Best Science Books for Children: A Selected and Annotated List of Science Books for Children Ages Five through Twelve.* **Washington, DC: American Association of Science, 1983. 271p.**

This national scientific organization has sponsored for many years a selected and annotated list of recommended children's books for use by teachers, librarians, media specialists, and others concerned with science teaching and science information sources. Published in 1959 as *The A.A.A.S. Science Book List*, revisions appeared in 1964 and 1970 (E/S 1945–75, pp. 43–44).

A supplement to the third edition was issued in 1978, edited by Kathryn Wolff and Jill Storey, with nearly 3,000 titles published from 1969 to 1977. The present volume gives annotations for more than 1,200 titles chosen from longer reviews which appeared in the Association's review journal *Science Books and Films*. The editors selected these as excellent books about areas of knowledge often unavailable to children, bearing in mind an audience of "the many children in school now who are gaining so little understanding of science and math that they will have great difficulty mastering both work and citizenship skills in a high-technology society." Entries are grouped under specific scientifically related categories arranged by the Dewey classification. A paragraph of careful descriptive and critical annotation is given for each. Bibliographical information supplied includes Library of Congress numbers and reading level designations. The conscientious selection and high-quality annotation makes this list an essential for all libraries dealing with readers of this age group, and it will be both useful and interesting to teachers, parents, and young readers.

407. Woolman, Bertha. *The Caldecott Award: The Winners and the Honor Books.* **Minneapolis, MN: Denison, 1978. 54p.**

Similar in objectives and treatment to the author's companion volume on the Newbery awards, this explains the history and significance of the Caldecott award, and includes a list of the winning and honor books, brief biographies of their illustrators, and questions about their books.

408. ———. *The Newbery Awards: The Books and Their Authors.* **2d ed. Minneapolis, MN: Denison, 1981. 84p.**

First published in 1978 as *The Newbery Awards: These are Winners*, this account of the prizes and their creators is intended "to spark the interest of the student and to make him want to read," and for teachers and librarians to use as a springboard for a variety of group activities. The preface gives a brief history of John Newbery and the establishment of the award. The arrangement of entries in the text is by author; biographical notices are followed by the winning titles, with incidents from the book cited in a question-and-answer format, and references which form clues for book talks or serve to motivate use by students. A second section gives further informational references about the authors. Title and author indexes are provided. The value of this booklist is in the activities framed around the Newbery award winners; the factual information can be readily checked in other sources.

409. Wynar, Christine Gehrt. *Guide to Reference Books for School Media Centers.* **2d ed. Littleton, CO: Libraries Unlimited, 1981. 377p.**

First compiled in 1973 by Christine L. Wynar (E/S 1945–75, p. 194), who supplemented it in 1976 with titles appearing from mid-1973 through 1975, the work in the new edition represents a thorough revision and updating, designed specifically to satisfy the reference and media selection requirements of the media specialists and library science professors who have used the work. "Effort was made to winnow the potential list of titles so as to retain outstanding reference books...while books of lesser quality or potential interest...were put aside." Except for the most significant, out-of-print titles were deleted. Nearly 2,000 entries reflect a wide range of subject areas represented in elementary and secondary school curricula, as well as those topics of special interest to young readers. The basic organization remains unchanged; entries are arranged under broad subject headings, with subdivisions, and are accompanied by a paragraph of descriptive and critical annotation. This edition's realistic restriction of titles included reflects dropping senior high school students from the clientele to be served, as well as the financial constraints now affecting school libraries. The current edition is an efficient tool which serves its audience well.

410. Wynnejones, Pat. *Pictures on the Page.* **(Lion Paperback). Tring, England: Lion, 1982. 175p.**

Written for parents and teachers, this wide-ranging survey of books for children from babyhood to teenage by a former primary school headmistress examines the personal values that books can give and their influence on the developing person. The author considers that "a book need not always convey an explicitly Christian message...but it must convey the feeling of life itself." A secondary aim is to suggest some guidelines in looking for books. The first part, "To Teach and Delight," examines the ways in which the written word can affect ideas and attitudes. The second part gives examples and illustrations from children's books, with frequent short textual extracts, and considers how these books can meet the emotional needs of growing children, stress being on early life. The third part is a personal choice. In addition, a list of titles mentioned is appended to each chapter. Optimistic and inspirational in tone, this guide will appeal chiefly to those who consider children's books as an aid to a religious upbringing.

411. Yates, Jessica. *Tudors and Stuarts.* **(Storylines). London: Library Association, 1977. 20p.**

One of the Youth Libraries Group's short bibliographic guides to periods of British history, this annotated list covers a period which has attracted many good British children's writers. It is selective, books not of an acceptable standard being excluded. The titles are chiefly of novels set in Great Britain—there are no Mayflower pilgrims—and are generally suited to the ten-plus age group. Arrangement is in chronological sections according to the reigning monarch. Descriptive annotations usually carry a closing critical sentence indicating suitability for a particular age group. There are supplementary lists of adult novels for further reading and of background information books.

412. Yonkers, N.Y. Public Library. Children's Services. *A Guide to Subjects and Concepts in Picture Book Format.* **2d ed. Dobbs Ferry, NY: Oceana, 1979. 163p.**

First published in 1974 (E/S 1945–75, p. 195), this helpful subject listing has been updated by the library staff to include titles up to October 1978. Some alterations have been made to headings used to reflect changing emphasis of patron requests, as well as changes in the types of books being published. The changes often reflect developing areas of social and personal concern, such as "Male-Female Roles" and "Single Parent Families." A bibliography of further readings is provided.

413. Zipes, Jack. *Fairy Tales and the Art of Subversion: The Classical Genre for Children and the Process of Civilization.* **New York: Wildman, 1983. 214p.**

This original and perhaps provocative study of how the fairy tale has functioned within the framework of civilization presents a thesis that has occasioned some scholarly controversy. The social history of the genre receives attention rather than actual publications for children, although there is careful analysis of some major writers such as Perrault, Grimm, Andersen, MacDonald, Wilde, and Baum. Socialization, politicization, domination, and liberating potential are among the concepts examined. Bibliographical references provided are mostly to scholarly research rather than to children's literature. This is a book about intellectual issues for students and thinkers, rather than for practitioners in the teaching and library professions.

414. Zippel, Mary Ella Holst, and Utt, Angie Henry. *Unitarian Universalist Contributors to Literature for Children: An Annotated Bibliography.* **New York: The Unitarian Church of All Souls, 1977. 22p.**

This privately printed booklist seeks to create an awareness of the contributions of individuals associated with the Unitarian Universalist movement and to stimulate research into the impact of the cultural values expressed. Seventy-five authors from the 18th to the 20th century are listed with brief biographical and bibliographical annotations. The list is not considered definitive, but includes some popular and recognized names in the children's literature field.

415. Ziskind, Sylvia. *Telling Stories to Children.* **New York: Wilson, 1976. 162p.**

The author tries to make this practical guide simple enough to appeal to the totally inexperienced teller of stories, and introduces practical means by which the reader can develop skill in the art of storytelling. Also described are "more advanced techniques and procedures for those who wish to become professional storytellers." Chapters cover selecting the story, learning the story, mastering technique, reading and speaking poetry, creative dramatics, and planning the story hour. A number of supplementary bibliographies are provided, including background books, periodicals, booklists, and indexes, and also "Where to look for stories to tell," "What to read to improve your skill," "What to use for language differences," and "Stories for maturer children." These lists make a thorough attempt to document the minimum in this extensive field, and together with the extensive citations and the index furnish a valuable checklist for library collections. It is also a useful textbook for the craft.

Subject Index

Compiled by Bunny Scott and Gillian Strange

References are to entry numbers, not page numbers.

Added Entry Index

Compiled by Bunny Scott and Gillian Strange

Includes joint authors, titles, organizations, and series. Authors and organizations appearing only as main entries are not repeated in this index; check body of text. Subtitles are used to distinguish identical titles, where possible. References are to entry numbers, not page numbers.